BEAST OF NEVER, CAT OF GOD

BEAST OF NEVER, CAT OF GOD

THE SEARCH FOR THE EASTERN PUMA

By Bob Butz

Foreword by Jay W. Tischendorf,
Founder and Director of the
American Ecological Research Institute

The Lyons Press
Guilford, Connecticut
An imprint of The Globe Pequot Press

To buy books in quantity for corporate use
or incentives, call **(800) 962–0973, ext. 4551,**
or e-mail **premiums@GlobePequot.com.**

The Lyons Press is an imprint of The Globe Pequot Press.

10 9 8 7 6 5 4 3 2 1

Printed in the United States of America

Designed by LeAnna Weller Smith

ISBN 1-59228-446-9

Library of Congress Cataloging-in-Publication Data is available on file.

For Gabriel

•••

"Though the world is shrinking daily, much of it is still unknown; the blank spots are disappearing beneath the unblinking eyes of satellites and the probing fingers of chainsaws, bulldozers, and the farmer's hoe, but great swaths of the planet remain a mystery to polite society, fit habitat for myths and monsters, a place where dreams can live."

Scott Weidensaul, *The Ghost with Trembling Wings*

"The wilderness is out there, quiet under the brief, rose-gray twilight before the sun rises again. But the wilderness is in myself, also, like a durable shadow. I prowl the region of flesh, my forest of blood, muttering and sniffing, turning many times in search of my own best place."

John Haines

CONTENTS

ACKNOWLEDGMENTS

There's an old saying that a story is only as good as its characters. And in that regard, it would be hard to top a more colorful, opinionated, and polarizing bunch than all the people I encountered while exploring the mystery of the eastern puma. Hard also not to admire the courage and passion most exhibited when expressing their positions and ideas. My thanks go out to anyone and everyone who shared their knowledge and insight with me, especially those unafraid to be identified by name, the ones who spoke up and spoke out despite knowing their words—their enthusiasm for finding out the truth and in some cases the lack thereof—would not be appreciated or embraced by all.

Thanks to my agent Richard Abate and his assistant Kate Lee who worked to find a home for this book; and to my good friends Doug and Anne Stanton who not only offered valuable words of encouragement but also some last minute editorial advice that helped strengthen the narrative; and to Kathy Erlewein and Matt McDonough for helping track down some key stats. Jeff Smith, editor of *Traverse: Northern Michigan's Magazine;* Susan Adams at *The New York Times;* John Snow at *Outdoor Life;* and Mark Wexler, editorial director for *National Wildlife*—I'm much indebted to these editors for the interest they showed when this story was first forming and, most of all, to my editor at The Lyons Press, Ann Treistman, who was able to look at what was originally a handful of magazine articles and a twenty-five word proposal and not only saw the "bigger story" here but was also able to keep me writing through insightful comments and her sheer enthusiasm during spells when I pretty much lost mine.

And finally, to my wife Nancy for her patience, faith, goodness, undying optimism, and joy for this life.

FOREWORD

A mong mysterious and fabled animals, few have endured like the cougar of the East. A vestige of our primitive past, this long-tailed cat, known also as mountain lion or puma, once ranged from the wave-pummeled coast of northeastern Canada to the windswept reaches of the Great Plains. Living large in legend this golden ghost persists in the talk of campfires, break rooms, bars, hunting camps, classrooms, and DNR offices across that same vast historic range. But are there really cougars in the East, a region often thought tamed, cultured, refined, and—at least in terms of its wildlands—safe? A growing number of credible reports and, indeed, even confirmed cougar evidence—video footage, track photos, scat, hair, blood, and DNA samples from New Brunswick to Nebraska—suggest there are. It would seem *Felis concolor,* adaptable and resourceful in its needs, thriving still among the redoubts of the mountain West, is poised for a comeback in the East.

Large predators like the cougar—powerful, capable, and stealthy—stir our collective imagination, even more so with the added element of uncertainty. And rife as it is with rumor, intrigue, and whispered warnings of conspiracy, the eastern cougar story is truly an uncertain one. This fascinating yarn blends folklore, fable, forensics, cryptozoology, historical ecology and detective work, modern wildlife management, human psychology, believers versus non-believers, and the incendiary contentiousness of endangered species and wide-ranging, potentially dangerous predators. I know, for as a biologist, veterinarian, and director of a wildlife research and consulting firm deeply involved with predators, I have been intently following this story for over a quarter of a century.

Michigan, both figuratively and literally, lies at the epicenter of this fascinating tale. A classic David and Goliath saga, pitting a brash, believing biologist and his small, independent group against the monolithic, unbelieving machine of the state Department of Natural Resources, the Michigan cougar clash has sparked an avalanche of outside interest in the possible continued existence, or the return, of eastern North America's largest wild felid. The burden in this battle, as always in science, is proof. Consistent, replicable proof. And impartiality. As Bob Butz discovered, the latter may be more elusive than the puma. I suspect Bob also discovered that it took courage to pen this book, for there are few in whom it will not incite some ire. Perhaps that is the measure of its success.

In terms of proof, the only thing more difficult than proving an animal exists, of course, is proving it doesn't. But even if one can confirm that an elusive species in fact exists, further proof is required to determine whether the animals are solitary wanderers or part of a viable breeding population. Today, most reasonable people agree there are at least a few of these tawny, long-tailed cats prowling our midwestern and eastern forests, fields, and streams. Unfortunately, while the critical question of a breeding population goes unanswered, many experts argue vociferously over whether or not the cat was ever really totally extirpated from the region. Even more unfortunate, such unproductive debate—probably both unknowable and immaterial in the big picture, tail-chasing in its truest form—takes away from an even more critical issue. Ironically, amid all this unrest and argument, the most important question of all—what collectively are we going to do to manage this large cat as it inexorably makes its return?—goes unanswered and in fact all too often unasked.

This, then, is the crux of the cougar dilemma. The fertile fields of folklore aside, is the bio-political and societal landscape of today prepared to sustain this large, lithe, and capable creature, *la panthère légendaire de l'est*? This book helps answer that question. It also serves to remind us that in developing a rational understanding and tolerance for the natural world around us, our greatest challenge will be achieving peaceful coexistence with the planet's most capable predator. No, not the cougar, but rather our own fellow man. It seems the great cat can adapt. Can we?

JAY W. TISCHENDORF, DVM
OCTOBER 2004
AMERICAN ECOLOGICAL RESEARCH INSTITUTE (AERI)
GREAT FALLS, MONTANA AND KENT, OHIO

BEGINNINGS

There is at bottom the only courage that is demanded of us: the courage for the most strange, the most singular, and the most inexplicable that we may encounter. That mankind has in this sense been cowardly has done life endless harm; the experiences that are called "visions," the whole so-called "spirit world," death, all those things that are so closely akin to us, have by daily parrying been so crowded out of this life that the senses with which we could have grasped them are atrophied. To say nothing of God.

Rainer Maria Rilke

A cold, creepy December drizzle fell steady for three days after my first meeting with Patrick Rusz. Hard against a deadline and suddenly unsure of exactly where to begin, I stood facing the window in my tiny cluttered office, watching the raindrops runnel the glass. An unexpected call from the doctor that morning was initially a welcome distraction. Now I had the feeling that an already weird story was fixing to get even more bizarre.

For three days I'd been thinking hard about cougars, and specifically the likelihood of what this man Rusz believed was true. Could it be that cougars, wiped out in Michigan and elsewhere east of the Mississippi River since around the turn of the twentieth century, were really just hiding all this time? Rusz, an anonymous PhD working on a shoestring for a little Lansing-based wildlife conservancy that likewise nobody had ever heard of, had publicity earned the reputation of a man who'd rediscovered a lost species—the eastern cougar—a find of downright monumental biological significance and a gravy assignment for any writer lucky enough to score some face time with the man. It was the kind of against-all-odds story that should have been able to write itself. So I why was I just standing there feeling snared by imponderables, staring outside at the gathering fog, placing one losing bet after another on the raindrops racing down the glass?

That's when the phone rang. It was Rusz.

"Remember how ridiculously easy I told you finding these cats could be sometimes? Well, I was wondering if you could do me a favor."

Quite out of the blue, that weekend Rusz had come up from his home office in southern Michigan to my neck of the woods ostensibly to investigate some big-cat sightings near my home in Lake Ann. He returned home to St. Charles to a phone message from a Grand Rapids deer hunter, a man who just happened to own property smack dab in the middle of my backyard, a place where Rusz believed at least one cougar, maybe more, were hiding out. I not only knew the general location of the property, I had pretty much taken Rusz right past it a couple of days before. After our little Q&A he asked if I had time to show him a little of the surrounding country. I jumped at the chance. And why not? What better way to learn more about my subject and the nature of his work than spending the afternoon riding around with him?

The message from the Grand Rapids hunter was all some strange bit of happenstance. Pure shithouse luck. According to Rusz, it happened like that sometimes. I would talk to the property owner afterward, and Rusz's rendition of the story checked out. The man had stumbled upon some strange tracks—what he thought were puma tracks, along with some peculiar-looking droppings—while up hunting deer the week before. Rusz had been making the rounds with reporters ever since going public with news of his work, and the man had seen one of the stories in the papers. He'd called Rusz's office then sent a hastily drawn map of the property, a map that Rusz faxed to me.

"I know it sounds crazy, but I think the guy's for real," he said. "I was hoping you might go check it out."

•••

Big rain was falling, dinging like gravel on the roof of the truck, when Wayne and I turned off the hardtop onto a dirt road. While I was getting ready to head out, lacing up my boots back at the house, Wayne had called reminding me of a grouse hunt we had planned that morning. I'd canceled on him once already earlier that weekend on account of Rusz's surprise visit. So I asked if he wanted to come along.

"Looking for mountain lions!" he said. "Okay. Sure. What the hell."

Good old Wayne, always up for an adventure. I never did know him to have a real day job. He sometimes mowed lawns or plowed snow over the winter months. That year he actually had a job playing Santa Claus at the local shopping mall. But most of the time he spent hunting and fishing as much as I sometimes wished I could, living on what he caught and killed like a poacher up there in his broken-down shack of a home, an uninsulated summer cottage that he heated with wood and rented dirt cheap from some retired downstate couple who never used the place. Wayne knew animal tracks probably better than me, so I figured he would not only be good company that morning but also serve as an extra set of critical eyes in the event we found anything.

When I pulled up in front and hit the horn, Wayne came stumbling outside wrestling with his red suspenders, which caught on something, the doorknob, *inside* the house. He pitched backward and slipped on the wet stairs, arms windmilling like Wile E. Coyote backsliding in a puddle of ACME bearing grease. His coat and gun case went flying.

A woman, a blonde in a long white T-shirt and no pants, appeared. I'd never seen her before. When she opened the door Wayne was free, running bowlegged through the rain with his hunting coat up over his head. Jumping in the passenger's seat, he sighed heavily and slammed the door.

"Damn near broke my neck back there," he said.

"Who's the lady?" I asked.

"Picked her up at my Santa gig at the mall," Wayne said, wiping the rainy shine from under his bloodshot eyes. "She's one of my naughty little helpers."

He cast a glance at me and smiled.

"And the gun?" I asked.

"Backup, Butzie. Case your mountain lion wants to get fresh."

•••

We found the dirt road leading back to the hunting property a couple of miles outside the town of Honor, north of the Dead Stream and Indian Hill crossroads, up from the bridge overlooking the Platte River where Rusz and I had stopped a couple days before to ogle some spawning salmon fresh out of nearby Lake Michigan.

Rusz made it clear from the get-go that he didn't much care for reporters.

"But I have a feeling about you," he said.

Standing there watching the giant fish finning lazily in the current, Rusz not only confided that he had reason to believe cougars were hiding out around here but also that he had a pretty good idea where. For the better part of the afternoon I listened to him go on and on about cougars. According to Rusz, my little corner of northwestern Lower Michigan was a veritable hot spot for sightings. The cats were close. Very close. While I heard variations of the same stories he retold, given that most of my life I've been afflicted by more than just a passing fancy with the outdoors, I had some doubts. Sometimes I think I know the woods better than I know myself. Eight years living up here and I had never so much as seen a track of the animal he described, and neither had my buddy Wayne, a local and probably the best woodsman I know. But then again, I'd never seen a wolf up here either. There are a lot of things out there I haven't seen, and that's nothing to be embarrassed of. One of the most alluring things about nature, aside from its ability to constantly surprise, is that nobody who loves wildlife and the woods lives long enough to see *everything*.

The pickup splashed down Indian Hill road, a countrified northern landscape of scattered trailer homes and dank houses with overgrown front lawns adorned with plastic birds and jolly gnomes, tractor tire planters, American flags, and laundered clothes hanging like sodden dishrags on drooping lines.

Turning off the hardtop down an unmarked dirt road, we easily found the place following the map. No house. Just a rusty iron gate across a grassy access road leading into the woods. Waiting for the rain to slow, I let the truck idle while I doubled-checked the contents of my pack: ziplock bags; my dog-eared copy of Olaus Murie's *Field Guide to Animal Tracks;* camera; Sharpie marker; a piece of window glass; and tracing paper, which Rusz told me to take along just in case I managed to find a good-looking track.

Another pickup, an old white Ford splattered with mud, rolled down the road behind us, slowing as it passed. The driver eyed me hard through the windshield, just staring, when I waved.

"Friendly," Wayne said.

We waited until the truck disappeared around the bend, then Wayne and I slipped out into the mizzling rain, ducking under the padlocked gate. The property owner's map that Rusz had faxed me showed a big X on the top of a little hill along a heavy black line that indicated the access road. The land itself was more or less an old farm field gone fallow, a wide-open grassy bowl surrounded by rolling tree-covered hills. After cresting the hill, I paused to consult the map. The valley below was socked in with fog, a hazy white mist. A couple more steps and I spotted the scat, an olive-colored coil marbled with white deer hair, partially covered with grass but impossible to miss there on the hump between the two tire ruts, exactly where the map indicated I would strike gold.

A pretty good pile. I'd never seen anything quite like it.

"Aw, now, come on," Wayne said. "What the hell is that?"

A rhetorical question, we both had a pretty good idea what it was. The real question was how it got there. The turd, if laid straight, was easily a foot long, and bigger around than my thumb; the dirt and grass around it were raked up, just a little, or just enough to suggest the pawing of a cat.

"You're not actually picking that up, are you," said Wayne.

"Well, that's why we're here," I said, sheathing my hand in a Baggie like somebody about to clean up after a pet.

Wayne called "Bullshit" and gave me a disgusted wave. He ambled off through the cold drizzle, down the road toward a copse of birch and aspen, his shape looking specterlike in the fog, leaving me to wonder if in fact I was being swept up in somebody else's folly or just playing a bit part in somebody's idea of a practical joke.

When I caught up with Wayne again it was exactly where the map indicated we'd find the tracks, the base of a clay bank where a patch of bare ground as big around as a dining room table was also pocked with dozens of deer tracks, coyote, the little hand-like feet of a raccoon. Wayne was standing off to one side, massaging the back of his neck, looking solemnly at a strange saucer-shaped track in the clay filled to the toes with rainwater. I knelt down for a look, judging it a week or so old at best.

Beyond that, Wayne was no help. And neither was Olaus. My first thought was black bear, remembering something I'd read about how the front foot of a small cub can easily be confused for the track of a puma. But black bear feet have five toes. This one only showed four. Yet I couldn't let myself jump to the conclusion that the impression before me was actually made by the front foot of a puma. So what else could it be? I've seen dozens of bobcat tracks, none bigger around than a silver dollar. This one was round as my fist. Coyote then? Common dog? No. The size and shape were all wrong. Up north these animal tracks are of the mundane sort, yet each very unique to its maker, like a signature I've come to know as well as my own.

But since I'm no expert on puma tracks, how could I say for sure? I remember a fleeting flutter in my stomach, an electrifying charge of childish hope—What if?—all of a sudden replaced by a hard, grown-up skepticism. Wayne was echoing the voice inside of me:

"C'mon! Could finding proof of the most elusive animal in the East really be as easy as following a dotted line to an X on a map?"

For the next five, maybe ten minutes, I crouched there consulting Olaus who seemed to be suggesting the impossible: that this was, in fact, a nearly textbook impression of a puma track preserved in the clay as crisp and deeply set as a child's hand pushed into newly poured cement. The track was nearly four inches across. It showed a lead toe of a front foot and that unmistakable heel pad with the three scalloped lobes at the rear, giving it the appearance of a pregnant letter *M*.

But there was only one decent track, and it wasn't exactly perfect. I found a few other partial impressions—a couple of toes, part of a pad—nearby in the clay, but nothing quite as good as the first. Skepticism was winning out. After all, Wayne was first to point out, a bear can put down a four-toed track if it happens to place its foot just right. I also knew from personal experience that I could take a snowy stroll behind my two Labrador retrievers and, if they put down enough tracks, find more than a couple that would certainly appear pumalike enough to fool someone who really wanted to believe.

But how to explain away the strange scat? Wayne still hadn't said a word. His face remained fixed, an expression of utter helplessness. He stood there wide-eyed then puffed his scruffy cheeks as I laid a tape measure down under the track for scale. After snapping a photo, I dug in my pack for the Sharpie, the plate glass, and a piece of paper for tracing, all the while unable to shake the deep-seated suspicion that all this was a setup. Wayne didn't have to say a thing. I caught him casting a squinty gaze toward the distance tree line.

"What are you looking for?" I asked. "The puma?"

"Naw. I'm keeping an eye out for your buddy. I bet he's watching us right now, laughing his ass off."

As I set about tracing the outline of the track, Wayne pondered aloud the possibilities: Maybe a puma really had passed through here. Maybe Rusz— perhaps even the landowner—was out here tromping around with plywood puma feet lashed to his boots. Wayne predicted, rightly it turned out, that even I might be suspected at some point of being in cahoots with the doctor and planting the evidence myself. He let the thought linger, then . . .

"Aw, shit. Who the hell's this?"

Beelining up the hill toward us came the hard glaring driver of the white pickup we'd seen earlier. A great big fat man with a formidable Jay Leno–like chin, the forehead under his Smith & Wesson ball cap oddly small and his dark, squinty eyes deeply set, giving his face the appearance of a bed pillow folded in half. Cigarette dangling from his thin lips, shoulders square, the man stopped like a gunslinger, hailing us from a distance, hands poised coolly on his hips.

"Who you?" he said.

"Who you?" Wayne shot back. I cringed. He was definitely not being helpful.

"I'm the neighbor and all this is private property."

As The Neighbor took a drag on his cigarette, waiting for our reply, I was hastily rolling up my sketch, cramming it into the backpack with the Baggie full of shit. The Neighbor's face softened a little, the crease over his eyes widening just a tad, when I mentioned we had come out here looking for puma sign.

"Like mountain lions?" he asked, palming the cigarette and blowing another plume of smoke. "Sure I've seen 'em. Couple times. Saw one just last week, just down the road, headed into the Dead Stream." The swamp.

"What makes you think it wasn't a bobcat," Wayne said.

"This weren't no bobcat," The Neighbor shot back, holding out his arms as wide as they would go. "Had a tail sproutin' out of its ass yea long."

Describing a huge reddish-colored cat with a long tail "about as big around as the mouth of a coffee mug," The Neighbor tossed his now smoldering butt to the ground. He was standing no more than a boot length away from the track and never noticed it. His eyes were too busy watching his toe working the butt into the clay.

"You see any other strange cars parked out here in the last couple of days?" Wayne said.

"Naw," he said. "Yours be the first."

With that he pulled open his tan Carhartt to reveal the black grip of a .45 holstered on his hip.

"I ain't never seen your truck before," he said. "So naturally I got suspicious."

"Well, you don't miss a thing," Wayne said, casting a glance down at the track on the ground then catching my eye with a look that said, *Let's get the hell out of here.*

The Neighbor accompanied us back down to the gate, where we found my truck blocked in by his white Ford. I tossed my backpack onto the floor at Wayne's feet and climbed into the cab, waiting as The Neighbor turned his rig around, saluting when I waved.

"Nice guy," I said.

"Yeah," Wayne said. "A real sweetheart. Fuck! Did you hear the dueling banjos when he pulled out that gun?"

Back on the main road, heading through the town of Honor, Wayne wanted to stop at the Sleeping Bear Lounge for a drink. But the bar was closed and this left him silent and looking forlorn. Wayne didn't say another word until we reached the railroad tracks a couple of miles short of the lane leading up the hill to his house. The brushy bottom, mostly Russian olive, jackpine, dwarf aspen, on either side of the tracks was always a good place to find grouse after the leaves were down. The sky overhead was white as a bedsheet, but the drizzle had stopped. Wayne wanted to try to get a bird for dinner. So I dropped him off. He slipped his shotgun out of the case, turned up the frayed collar of his hunting coat, and before slamming the door of the cab smiled and said, "Hope the cougar don't get me. Har! Har!"

Driving home I kept thinking, What in the world was I getting myself into? Maybe Wayne was right. Maybe Rusz was a wacko with a warped sense of humor. But what if he wasn't? I decided to play it cool, tell the events as they happened, and just let the story play out. Back at the office I got Rusz's machine and was partway through leaving a message when he picked up.

"So you really found something," he said. "No shit."

I listened hard, trying to detect some verbal shred of betrayal in his voice, but he sounded genuinely surprised. He wanted me to tell him more but I demurred, promising to box everything up—the scat, the track tracing—and drop it that day in the mail. Rusz told me he'd call when the package arrived. But I missed him the next day, returning home late in the afternoon to a message on my office phone.

"Yeah, this is Pat. Call me," he said, "I think you may have found yourself a cougar up there."

BEAST OF NEVER,
CAT OF GOD

ENTER THE DRAGON

We need stories that take note of our frailty and foolishness
and yet honor our deepest longings and highest aspirations . . .
that will heal our wounded imaginations.

Alan Jones, *The Soul's Journey*

O n the morning of December 31, 1906, far away in the big
woods of Michigan's Upper Peninsula, two men set out through
the gray gloom and snow from their hunting camp to check on
a few traps placed out overnight. Cool winds blew in from Canada, over Lake
Superior where steamships plowed through rolling whitecaps loaded with
lumber and copper ore coming and going from the mills and mining towns
salted all along the rocky northern coast. By all accounts it was a mild start
to winter. Light snow mixed with rain fell from the skies for the week after
Christmas. Most of the hunters at Deerfoot Lodge passed the holiday hunkered around the fireplace looking forward to New Year's and, after that, the
wagons and trains that would take them home. Game was scarce, and—given
the unseasonably warm weather—what little there was seemed disinclined to
move. That morning Chase Osborne and Ted LaLonde debated over breakfast about who should carry the rifle, or if they should take it at all. They
pocketed only three cartridges before disappearing into a misty curtain of
trees. The wind switched to the south. The sky, gloomy gray, looked like rain.
And one trap after another was discovered empty. Until the trappers came
upon the last.

A cubby-style set sided and roofed with logs with an open portal at one end had the bait placed in the back and the trap at the door concealed under the snow. A No. 4 Newhouse is a heavy, steel-jawed trap big enough to catch wolves, all but exterminated in Chippewa County by the turn of the century. Nearing the site, though, Osborne and LaLonde found the broken brush and kicked-up snow hinting of something just as formidable caught inside.

The big cat materialized in the shadows, backed into a dark pocket underneath one of the cubby's logs, needling eyes watching, a front leg outstretched, the melon-sized foot held fast by a massive steel trap. Realizing the catch was rarer than even a wolf, Osborne and LaLonde snapped a few photos of the animal before trying to dispatch it. But then came three bungled shots with the rifle, probably a .22 caliber. Out of ammunition and with the cat wounded and thrashing, the two hurried five miles back to camp for help. When the men returned, a second barrage finally finished off what the *Sault Ste. Marie Evening News* described as a reddish brown "catamount," standing as high as a large dog and measuring five feet six inches in length . . . what a century later is held to have been the last wild puma in Michigan.

• • •

Soon after moving up north I heard whispers of a mysterious creature prowling the dark swamps and forests surrounding our small town. The sightings were rare and usually happened at night, a handful of close-range encounters with a long-tailed catlike animal caught in the headlights ghosting across some desolate country road. One tale told of wailing midnight screams; another, a foggy-morning glimpse of a huge honey-colored feline sulking along the woodsy edge of a corn stubble field. Local knowledge held that it was a panther. That's what the townies who would talk about it believed.

Michigan was new to me then. And so big. After college and through some bit of luck I got a job in Traverse City, what passes as a city by this region's standards, a sprawling, trendy mishmash of beachfront hotels and fast-food joints, Indian resorts and casinos, and a main-street shopping district that in summertime bustled with lobster-fried tourists up from downstate.

I lived in country along the perimeter, an almost half-hour winding, back road commute (longer in fall when you had to be mindful not to splatter the occasional deer or procession of wild turkeys crossing the centerline) to and from the tiny village of Lake Ann. That's in the northwestern Lower Peninsula to be a little more exact, way up high near the forty-fifth parallel where the hardwood hills and piney forests ripple up from the flat farm country of the south. It's a vacation destination renowned for its golf courses and ski resorts, cherry orchards and vineyards, secluded Caribbean-like beaches, and, to a lesser degree, its wine.

I used to dream of becoming a mountain man and was on my way to the Rockies, my heart set on Montana, when I'd heard about the woods and the hard winters up here. Something about the deep forest, snow, and frigid cold—the word *North*—has always conjured in my mind an ideal backdrop for solitude. I'd never seen the Great Lakes before and was unprepared for the disarming immensity of so much water so close to home. Michigan is virtually surrounded by these vast inland, freshwater seas: Lake Erie to the south, touching up against Detroit; Lake Huron running along the rest of eastern shore; Lake Superior—the biggest, coldest, and deepest freshwater lake in the world—between here and Canada; and to the west Lake Michigan, what a grade school teacher once taught me to remember by its "spoon" shape but, as boys will be boys, seemed easier to recall given its striking topographical resemblance to a flaccid blue penis.

The waters are wide, unbelievably so to anyone gazing at them for the first time. My first time standing alone on the coast of Lake Michigan staring off in the direction of the setting sun, I remember feeling a cold chill of disconnectedness, an overwhelming sense of watery isolation, as if I were both a castaway marooned on a lost island and an explorer stepping upon the long shores of a new world. That day I made for the beach to watch the sunset even before unpacking my things. Down a dirt road past a DEAD END sign where I parked the truck and followed a footpath through a dark forest of tall maple, white oak, aspen, and stony gray American beech, heading toward the sound of lapping surf, over the barrier dune bristling with prickly, knee-high grasses, then onto a secluded sandy beach. There I found a sunny ocean view and a watery skyline, an emerald-colored sea near shore fading into deep-water blue. I sat for a while watching two sunny children flying red and yellow kites, their mother and father shooing away from a picnic basket a pair of gulls hovering overhead on a gentle inland breeze. And the water . . . The only thing I spied in my binocular was a lonely sailboat rising and falling in the crests and troughs of the white-topped waves until finally its milky sail dropped over the edge of the earth, shimmering in the mirage.

•••

The best thing about living in a tourist town is that after the first hard frost all the riffraff scurry home. While the streets aren't necessarily quiet again, there is a lot less tailgating and angry blaring of car horns. Up north whole businesses shut down over winter. One sign in the window reads CLOSED FOR THE SEASON . . . THE REASON: IT'S FREEZIN', while out on the strip marquee signs that during summer advertised tanning lotion, discount sunglasses, and free HBO suddenly announce CARHARTT, WOOLRICH—LOWEST PRICES IN THE NORTH, SMOKED WHITE FISH, JERKY, and GOOD LUCK DEER HUNTERS! to us, the hearty locals who dared to stay on and winter here. That cutoff, otherworldly feeling of the place was more keenly felt come the first hard snow. I loved how that first year it snowed in October and kept snowing until May.

And did I mention the fishing? Michigan has more than eleven thousand inland lakes, blue-ribbon trout streams galore, and rivers that every autumn teem black with millions of salmon nosing upstream to the natal waters from those vast inland seas of the Great Lakes. Just like the West, Michigan was every bit a land of imagination and myth. I remembered after reading Hemingway's Nick Adams tales and Longfellow's story of Hiawatha, I wanted to catch brook trout in the Big Two-Hearted and paddle a canoe in the big lake called Gitche Gumee. Other books revealed that the state had more old-growth forest and—with its moose, black bear, elk, otter, beaver, marten, fisher, coyote, lynx, and bobcat—arguably more wildlife diversity than any other in the East. There were more than three hundred wolves in Michigan at last count, almost twice as many as Yellowstone National Park. And what history! I loved all the stories of tall timber and lumbermen, grizzly French trappers and wild Indians. For a boy growing up in a sanitized hemmed-in suburb of eastern Pennsylvania, the great North Woods seemed a faraway and exotic land, a right place to stop over and explore, maybe settle down for a while and see for myself if the country today lived up to the poetry.

But after six years, a marriage, a mortgage payment, and a baby on the way, I still felt like an outsider here. Maybe that's why the rumor of ghost cats eventually came to fascinate me so: The beast was something of an outsider, too. Shy. Solitary. Misunderstood. A creature that moved among us, yet apart from us. I liked the way the mere mention of mountains lions always got people talking, even complete strangers. In that regard the animal spoke to my story-loving soul: a creature that embodied the spirit of true wilderness and that soul-stirring sense of mystery that helped draw me here.

Then came a newspaper article. The doctor claimed (at last!) real proof, DNA extracted from scat—panther shit—found across three Michigan counties in the Upper Peninsula. Intrigued by the very real possibility that here a lost species might finally be raised from the list of the missing and the dead, I read the story twice. Three times.

At the time, I didn't know much about panthers or cougars or whatever you want to call them, only that east of the Mississippi right-thinking people regard them as nothing more than a myth, a modern-day beast of never that only exists wild and free in the feeble minds of those also preoccupied with tales of Bigfoot and Loch Ness. If true, Dr. Patrick Rusz, along with a little twenty-first-century science, had essentially slain a dragon with a pooper-scooper instead of a sword. But comments from so many wildlife officials here were anything but hopeful and inspired by the news. Rusz (I remember thinking the last name was pronounced *rooze* or *ruse*, a mispronunciation that struck me as prophetic given his claim) came off sounding like a caricature. I pictured a pale and spindly-legged old duffer clad in safari shorts and a pith helmet and plagued by nervous tics, looking over his shoulder and muttering conversations with himself. The article ended without resolution, stymied in a frustrating tangle of bureaucratic questions hinting deeper concern for the man's nefarious motives than for all the amazing possibilities, the great "what ifs," in a word, the cat.

The naysayers all wanted the kind of certainty—ironically, a proof of life—only a body could provide. And to tell the truth even I remember thinking that instead of a fistful of panther plop I would have rather seen proof in the form of a photograph of the scientist standing over a sprawling corpse. And with that I tossed the paper into the tinderbox and later that chilly November evening fed wishful thinking to the fire.

•••

Catamount, panther, cougar, swamp screamer, mountain lion . . . I soon came to love all the names—one source claimed nearly hundred in all, supposedly more than any other animal on the globe and, for that matter, any other entity in our human consciousness this side of God. But before I go any deeper into this I think it important in the order of things to settle on just one. After all, how can we begin to know what might be out there if we can't even agree on what to call it?

New World pioneers called them "sneak cats" and "mountain devils." What Teddy Roosevelt dubbed the "lord of stealthy murder" was the "lord of the forest" to the Cherokee. One name calls us to gaze at the woods with starry-eyed reverence; the other is a four-fanged killer lurking amid moon shadows and thorny black forests.

There's so much about this animal that we don't understand. And everything we think we know is changing. Taxonomists once believed there were as many as thirty-two different subspecies of Pan-American lion, fourteen in North America alone. But recently geneticists working at a molecular level have determined this to be incorrect; in fact, the cats are all so closely related that there are no significant differences among animals here in the United States. What the Chickasaw revered as "the cat of God," the Society of Mammalogists renamed *Puma concolor* in 1993. I am not a scientist, but I like the name. *Puma*: It's simple, not sinister. "Easy to spell," says author-expert Harley Shaw, "while at the same time recognizing the cat's unique New World origin."

Often described as secretive, solitary, and elusive, the puma is a silent and opportunistic hunter that can and will eat almost anything it can catch. From rabbits to raccoons, wild pigs to porcupines. An adult puma can take down prey as big as an elk, yet prefers a steady diet of white-tailed deer, up to one a week say biologists. A highly evolved deer killer down to its teeth and bones, an adult puma's skull has upper fangs spaced exactly two inches apart, perfectly grown for slipping between the vertebrae in a whitetail's neck and severing its spinal cord. Pumas kill at close range by stalking or ambushing. Weighing in at upward of 150 pounds and stretching up to seven feet from nose to tail, pumas are built for short, hurtling bursts of speed. They are startlingly efficient hunters; it's been said that when a puma slips within forty feet of its prey, it will successfully kill an average of eight out of ten times.

"A lion can pounce twenty feet or more from a standstill," wrote Bill Heavy in a recent article for *Field & Stream*. "Lions have been observed dropping sixty-five feet from a tree to the ground without injuring themselves. This is partly because a mountain lion's entire dismantled skeleton would fit inside a hiking boot box. The creature is all muscle and sinew."

Instead of a roar, pumas are said to caterwaul or scream. When content they can purr like an ordinary house cat. And sometimes they whistle and chirp like a bird.

As testament to the puma's elusive nature, even in country where they are plentiful pumas are so rarely seen in the wild that biologists have yet to figure out a way to accurately tally their numbers. In fact, pumas are so hard to detect that most experts go their entire careers without ever having seen one in the wild that wasn't at bay in a tree with a Day-Glo tranquilizer dangling from its butt.

Depending on the source, the nationwide population estimate ranges anywhere from thirty thousand to fifty thousand. That's a margin of error of almost 50 percent. The only surefire way to count pumas is to slap radio collars on them after laboriously running them one by one up trees. Like they did in South Florida, home to around 100 cougars, and in the Black Hills of South Dakota, where the count is now at 150 and growing.

The fuzziest population figures come from the western states. In Oregon estimates range anywhere between four thousand and six thousand animals. Same guesstimate in California. Arizona, New Mexico, Utah, Washington, Montana . . . Best guess is that one to four thousand pumas inhabit the rest of the western states straddling the Continental Divide. But really, nobody knows.

A cunning and wary creature that buries its kills and droppings, hunting alone and mostly at night across a territory that can span hundreds of square miles, the puma hardly ever leaves behind any evidence of its passing, except for the occasional track. Pressed in soft mud or wet, slushy snow, the impressions are easily recognized by experts as palm-sized, three to four inches wide and almost round, showing three distinct lobes on the back of the heel pad, a pronounced "lead toe," and, unlike the oblong footprints of a canine, rarely if ever showing any claws.

The puma is also an occasional eater of livestock and killer of humans. Remember the wolf? The grizzly bear? Looking back through history, it's pretty much the same old miserable story from here. Before European settlement the puma was the most widely distributed carnivore in the Western world after humans, ranging from the Atlantic to the Pacific, and from the Yukon to the tip of South America. Pumas are now being reported with increased frequency as far north as Alaska, along the Kenai Peninsula, where one was killed near the town of Wrangell in November 1989 and another, two years later, was snared by a wolf trapper on South Kupreanof Island, across the Wrangell Strait.

The big cat Columbus called a "leon" once lived in the thin air seventeen thousand feet up in the Andes and in every tropical jungle, coastal swamp, and prickly pear desert in America. In Michigan and elsewhere east of the Mississippi, the puma just barely outlasted the pioneers' slaughter of elk, moose, bison, woodland caribou, and the passenger pigeon. Historical records show that, in the region, pumas held on longest in the Appalachian

Mountains and here in the North Woods of the Upper Midwest, what was then the edge of a wild frontier and a fitting place for such a dark and terrifying creature once described in colonial Boston as having a "Tail like a Lyon, its Leggs are like a Bears, its Claws like an Eagle, its eyes like a Tyger, its countenance is a mixture of every Thing that is Fierce and Savage."

Now everything on the books says that west of the Great Plains is the only place in America that pumas are not considered endangered and that save for roughly a hundred living in and around the Florida Everglades—the only officially recognized breeding population left in the East—the second largest cat in North America after the jaguar and the fifth largest cat on the planet was totally eradicated east of the Mississippi around the turn of the twentieth century.

••

As anybody who reads the papers with an interest in wildlife and wilderness knows, for as long as the puma has supposedly been extinct here, everyday folks from the backwoods of Maine to the so-called Third Coast of Michigan, from the foggy hills and hollows of New England to the boggy swamps and bayous of the Deep South, have persistently encountered the creature over the years. The controversial amateur puma sleuth John Lutz of the Eastern Puma Research Network claims to have compiled over six thousand sightings throughout the region, more than two thousand of those since founding the group in the early '80s. So many run-ins with pumas, including a surprising number of mothers with young cubs, have many amateur investigators leaping to the conclusion that the animals are already established here. West Virginian Todd Lester of the Eastern Cougar Foundation in 2000 tried unsuccessfully to petition the Department of the Interior Secretary Bruce Babbitt for better protection of what the environmental policy makers in Washington contend is nothing more than a ghost.[1]

Closer to home, Mike Zuidema—a retired forester for the Michigan Department of Natural Resources on the trail of the puma the last twenty years—has compiled nearly a thousand encounters, most from just five Upper

Peninsula counties. Ironically, after spending years assuring concerned citizens that they were mistaken whenever they rung his office phone to report a puma sighting, Zuidema himself allegedly witnessed a puma bound across the road in front of his truck in the Upper Peninsula back in 1981.

In the northern Lower Peninsula, where most of my wanderings took place, sightings would prove even more common. Everybody but me seemed to have seen one, or knew somebody who had. When you fancy yourself something of a been-there-done-that, take-it-on-the-chin outdoorsman this can smack of an affront. Like my buddy Wayne once said, people who can't even tell their ash from an elm will tell you they've seen a puma. And the thing is, sometimes they really do. How do you separate the facts from fantasy?

My neighbor, a grade school teacher who couldn't care less whether pumas are here or not, insists that one ran in front of her car the other year right down the road. The burly dude who fixed my furnace last winter told me of an encounter with a "sooty gray" puma that passed under his tree stand on the opening day of deer season. Twice he drew his bow, setting his sights on the animal's shoulder. But afraid he'd miss or wound the animal— "I figured if that bugger spotted me up there my ass would be cooked"—he lost his nerve when it came time to shoot.

I met a postman who recounted a Disneyesque encounter involving a mother puma and two cubs "sunning themselves" in a field along his route. Over his lunch hour he watched them through a binocular, a vision so clear he could see the kittens chasing around a monarch butterfly before turning their attention to the wriggling tail of the mother dozing in the grass on her side. A fly fisherman I crossed paths with on the nearby Boardman River, just twenty miles outside Traverse City, remembered another sighting from roughly a decade ago. He and a buddy were up at a place called The Forks sitting on the bank one warm June evening waiting for the bugs to rise. As the sun started down, a drake mallard and hen drifted past them on the current, hugging the far bank.

"I didn't pay them much mind until they disappeared around the bend and I heard this explosion like a depth charge going up."

The hen mallard came winging up past them and both anglers spun around, gawking downriver, where their eyes fell onto a puma standing up to its chest in the river not twenty-five yards away.

"Just like a Labrador retriever. 'Cept this wasn't no dog. It was a fuckin' cat. And you better damn well believe I don't go up there anymore."

I heard stories coming from the mouths of preachers, police officers, a state representative, and a judge. An average cross section of seemingly credible people, all claiming a fleeting brush with something extraordinary. In fact, everywhere I looked it proved more unusual to find someone who had never seen a puma in the wild than coming across the occasional oddball who had.

Wishful thinking, or that peculiar human desire to bear witness to something nobody else has seen before? Have pumas really been here all along, fooling us, or are we fooling ourselves? Contrary to the multitude of sightings, even the casual outdoorsperson knows there isn't one place from the Adirondacks to the Ozarks that's overrun with potentially man-eating wildcats. Like most conservation officers who have experienced firsthand far too many panicked calls of menacing black bears that turn out to be clumsy raccoons, most reasonable believers concede that probably nine out of ten sightings are innocent misidentifications of a bobcats, coyotes, and lost hunting dogs.

Even more frustrating for anyone interested in real research and serious debate are those nagging parallels to the hunts for sea monsters and big hairy upright apes. A certain subculture believes the puma, like Bigfoot, is the harbinger of the supernatural, a spirit cat—a sort of "paranormal puma"—that wanders between this dimension and the netherworld. Another claptrap of kooks blames wildlife agencies for secretly stocking wild pumas in an effort to control expanding white-tailed deer populations. Others say the government has long known that wild pumas are out there and that a massive, interagency cover-up is at work.

Eventually I met John Castle, an ex-newspaperman who spent a considerable portion of his life trying to prove that Michigan harbors a wild population of big cats. Castle has special interest in "black panthers," another name for a rare color phase of Asiatic leopard, and has documented several hundred sightings across the state since starting his work in the 1950s. Believers in black panthers, which include John Lutz of the Eastern Puma Research Network (and, I would soon discover, Patrick Rusz), advance perhaps the wildest theories of all to explain persistent sightings of these animals. Lutz, for instance, gives credence to claims that the black cats seen today are descendants of those brought over by slave traders in the 1800s who supposedly shackled the animals belowdecks for the purpose of intimidating their human cargo during the long voyage across the Atlantic. According to Lutz (known also for his penchant for tales of Bigfoot, UFOs, and spontaneous human combustion), after slavery was abolished the leopards were turned loose into the Southern Appalachians, where they spread to every corner of the East and survive in small numbers today. Some say these animals are the offspring of circus cats escaped from Depression-era train wrecks. Others, like Castle, wonder if persistent sightings of ghosty black felines can be traced back to pets brought home by veterans of the Vietnam War and/or to members of the 1960s-era Black Panther political movement, whose members were rumored to have kept black panthers as symbols of black power and mascots for the cause. And still another theory—one I later learned that Rusz subscribes to much to the detriment of his credulity—gives credence to the idea that these might not be melanistic leopards at all but perhaps "black mountain lions," a color phase of puma never documented in modern times save for one dubious, and unconfirmed, photograph of a specimen supposedly killed in 1959 in Costa Rica.

Theories to explain sightings of big wild cats, black or otherwise, abound. And it's not always easy to tell crackpot from clear thinker.

For all the fuzzy pictures and shaky home videos, certainly the most aggravating to everyone searching for real proof must be the growing number of encounters backed up by stunningly clear photographs, plaster casts of puma tracks, and, more recently, some unmistakable backyard video footage. Along with eyewitness testimony, this is the kind of hard, physical evidence that—while perfectly admissible in a court of law as many eastern puma proponents complain—means little to science and the majority of wildlife policy makers who routinely dismiss these, too, as inconclusive and meaningless encounters with escaped or illegally released exotic pets.

Unlike the hunt for Sasquatch, where skeptics would be quieted if just once a body would turn up, in the hunt for puma in the East recent history proves that even a corpse has failed to inspire much agency interest. In the spring 2002 issue of the *Wildlife Society Bulletin,* in an article titled "The Eastern Cougar: A Management Failure?," James E. Cardoza and Susan A. Langlois noted that there have been at least fifteen pumas killed in eastern North America, north of Florida, since 1950. Most of these pumas—some declawed, defanged, and sporting identification tattoos—were obviously once captives. But what to make of the ones that were not? And for that matter, what about the many escaped and illegally released pets, the ones that after a string of sightings and a string of hysterical evening news reports, seem to vanish, never to be seen again?

Two such cases that have baffled biologists: In June 1997 a Kentucky motorist traveling on Route 850 in Floyd County struck and killed an eight-pound cougar kitten that was following another kitten and a larger cat across the roadway. The carcass was turned over to game and fish department officers, who found all its claws intact and no other indicators commonly associated with cougars kept as pets. Subsequent DNA testing revealed that at least one of the animal's parents was South American in origin even though it's still a mystery where these animals came from and why the mother and surviving kitten were never seen again.

In Illinois back in July 2002, near Fort Kaskaskia State Historic Site in Randolph County, a 110-pound male puma carcass was found on the railroad tracks, apparently killed—nearly decapitated—by a train. *Southern Illinois Outdoors* reported that the results from DNA tests revealed the cat to be at least four to six years old and having the genetic makeup of a North American strain of cougar, not Central or South American as is common in cougars sold as pets. A necropsy showed that the puma was in good health, had all its claws, and exhibited no signs consistent with cougars held in captivity. Stomach contents revealed the cat's last supper: the remains of a white-tailed fawn.

Here in Michigan officials insist that never has a puma that didn't turn out to be someone's pet been hit on the road or killed during the state's deer season, when an estimated one million hunters are out there thrashing the brush. Pieces of bone. Puma hair picked off a car bumper. Actually, a century has gone by and there's never been a whole body turn up. Michigan also has a dedicated cult of bear and bobcat hunters, yet there's never been a reliable report of a puma being treed by a pack of hounds. Believers counter that even though there are tens of thousands of fisher, black bear, elk, moose, and bobcat in the state, it's rare to hear of any killed on the road. Everyday hunters have, in fact, been responsible for many of the best yet chronically ignored sightings over the years. And finally, so say the puma people, Michigan houndsmen and their dogs have no experience running these wide-ranging and crafty animals. Like most eastern game wardens, so the hopeful reasoning follows, most houndsmen here would have a hard time telling a puma track even if they cut across one in the snow. Or maybe they're simply not hunting where the pumas are. Believers say it takes only a map and a little imagination to see that Michigan's big woods are still so vast and impenetrable that a minuscule population of ultrasecretive, nocturnal carnivores could survive here without widespread detection. And that might be true.

Michigan's Upper Peninsula is roughly the size of New Hampshire and Vermont, yet fewer than four hundred thousand people live there. Marquette County alone is the size of Rhode Island, yet, to look at a map, it's entirely conceivable that hikers could bushwhack northward from the bottom of the territory all the way to the cold rocky shores of Lake Superior without their boots ever touching more than a couple of hardtop roads. The northern Lower Peninsula, a trendy summer destination where prime waterfront real estate can fetch as much as ten thousand dollars a foot, is still largely underdeveloped between towns.

People who want you to believe that a 150-pound, wide-ranging carnivore like the puma could avoid widespread detection in this modern age like to point to that other touristy, peninsula state—Florida—where biologists didn't radio-collar their first wild puma until 1983 after nearly a hundred years' worth of sightings were met with doubt and bureaucratic denial. After a multimillion-dollar recovery program was launched by the state, these reports were later found to be attributable not to escaped circus cats and drug dealers' pets, but instead to a remnant population of less than fifty wild animals hiding out in the mucky bug-infested palmetto jungles in southern Florida's Everglades and Big Cypress Swamp.

•••

In my heart I want to believe pumas are here. I do. The dreamer, the artist, the right-brained gorp-eating tree hugger in me has always been fascinated by the possibility of big, toothy predators lurking out there just beyond the campfire glow. But the left-brained cynic, that overbearing voice of reason, knows that there comes a time when faith must be reconciled. The question of whether wild pumas live secretly in our midst has confounding political and cultural implications. It's one of our greatest wildlife mysteries, an issue steeped in weird and wonderful controversy. But since the final word on the matter rests with the same state and federal agencies either unwilling or uninterested in conducting any meaningful research of their own, it's a question not liable to be answered in the East anytime soon.

In his book, *Where Bigfoot Walks*, Robert Michael Pyle wrote of the mindset I seek in trying to understand Sasquatch's mythic eastern cousin: "What I want is a state of brain aloof from arrogant dismissiveness, free from superstition, and rich in question." As with Bigfeet, to paraphrase Pyle, right now only one thing is for sure: The phenomenon of the puma is something definitely very real. What does this say about both the skeptics and the believers? What is this creature that the writer Donald Schueler said "works such a strong magic in the minds of many Americans . . . a renegade presence, the sign of everything that is remote from us, everything we have not spoiled"?

The Michigan case is, I think, the perfect microcosm for examining the mystical hold the puma has on all our civilized minds. More important, it also offers a preview of all the political pitfalls in store for other eastern states as puma populations drift ever eastward following hoof-trampled game trails and invisible, wafting tendrils of prey scent to reestablish a foothold in their old hunting grounds, as ultimately most western experts agree they will.

For some this predator will always be nothing but a man-eater and a sheep killer better off dead and gone. To others who long for wildness in a sprawling suburban landscape fungified and homogenized by housing tracts, Red Lobster restaurants, and Wal-Mart stores—a dishearteningly fragmented country where true wilderness is no longer believed to exist—the animal symbolizes a paradise lost, a wilderness Eden . . . hope.

I am interested in the characters as much as the cat. Like bearing witness to miracle or epiphany, what some see or think they see has the power to alter destinies, maybe even give meaning and purpose to otherwise humdrum lives. Plenty of self-appointed experts have invested their time, money, and reputation trying to convince uninformed naysayers that pumas inhabit the East. It would be absurd, horribly naive, and wrongheaded to set out thinking the following pages might come any closer to proving what all that collective effort has not. That is not my intention.

In autumn 2001 Dr. Patrick Rusz told the Associated Press that he believed the puma population in Michigan was likely a small, inbred, "genetic bottle neck" of maybe twenty animals in the Upper Peninsula and fifteen in the deep woods very near the small town where I lived. With a case buttressed by unbroken chronology outlining seventy years' worth of sightings, a compelling dossier of hard empirical evidence, and a handful of scat samples reportedly testing positive for puma DNA, Rusz appeared well on the way to proving it.

While at first my heart swam in a river of possibility, into my head soon poured a cascade of obvious questions: Where did these animals originate? Are they a remnant population, transient animals from parts west, escaped pets that are managing to live wild, or a mongrel mix? Or was Rusz a flim-flam artist perpetrating a fraud?

I went into this wondering where the myth and reality of the puma merge, if at all. Does wilderness exist anymore east of the Mississippi? I'm talking true *wild*, in what the writer Grant Sims called "its old Teutonic infancy": uncivilized, ungovernable, unartful, chaotic, beyond control. When I think of it that way, the eastern puma—if it is out there—might possibly be the last true wild thing left: a beast that comes and goes silently and without asking, surviving without our help and despite our indifference, and evading us all, even the dedicated seekers crawling around in the brush searching for real proof—following tracks, seeking out hair, picking up shit and bagging it for the lab—all trying to find meaning, perhaps truth, despite laws and politics and the blank faces of the skeptics who would rather not be bothered by the implications of what might be out there.

This book is a reckoning, a chronicle of the hunt playing out in this not-so-faraway corner of the East, deep (and in some cases not so) in the woods of my adopted home state where amateur sleuths and one bona fide scientist appeared to have come the farthest in proving that a dragon has long been living secretly among us. It's a story about people, politics, and, of course, the search for pumas that may or may not exist out there, perhaps only barely hidden on the fringe where myth and reality converge—if only we had the willingness to see.

THE GREAT DIVIDE

Obsession doesn't need reason or rationale, it simply requires an object of desire, the less attainable the better.

Scott Weidensaul, *The Ghost with Trembling Wings*

From where Patrick Rusz discovered the deer—a carcass of a doe hidden along the tree line in a clump of shady cedars, partially covered with pine needles, black earth, and leaves—he could see the waves of Lake Michigan peeling up onto a remote stretch of sandy Upper Peninsula shore.

Rusz recalled that the May afternoon in that summer before we met in 2001 was sunny and bright and the kill was only a couple weeks old, judging by the smell. A short distance away, flies buzzed circles over what the predator had pulled from inside, a spaghetti pile of innards minus the heart and liver. White belly hair lay in a starburst around the bony remains, and Rusz, a blue-eyed two-hundred-pounder with the rounded, muscular build of the ex-college-wrestler he is, knelt down, took a pinch of hair, and considered it.

Rusz had told one reporter that this was actually the third carcass he, his son, Mark, and a handful of volunteers found on the beach at Seul Choix (pronounced *SIS-shwa*) Point that day. The kill he described as oddly neat and lacking the frenzied mess of a coyote or wolf pack attack. To him, everything suggested a textbook puma kill: the concealed carcass; the toothy punctures two inches apart on the back of the deer's broken neck; the neat shearing of the rib cage; the guts (minus organ meat) pulled neatly out of the deer's chest cavity and moved off to the side.

I read a handful of news accounts before meeting him face-to-face, and the details of the story never changed. Rusz scanned the scene for more evidence and found it, a footprint measuring a hand width across and showing four staggered toes in the sand, likely a puma track. From his day pack, he pulled a camera, tape measure, and notepad. He moved carefully around the kill, snapping photos, scribbling notes. Then his eye spied the evidence he sought.

Droppings. A pretty good pile. The scat was long, an inch and a half in diameter, and consisted of mostly deer hair and small glittering pieces of bone. Rusz reached into his day pack again and pulled out a plastic bag. He snapped another photo with the tape measuring a ten-inch segment. Then as he had done for a couple of dozen other likely-looking specimens that afternoon, he bagged the scat and placed it in his pack.

A partially eaten doe. A tidy pile of guts. A fresh turd with just the right look. For Dr. Patrick Rusz this made for a pretty good day. A nearly unbelievable day I would soon discover, considering that all this happened in the opening hours of Rusz and his crew actually heading out into the woods.

•••

Seven months later, December, I sat waiting for the man who, by all accounts, had solved the greatest wildlife mystery of the century to finally walk through the door.

They don't serve anything but breakfast at the L.A. Café on Sunday. Steaming black coffee, heaps of homemade corned beef hash, a side of eggs, and—should your faith require a weekly tune-up at the tiny Methodist church next door—sweet salvation can all be had within a block of each other in the tiny village of Lake Ann. Seated at the window watching the comings and goings out on the street, I half considered something called the "American Skillet," new to the menu after September 11, as neighbors whose sunny faces I recognized began filing into the diner all done up in dresses and ties. True to the town motto "Small, but friendly," the diners exchanged courteous nods and a few *good afternoon*s. My adopted hometown has always had a quaint Mayberry feel, a certain delightful sense of familiarity that comes from being able to sit in one spot and at a glance see every corner of the place you call home. Looking through the glass I could see the brick firehouse, the township building, the tiny post office just a short stroll through a shady little park, and the always bustling Lake Ann Grocery, our general store. Yellow ribbons tied around every tree. Red, white, and blue. I noticed, too, on this uncharacteristically cool December day—downright balmy by northern Michigan standard so close to Christmas—that when the boughs of the windy willows, white pines, and red pines that line the town's main street blew and bent just so, I could even see the north end of the big blue lake, a sliver of tranquil turquoise water that lends this place its name.

Sitting there, I remember thinking how it's not every day you plan on meeting someone who could quite possibly change the way you look at the world, or in this case the woods just beyond my neighbors' well-manicured lawns. I wanted to meet the man and look into his eyes. I wanted to see firsthand the proof since if he had indeed figured out a way to prove that pumas were real, it's not a stretch to say that everything I thought I knew about the woods would be irrevocably changed. Somewhere in the back of my mind, I suspected this might ultimately take an actual firsthand glimpse of some puma sign. Patrick Rusz never actually said he'd show me a puma, but he did offhandedly mention that if there was time after our meeting that maybe I could tag along with him for the afternoon while he poked around looking for tracks.

•••

For weeks after first reading about Rusz in the paper, I couldn't get this man, or the puma, out of my mind. Everywhere I looked, from national magazines to big-city papers, there were all of a sudden stories about eastern pumas inspired by the Michigan goings-on. Rusz's announcement had also caused a minor flap among puma enthusiasts on the Internet, where many believers began calling him a hero for finding the kind of proof no government agency could ignore. For me the stories seemed the perfect little diversion to take the mind off the rubble in New York—those two towers, two fiery planes, and talk of war in Afghanistan—in other words, the real news of the day. So I read everything I could.

Hanging out with this guy would be a kick, I thought. An editor at a magazine I occasionally write for agreed. We settled on a simple assignment, no more than a couple thousand words, a sort of day-in-the-life chasing will-o'-the-wisps in some forgotten corner of the state with a man who, by all accounts, sounded like a crazy cat himself.

So the puma was actually secondary at first. I can't really admit to being a cat person. I've dreamed of bears and wolves and big antlered bucks. I've dreamed of catching salmon on Russian rivers I've never fished and standing eye to eye with snowy white Dall sheep on a treeless mountainside in a part of the Yukon Territory I've only ever visited in books. But I've never been haunted by pumas. Never even seen one in the wild. Never been stalked, at least not that I knew. Never once had a puma come to me in a dream. Pumas were never really part of my mindscape except on the periphery when hunting and hiking in the mountains out west.

Once while chasing ruffed grouse in a green, misty valley in northwestern Montana, a friend who lives in a tiny cabin in the woods up there pointed out the fresh track of a puma stamped in mud along the berm of a mountain road. Curiously unlike in the East, where I found that almost everybody has a puma tale to tell, few of my western friends have ever seen them. Tim is a full-time hunting and fishing guide, which means he spends almost every day of the year either on the water or in the woods, and even he had only ever seen a handful of pumas himself. And most of these were dead ones killed by houndsmen who occasionally barreled through town with a cat sprawled in the open bed of their rickety pickups.

I still vividly recall the sharp ridges and deep valleys of the track. Like the western landscape, it was an intoxicating topography to behold. I reached a finger down to trace the delicate impressions of the teardrop-shaped toes, but I couldn't bring myself to touch it. The track looked so fragile, the lines so sharp. I remembered puzzling over the meaning of the track, as if trying to comprehend the hidden message in a poem. For me, it signified a sort of defiance I've always associated with the mountains—Schueler's old "renegade presence" again—purposely laid down by the maker to harden in the mud and serve as a warning to any who would come: *This is my country. Fuck off.*

Snapping a picture, I wondered aloud how exciting seeing a live puma out there in the true western wilds would be. And for years that's as close as I'd ever come to a wild puma: a photograph of a track and a mention of unrealistic ambition. Through the camera's eye it felt like I was a spectator gazing up at the Great Divide, a snowy summit of a mountain range I thought I'd never really get the chance to climb.

•••

By the time we met I knew the doctor's research was taking on a new direction, specifically south into the northern Lower Peninsula. Rusz had hinted in the papers that he was close to finding evidence of another lost colony of pumas living here, too. All the better for my little story if he happened to do it while I was along. So I called him up, identifying myself as a writer working on an article about the mystery of the Michigan puma.

"Another writer." He snorted. "Why don't you write this down. There ain't no mystery. Not anymore."

I heard the angry shuffling of papers in the background. A long, uncomfortable pause.

"Twenty calls a day, and no one yet has gotten it right."

He told me how he was reconsidering talking to newspaper reporters; reporters were the reason what little hair he had left was gray.

"Yes . . . well, I'm a magazine writer," I stammered, groping for something more to say.

"Oh, there's a difference? Well, here's the story everybody's afraid to print: how the Michigan Department of Natural Resources—an organization supposedly based in science—can get away with ignoring what the scientific evidence clearly suggests."

•••

Michigan puma lore traces back prior to the 1930s, when naturalists and reporters began citing reliable sightings from game wardens, trappers and hunters, naturalists, and backwoods logging men to question whether pumas were truly vanished from the state. In a 1948 scientific paper on the wildlife of the Upper Peninsula's Huron Mountains, R. H. Manville lent credence to several of these sightings and a handful of instances where puma tracks were found.

Throughout the Upper Peninsula, the legend was kept alive during the 1950s and '60s with periodic stories about a "mystery cat" that lurked in the North Country's black forests and swamps. Tales of "blood chilling screams" in the night and the occasional attack on livestock. Another "last" Upper Peninsula puma may have been killed by Elmer Larsen, a trapper from Ford River, in 1968. In an interview with Mike Zuidema, Larsen described the animal as a "lactating female" and a "rack of bones." He recalled taking the carcass of the cat to the nearest Michigan Department of Natural Resources branch office, where conservation officers examined the carcass, told him it was probably an escaped pet, then let the trapper go home with the body. Believing the hide likely worthless, Larsen said he buried the carcass out in the woods under a brush pile.

Nobody really knows when the last puma was supposedly killed in the Lower Peninsula. In his definitive work *Michigan Mammals*, Rollin Baker mentions a report of a puma killed in 1875 at Pleasant Lake in Ingham County and, later, another treed by dogs near Stanton in Montcalm County in 1885.

A recent issue of the *Oscoda County News* featured an article by Alcona County historian Nelson Yoder, who recounted a story from 1940 involving "a hunting party of railroad men from Bay City" who killed a puma in Horton Township that year, a cat estimated at 165 pounds by one witness, Ruth Taylor, who recalled how one of the hunters "posed with the cat's front feet pulled over his shoulders . . . the back part of the animal [dragging] on the ground."

In 1966 an archaeological excavation in Saginaw County near the Flint River was sifting through the dirt of a pre-Columbian Indian grave site and stumbled upon the earliest known record of pumas in the state—a skull—now kept at the Michigan State University Museum. Oddly, pumas proved scarcely worth a mention in the journals left by Michigan's early pioneers. That or the settlers simply talked of "wild cats," reflecting no distinction among bobcats, lynx, and pumas. Many of the old records were undoubtedly destroyed in the great forest fires that swept shore-to-shore over Michigan off and on for a decade after 1871. I read any and everything I could find on the history of pumas in Michigan, but the sparse written records left by the trappers, farmers, and lumbermen who settled here revealed surprisingly little detail about the decline of the cat in the region—an omission I took as suggestive that nobody seemed very sad to see them go.

Old newspapers, on the other hand, reveal an uninterrupted time line of encounters—stories of sightings and livestock attacks chalked up to pumas—that go back as long as the animal has supposedly been extinct in Michigan. I read dozens of tales filled with "blood curdling screams in the night" and tracks, described in one story, "as big as a Guernsey cow's." Historian Nelson Yoder found stories going back to the 1930s, one particularly interesting tale involving a puma track discovered by an Oscoda County farmer one winter after a string of sketchy sightings. After carefully chipping the impression out of the frozen crusty snow, the man kept the track on public display in the icebox at the general store, where customers paid twenty-five cents to see it. Another recollection told of a puma blamed for thirty-five sheep killed during the summer of 1967 on an Alcona County farm belonging to Norma Jean Ryckman.

"The sheep carcasses were lugged up under an apple tree that grows along a ditch in the pasture," said Ryckman, who also claimed she got a glimpse of the reddish brown cat, a color she described as "almost like newly turned oak leaves when they change color in the fall." I found hundreds of these kind of old news clippings. Yet biologists from the MDNR have never wavered in maintaining that wild pumas are extirpated here.

Gone.

In 1966 Francis Opolka, then a conservation officer with the Michigan DNR, was traveling in a car with another officer late one rainy night when they saw a puma cross the road in front of them. From about fifty feet, Opolka and his companion turned a spotlight on the animal, and the two officers watched as it walked slowly away across a plowed field. Returning to the scene the next morning and locating the cat's tracks in the dirt, Opolka made a perfect plaster cast that showed a distinct lead toe and three-lobed heel pad, a textbook impression of a puma track. Opolka later went on to become the deputy director of the MDNR, but never wavered from the story of what he saw.

In 1977 David LaPointe, then assistant park manager of the Porcupine Mountains State Park and a graduate wildlife biologist, wrote of finding cougar tracks in *Michigan Natural Resources Magazine*—an official publication of the MDNR. In 1984, just prior to the federal law protecting the puma from killing and harassment, a deer hunter in the Wilson area of Menominee County wounded a puma that passed by his deer blind on opening day. The cat escaped, leaving blood and bone fragments from a damaged right leg, evidence that was later sent by Mike Zuidema to Colorado State University's College of Veterinary Medicine and Biomedical Sciences. There high-resolution electrophoresis determined a "positive identity to mountain lion."

That same year a deer carcass was discovered in southern Marquette County by amateur puma buff, John Mauer. Mauer, now deceased, sent pictures of the kill to nationally known puma expert Harley Shaw, who, after examining the photos, measured his words: "If I had received the information you have provided from any part of Arizona, I'd immediately say lion kill. All of the characteristics are right and the tooth mark is the right size. The only alternative I can think of for your country would be lynx, and I know nothing about them. Off hand, I'd say you have a lion."

Closer to my home in the Lower Peninsula, a crystal-clear photo of a puma appeared in the September 13, 1997, issue of the *Detroit Free Press*. Dubbed the "Alcona County Cougar," this was believed to be the same animal caught on videotape by another area citizen a couple of months before. Others suspected this was one of many, namely area historian Nelson Yoder, who traced sightings and encounters in the county that went back decades. In his search, Yoder also discovered another perfect photo of a puma taken by a deer hunter from his blind in 1993, less than ten miles from the spot where the *Free Press* photo would be taken four years later. Conservation officers dismissed the Alcona County Cougar as a probable lone, escaped pet that would almost certainly not survive the winter.

But the following summer this particularly resilient survivor was spotted again, this time at close range by conservation officer Larry Robinson while out on patrol. Rounding a bend on a woodsy two-track, Robinson ran headlong into the puma coming loping down the road from the other direction. The cat turned and bolted, leaping into the brush and leaving only a track behind. In an interoffice e-mail to his superiors that Mike Zuidema uncovered years later, Robinson (having been hounded by the press during the spate of sightings the year before) sounded less than thrilled by this once-in-a-lifetime encounter:

"This is a note I absolutely dread writing," the Robinson memo begins, "but I had the terrible misfortune of seeing the Alcona C. cougar. What do I do to get the pictures [of the tracks] and info to our division's files without this getting out to the media?"

That same year, 1998, reporters picked up on a story in the Upper Peninsula that involved a puma photographed by a couple weekending at a bed-and-breakfast near Seul Choix Point, on the edge of the half-million-acre Lake Superior State Forest in Mackinaw and Schoolcraft Counties. But after being flooded with calls from the press for more information, then wildlife chief George Burgoyne pooh-poohed suspicion that the cat was part of a wild population:

> Over my time as Wildlife Chief, I did interviews with reporters, including U.P. reporters, discussions with hunters and other outdoor enthusiasts, staff, etc., in which I emphasized that with all the cougar reports from apparently reliable observers, including department field staff, at least some of them had seen exactly what they reported, a cougar. However, we did not have any evidence of a breeding or

self-sustaining population. . . . Therefore it was most likely that misguided cougar owners were occasionally dumping their unwanted pets . . . likely declawed, these pets probably did not survive long.

End of story as far as Burgoyne was concerned. And with that, the final word on the matter, the issue was couched. The press went quiet and pumas seemed to slip back into hiding until Rusz started stirring things up again in 2001. I found this information and more in a promised package sent to me by Patrick Rusz and, taking him up on his challenge to double-check the historical record myself, spent the next week bleary-eyed in the library poring over old microfiche and out-of-print wildlife reference books.

It was all there, like a circumstantial case for murder so far lacking only one critical piece of evidence—a body. Rusz had spent the last two years documenting almost everything having to do with pumas in Michigan in the hope of convincing biologists that the state was home to a remnant population. I found one book he overlooked, however, a newer text from 1994—four years before Chief Burgoyne's stab at setting the record straight—containing a section about pumas that suggested maybe he needn't have gone to the trouble.

If pumas weren't truly wild and reproducing, as the MDNR insisted now, how was it that they kept reappearing decade after decade long before crazy Detroit drug dealers and dot-com exotic pet sales? I had just made a note to ask that question of a biologist in Lansing when it came time to get some sort of official reckoning.

Turning back to the book *Endangered and Threatened Wildlife of Michigan*, I paged through until finding the section about pumas. This particular text was unique, the only reference book in my towering stack largely funded by the state's Non-Game Wildlife Fund. Compiled by wildlife ecologist David Evers with input and oversight by the MDNR's biologists assigned to Michigan's Natural Heritage Program (the office in charge of managing the state's endangered species), the puma's current status in Michigan was explained as follows:

In recent years, reports of cougars have become increasingly more frequent and believable in Michigan and the upper Great Lakes region. . . . In 1984, confirmation of a Michigan cougar (through a blood sample) was obtained for the first time in Menominee County. There also are encouraging signs that the Michigan cougar is not transient but occurs in a self-sustaining population. . . . Since 1982, sightings of cougars have been reported from most Upper Peninsula counties with breeding evidence reported from Delta, Marquette, Menominee, and Schoolcraft counties. . . . Whether individuals are from a small, remnant population that survived human pressures through the last two centuries, transients from the western Great Lakes region, or privately released (or escaped) western subspecies, the cougar needs to be recognized, protected, and studied in Michigan's Upper Peninsula.

Not only did this flatly contradict the stance taken in Chief Burgonye's memo, this passage didn't jive with anything the DNR was saying now in regard to the status of wild pumas in the UP. Looking back, I would later recognize this as the point where I first got an inkling that the mystery of the puma might be one more of words than what actually lurked out there in the woods.

That passage from Evers's book wasn't exactly a ringing indictment of agency policy, but if true it certainly suggested a shift. Was the DNR being less than forthright about what they knew? Or were they simply so disorganized that one department did not know what the other was saying? I wrote these questions in my notes. Considering the fate of the pumas that may be here, neither left me feeling very hopeful about where all this seemed to be headed.

PROFESSOR PLOP

Scientists don't sit around in their labs trying to establish
generalizations. Instead they engage in mystery-solving
essentially like that of detective work, and it often involves
a creative, imaginative leap.

Burton Guttman

Professor Plop. The Sultan of Squat. This is what I learned snickering
skeptics call Patrick Rusz behind his back. *Rusz* rhythms with *buzz*
and Pat, or Doctor Dung depending on whom you're talking to, is
not a big man. Still, you can tell by the way his shoulders slope, the trapez-
ius muscles coiled around his neck like giant fists, his arms hanging with the
palms facing backward cavemannishly, that somewhere in his fifty-odd years
he used to lift a lot of weights.

The first time we met face-to-face, that morning in December at the L.A.
Café, Rusz came bullying through the door of the diner, stopping for a moment to scan the crowd and wearing what became a familiar scowl. I recognized him from the pictures in the paper, snapshots that I thought made him
look a little like an angry Don Rickles in the face. He didn't look anything
like the mad scientist I expected. Nor did his dress strike me as that of a
woodsman: white tennis shoes, blue jeans, and a sweatshirt advertising Tim-
berland boots or something with a silkscreen image of a mountain scene and
the words GREAT EXPLORER on it.

Tagging along was Rusz's son, Mark, a clean-cut, athletic-looking senior similarly clad in a gray Michigan State University sweatshirt. Mark, too, I soon learned, was a top-notch college wrestler, just like his old man. A physical education major, Mark also carried a minor in biology and was one of Rusz's main field volunteers who, by his father's own admission, had been instrumental in finding some of the Michigan Wildlife Conservancy's best puma evidence to date.[2]

I waved them over to my table and extended a hand. Rusz's paw felt meaty and soft, which is to say I didn't like his handshake. Nor did I like the way he mumbled hello, not meeting my eyes as if he were consumed at that instant by some pressing, very important, profound life-altering question: *Did I run off and leave the coffeepot on?* I chalked this up to Rusz being something of an eccentric. Given that he held the secrets of discovering pumas, he probably did have a lot on his mind. As far as Rusz not seeming all there, I probably would have been disappointed if he wasn't a little aloof.

As the waitress brought fresh coffee and poured, he took a noisy sip and suddenly snapped back.

"I brought you all my best stuff," he said. "The good stuff. Pictures, too."

Mark sat quietly looking around while Rusz busied himself clearing the table of menus, ketchup, and mustard to make room for an armload of manila file folders. He fingered through the papers and pictures, squinting at a few of the images before pursing his lips and moving onto the next, all the time shuffling with the sort of childish intensity that reminded me of a boy about to show me his baseball cards. When finally he seemed to settle on the order of things, he took another big swig of coffee and launched right into his case.

"Deoxyribonucleic acid, or DNA, is the essential hereditary substance consisting of two long chains of chemicals called nucleotides that are wound around each other to form a double helix consisting of pairs of chemical bases joined by weak hydrogen bonds that when heated break into separate strands, each half serving as a template for making a new strand, which forms the basic genetic code that determines every defining trait of the animal."

Rusz told me the line came straight out of a field manual he was working on—*Detecting Cougars in the Great Lakes Region*. As he took a sip of coffee, I couldn't help but mention being struck by the irony that here he was literally writing the book on pumas in Michigan even though he admitted never having seen one in the wild for himself.

"Don't get me wrong," he said, "I'd like to see one. But it's not integral to my research."

Moving right along, Rusz rattled off the dime-novel version of how he, quite unwittingly by the sound of it, all of a sudden found himself involved in this big, nasty puma controversy. To hear him tell it, he was simply doing his job.

After studying fisheries and wildlife at Michigan State University, where he also carried a minor in environmental law, Rusz went on to get a master's, then a doctorate, in wildlife ecology with a thesis titled "Water Bird Responses to an Open Water System." He did time as a college biology professor and a faculty administrator at Grand Valley State. He remembered the seventies and early eighties as time spent bouncing around working as a freelance consultant building and maintaining wetland habitat for private conservation groups in more than a dozen states throughout the country and once overseas on a short stint in Australia where he headed a project looking into wild bird mortality caused by high-tension power lines in an environmental impact study involving a nuclear power plant outside Sydney.

"There are not many places to go with a biology degree," he said. "I mean, you either go and teach, work for some government agency, or go into the private sector."

That seemed like a good smattering of choices to me. How about the DNR? Did he ever consider working for it?

Rusz said that in fact he had only to bow out halfway through the interview process because, he remembered, "It never struck me as a good environment for independent thought."

Rusz finally settled down with a full-time gig with the Michigan Wildlife Conservancy in the mid 1980s. Years of toiling around with various habitat development and restoration projects mostly to benefit benign species of birds, reptiles, amphibians, and fishes (and a few heated controversies with the Department of Natural Resources he would fill me in on later) took what seemed to be an odd and more high-profile turn in 1998 when board members for the Michigan Wildlife Conservancy[3] wanted to reexamine the question of whether or not wild pumas roamed the state. They had listened to many reports of sightings and, according to Rusz, were "dismayed other citizens were being laughed at and called liars by the DNR."

"At first I was intrigued, but skeptical . . . probably like you," he said.

Working as the conservancy's director of wildlife programs under Dennis Fijalkowski—MWC's first and only executive director, whose personal interest in pumas I later found traced back to 1976 and a failed lobbying attempt to have the puma added to Michigan's list of endangered animals—Rusz began the search by compiling a historical summary outlining a century's worth of physical evidence of pumas in the state.

Over the next two years, *The Cougar in Michigan: Sightings and Related Information* grew to more than sixty-four pages and sought to answer the question of whether enough tangible proof existed to warrant the expense of an on-the-ground, conservancy-funded search for wild pumas. Anybody could go to the MWC Web site and download a free copy of *The Cougar in Michigan*. Interested reporters like me got their copy direct, part of what Rusz called "a standard press kit."

"You read the thing. The seeds of discovery are all right there, like a road map," Rusz said, tangling his metaphors.

By pooling the most compelling puma evidence from throughout the state over the last hundred years, the research revealed clusters of recurring puma activity—hot spots—from the same locations in the Upper and Lower Peninsula where Rusz now believed he had found solid proof of survivors.

He heaped credit on Mike Zuidema, the DNR forester from Escanaba whose twenty-year-old file of puma sightings was primarily responsible for leading Rusz's team to the beach at Seul Choix Point. On cue, Mark produced a book of maps from under the breakfast table to give me a visual.

Roughly forty miles west of where the supposed last Michigan puma was killed by trappers in 1906—and according to Rusz the center of hundreds of close-range, day- and nighttime encounters, including the 1997 incident involving that vacationing couple and the fuzzy puma picture that prompted a memo from George Burgoyne—the sandy shore at Seul Choix skirted a massive forest and swamp stretching unbroken for more than twenty-five miles along Lake Michigan. The place straddled the border of Mackinaw and Schoolcraft counties, the heart of the country mentioned as a territory where pumas might be breeding in that passage in David Evers's book.

Rusz tapped a finger on the map. "Downing said that to make a rudimentary detection of pumas, you need a trackable surface of at least twenty miles."

Robert Downing, a U.S. Fish and Wildlife Service biologist and Syracuse University professor emeritus, conducted the only federally sponsored puma inquiry ever in the East. In the late 1970s, several environmental groups had threatened to sue the USDA Forest Service unless it stopped timber harvests in the remote forests of North Carolina and Georgia where pumas had occasionally been seen. The suit prompted a cooperative effort between the USFWS and the Forest Service, led by Downing, who searched five years for tangible evidence over a wide area stretching from Virginia to northern Georgia, primarily along the Blue Ridge Parkway, the region's most popular scenic route.

Although a number of possible scats, territorial scrapes, and deer kills were found, Downing's final report, *The Current Status of the Cougar in the Southern Appalachian*, fell short of providing substantial evidence that a population of pumas actually inhabited the region. Or, he concluded, if they did so the animals were in such small numbers as to be virtually undetectable.

Downing was especially baffled by the overwhelming lack of track evidence—the primary means by which western biologists locate pumas—but acknowledged in his final report that a wide range of unfavorable conditions made finding a good track somewhere between vexing and impossible in the areas he tried to search:

Much of the dirt tracking I have done has been in the piedmont and coastal plain because conditions are rarely suitable in the mountains. Road surfaces are soft enough to register tracks in the mountains only during spring thaws. At night, when cougars usually prowl, these roads usually freeze hard again, preventing further tracks and deforming those already present.

After warm-weather tracking proved futile (Downing noted the presence of too many paved roads and dirt roads that seldom provided a useful tracking medium "due to their hard, rocky composition"), Downing naturally turned to looking for tracks in the snow. But even that yielded nothing:

> Snow was not nearly as good a medium as I had hoped. Snows here often occur only at high elevation and usually are followed by several days of high winds and bitter cold. Deer seem to know this and move to lower elevation where it does not snow often. The majority of deer also do their feeding before and during the snowstorm, not in the fresh snow afterward. It often takes two days or more for deer to become active again, and by then the snow normally has either blown away, melted, or developed a hard crust. Bobcats do a great deal of walking in the fresh snow and I'm told cougars do, too. However, as I attempt to explain why I have not seen cougar tracks, I suggest that this may be true of cougars only where the snow cover is widespread and of long duration. Where it normally occurs only at higher elevation or for short duration, the cougars may wait several days for the snow to melt or the deer to begin moving again.

While Rusz hoped Michigan's coastal beaches might offer a perfect medium to find the tracks that had eluded Downing, more intriguing to him was what the puma's trail might lead to. The shoreline at Seul Choix Point ran parallel to the Lake Superior State Forest, some five hundred thousand acres with very few improved roads and where dense coastal cedar swamps—white cedar offering both cover and food in an otherwise naked and windswept winter landscape—were a draw for white-tailed deer during winter, deer that gathered in large herds, or "yards," that also attracted predators such as wolves, coyotes, bobcats, and, if Rusz's theory held up, maybe pumas.

"The beach up there was both a killing field and a giant litter box," said Rusz, adding that the spring snowmelt, combined with a relentless coastal wind, helped him uncover dozens of promising-looking scats that had been buried and preserved under snow and sand since the preceding winter.

In addition to the first deer kill—which he had no problem telling me was found within ten miles of the truck—Rusz said he and his volunteers plodded over some thirty-three additional miles of beachfront on foot, a trek that netted dozens of tracks, a few territorial scrapes, and at least two other intact deer carcasses that by his estimation had the telltale markings consistent with a puma attack.

"The cougar kills were all found stashed under evergreen branches back along the tree line," Rusz added, further theorizing that the sign—tufts of deer hair, tracks, furrows in the sand that looked to him like drag marks— seemed to indicate that the actual attacks happened right out in the open. Using the rocks, trees, and barrier dune as cover, Rusz believed the pumas were emerging from the deep swamp at night and ambushing deer as they headed from cover down to water to drink.

All this Rusz had gleaned from the sign. He made it seem so dazzlingly elementary. Rusz painted a vivid picture of a puma's pounding rush across the open beach. The paralyzing tackle. A neck-breaking bite. The deer bowled over in blurry tangle of hooves. The pumas, he continued, would then drag the deer back into cover where, out of sight of scavengers and other predators, they could feed. And it was here Rusz discovered the carcasses and what he described as "the next best thing to capturing the puma itself."

...

A practical alternative for the underfunded seeking proof of large predators where conventional thinking assumes they don't exist, fecal analysis and the DNA extracted from it had been one of the methods amateur researchers used for years to try to convince wildlife officials that grizzly bears still inhabited the San Juan Mountains of western Colorado. DNA has been used to confirm the presence of lynx in northern Minnesota and Yellowstone National Park. In Maine and Minnesota, DNA from hair samples has likewise recently been used to verify that bobcats and lynx are actually crossbreeding here, a hybridization phenomenon never before documented by modern science.

Meanwhile, in the realm of amateur eastern puma research, a scat found to contain puma "groom" hairs was discovered in 1994 in the woods near Craftsbury, Vermont, after an eyewitness reported seeing a mother puma traveling in deep snow with three cubs. Three years later, in the mountains surrounding Quabbin Reservoir in Massachusetts, another scat was found by amateurs and tested positive for puma DNA. These finds stirred enthusiasm among puma proponents for a while, the hope being that these cold, coiled turds would somehow inspire more organized and government-funded research. But more than a decade later, these findings are hardly more than curious and controversial footnotes.

Every wildlife agency in America uses the same forensic evidence to prosecute poaching cases every day. So the science Rusz was using was not exactly new; people searching for irrefutable evidence of pumas in the East had just never extensively tried it before.[4]

Rusz went to the papers claiming to have discovered the same stuff collected in New England—bona fide puma droppings—but in a much larger quantity spread out over Mackinaw, Houghton, and Schoolcraft Counties (Seul Choix Point). Such a huge territory, Rusz believed, was suggestive of more than just a single, roving animal. With a couple of decades' worth of hard physical evidence, along with puma sightings from the very same country now producing their scats—and knowing that the life expectancy of a puma is roughly twelve years in the wild—Rusz pushed his multiple-puma theory even further by publicly announcing that the cats in the Upper Penin-sula not only were breeding, but were also the lost survivors of a population that had never been completely wiped out.

•••

Back in the diner, as the waitress cleared our plates, Rusz dropped a file in front of me filled with copies of unanswered letters sent to the same MDNR spokespeople now challenging his theories in the press. Of the many charges leveled against Rusz and MWC, one maintained that they had been unwill-ing to share their findings with state biologists before going public. This naturally led to agency suspicion that MWC's controversial proclamations—something Rusz and Fijalkowski knew full well would put them at odds with the MDNR's long-running response to questions about pumas (that they're all former, escaped, or released captives, or FERCs in puma-speak)—was a blatant self-promotion ploy specifically engineered to publicly blindside and embarrass the department. In other words, Rusz was acting as point man on a campaign to draw serious biologists from the MDNR into a nonsensical and divisive public debate about pumas based on a litany of half-truths, astounding leaps of logic, and outlandish conclusions based on incomplete scientific data.

"We tried for months to work with them on this, but they wanted no part it," Rusz said with a grin, clearly pleased by the direction the conversation was going. "Look here."

With that he produced more papers, copies of letters showing that he had, in fact, tried repeatedly to coordinate with department biologists before and after going public. Rusz had sent copies of *The Cougar in Michigan* along with the results from their DNA scat analysis performed independently and out of state by the Wyoming Game and Fish Laboratory in Laramie, a foren-sic lab that was chosen for its experience dealing with microscopic examina-tion of scat. Other letters he dealt out read like open invitations asking for any uninformed biologists to accompany Rusz into the field to see the track and scat evidence for themselves and scrutinize how he collected it.

When I would later be in a position to ask MDNR spokesmen about these letters, I was told they were viewed by the department as thinly veiled threats. In other words, *Go along with what we're saying about pumas or we'll take this debate public.* But I didn't see that in the language of the letters. Where I had seen it was is the running insinuation alluded to by department biologists and, especially, some commentators in the outdoor "hook-and-bullet" press where Rusz and MWC were characterized as a bunch of self-serving, loud-mouthed environmentalists who were simply trying to browbeat and bamboozle the department into sweeping government action that would ultimately infringe upon the rights of sportsmen. This paranoid picture didn't at all mesh with what action Rusz thought his findings warranted.

So I asked him, "What do you want out of all this?"

Rusz had another unanswered letter spelling that out, too. In addition to a formal acknowledgment that Michigan was home to a wild population of pumas, the document asked for "a modest research effort by the state." Asked to elaborate what that meant exactly, Rusz explained that he would like to step aside and see state biologists pick up searching for pumas where MWC had left off.

"We did our initial field study with a grant of only three thousand dollars," he said. "With the state's resources, they could cover twice as much ground for—and I'm guessing here—as little as five thousand."

That's it?

"That's it," Rusz said, leaning back in his chair and, with a reassuring glaze from Mark, added that this was a conservative budget for such a high-profile predator every bit important to what he called "Michigan's natural heritage" as the wolf, a predator the MDNR has dumped millions into studying over the years.

Just like the wolf, Rusz reasoned that state recognition that wild pumas roamed Michigan would serve to boost public education and awareness, thus paving the way for the cat's ultimate recovery and survival.

But wasn't the puma—a federally endangered mammal in the East, which includes Michigan—already recognized and protected?

Rusz let the question linger a beat before answering that he believed the puma deserved *better* protection than was already on the books. While Michigan's practice of paying bounties for dead pumas stopped up in 1967, it wasn't until 1987 that the cat was unceremoniously added to the state's list of protected species. Furthermore, Rusz contended that, as in every other state in the East, our DNR's current position on pumas was so vague that common citizens didn't even know the animals were real, let alone protected.

With that came another flurry of paperwork. Rusz pointed to the one sentence of fine print buried in a rules-and-regulations booklet issued to licensed hunters every year warning them that—along with ospreys and eagles and albino deer—it's illegal to kill a puma in Michigan. Rusz insisted this amounted to no real protection at all.

"Why are cougars even on the state's endangered species list if the mantra of the past fifty years is that they don't exist?"

He rolled right from this into another theory, one that for him explained perfectly why pumas were so rare. In a word: Poachers. Pumas were being killed illegally in Michigan, and Rusz claimed he was close to proving that, too.

Really? Well, that was certainly a twist.

"This combined with inbreeding are probably two of the main contributing factors keeping the cougar population from exploding here," he said.

Since in the last hundred years there has never been one concrete example of an actual dead body turning up in Michigan, I wanted to find out more about what proof he had that pumas were being killed indiscriminately here.

But there was something I was beginning to notice about Rusz. His fondness for theorizing and propensity for unscientific digression was matched by what can only be described as a politician's knack for changing the subject. That or he would answer a question he wished he'd been asked. Yet I noted a deep conviction, a forceful edge to his words. He could quote from scientific texts from memory. He made the unbelievable seem unremarkable.

I'll admit being dazzled by some of his theories at first. Imagine! Pumas out there. Deep down, I really wanted to believe. But at this point I was still serving purely in the capacity of a curious but cautious skeptic, a reporter pretending to myself that I was above the story looking in. Later I would find myself unwittingly a part of the hunt, a piece of my heart clearly vested in the chase, and wanting real answers I found Rusz a lot like the puma itself . . . a tiger nearly impossible to catch by the tail. He was quite a talker. But I always had the impression that he really believed everything that came out of his mouth. A frustrating interview at times, but in hindsight sometimes it was really amazing to hear his mind work. Ask a direct question, a hard question, and Rusz could weave an explanatory tapestry riddled with so many qualifiers and trapdoor caveats that my note-taking hand would seize up trying to get it all down, only to later look back over the conversation and realize he hadn't explained a damn thing. Sometimes he'd drone on so long I'd even forget what the hell the original question was.

But I'm getting ahead of myself. I really wanted to find out more about those hayseed hicks and country bumpkins out there whacking pumas. But Rusz wanted to talk about the MDNR. The biologists down there in Lansing are the animals that really seemed to baffle him.

As troubling to him that pumas were being killed was that the agency had a long-standing and built-in bias that every reliable piece of evidence related to pumas that came into department hands was dismissed as coming from once-captive animals. Such prejudice had long stymied serious inquiry by halting the kind of valuable physical evidence Rusz had collected from ever advancing up the chain of command.

Backing up the accusation in a torrent of paperwork and photographs—other diners in the café were beginning to cast sideways glances at us—Rusz pointed out that you need look no further than how the MDNR had handled every ounce of evidence received on pumas to date to see that current protocol had to change.

A picture of the plaster cast Frank Opolka made in 1966. Rusz found the original cast tucked away in the attic of a wildlife biologist, who had taken the hunk of plaster for a keepsake upon retirement.

"One of the most valuable pieces of evidence that has ever come into the hands of the DNR," said Rusz, "and some biologist was using it as a paperweight."

Rusz flopped down the 1997 *Detroit Free Press* photo of the Alcona County Cougar.

"Look at that." Disgusted.

A stellar image of a puma lying in the ferns. No doubt. But before I could ask more, he dealt a series of images on the table taken from a video shot the winter before by a woman in nearby Mesick, a forty-odd mile drive from the diner where we sat.

"Some DNR biologists told her this was a house cat."

Unlike the newspaper photo, these required a little interpretation. The blown-up pictures, while definitely depicting a deer-colored feline sulking through the woods in deep snow, were fuzzy and out of focus.

"That's the classic silhouette of a cougar." I had to take his word for it. Rusz described the long, cylindrical tail and blocky body topped off by a proportionately smallish-looking head. As he marveled at the picture I couldn't help thinking of the Patterson film, the grainy image of that well-endowed female Bigfoot mugging for the camera over her shoulder as she casually strolled away. But I kept this to myself.

In one frame, the cat passed behind a large tree with a broken limb midway up the trunk.

"I ground-truthed this one." *Ground-truthing* was Rusz-speak for going to the actual site where the video was taken. There he recounted a tale of interviewing the woman himself. He then located the same tree with the broken limb and found that it reached almost to his waist. Taking on-site measurements of the tree's diameter and height, Rusz alleged that the cat in the photo was around thirty inches at the shoulder and almost six feet from nose to tail.

"That ain't no barnyard kitty."

My pen was having a hard time keeping up when Rusz then launched into another puma mystery from June 2000, when a Tower City man, Dale Willey, had a full-grown Belgian draft horse attacked after he left the animal out in the pasture overnight.

More photos. One a picture of the mare with what appeared to be scabby claw marks on her back. Willey told Rusz that he had seen a puma sulking along the edge of the pasture only a couple of weeks before the attack. Naturally, he suspected this animal was the culprit.

There was also the matter of a missing foal the mare had earlier given premature birth to. I later verified Rusz's rendition of events with Dale Willey, who told me that the foal was stillborn yet turned up missing the next morning when he went out to bury it. He found the partially eaten body a couple of days later in the brush outside the pasture fence. Rusz theorized that the puma had come, lured by the smell of fresh meat, scooped up the carcass, and jumped the wire to dine in the bushes.

Two weeks after finding the mangled foal, after conservation officers without finding one shred of conclusive evidence declared the killing and the attack on the mare as respectively the work of either a black bear or an accident with a barbed-wire fence, Willey, who described himself to me as an experienced houndsman, located a feline track four and a half inches wide in the dirt along the pasture fence near where he had found the partially eaten foal. He telephoned Rusz, who arrived the next day, photographed the track, made a plaster cast, and with the help of New Mexico–based puma expert Harley Shaw concluded that the track in the photo had indeed come from a puma.

Rusz ended the Willey saga with a copy of the note from Shaw saying that the impression in the photo was "about as big a [lion] track as you'll ever see."

There was also the matter of the MDNR's own Web site—where citizens could report encounters with bear, moose, elk, bobcat, lynx, and other rare species of Michigan wildlife for the purpose of investigation and study—which had no place for citizens to report pumas. (The department would quietly add the puma a couple of months later, in January 2002.)

"Am I the only one who finds it troubling that people who chose wildlife as a career appeared less than thrilled at the prospect of this beautiful, powerful predator surviving in Michigan's forests? Wouldn't their own curiosity, not to mention the potential danger to citizens and livestock, lead these people to act?"

Good questions. I jotted them down.

I then asked Rusz if his research plan included running a puma up a tree and radio-collaring the animal for study.

Rusz's eyes flashed. "I'm beginning to think a more interesting study would be to put a radio collar on one of our DNR biologists just to see how far they travel away from their desk in a year."

The response was meant to sound spontaneous, but a gleeful smirk suggested the quip was prepared. Contrary to virtually every other biologist in the history of puma research, Rusz told me he believed radio-collaring was a waste of time. He called this "old science," a stunt used by biologists to get their pictures on the front page of newspapers, which helped them get more funding for their research.

Again, the irony of his words seemed lost on him.

But surely, I asked, wouldn't it help to silence the skeptics once and for all?

"There are some people who regardless of the evidence are never going to believe," he said. "Unfortunately, we're finding out some of those people are in charge of managing our wildlife resources."

And that's how it was talking to Rusz; all at once the whole controversy seemed to amuse and infuriate him. While he was careful never to mention the words *cover-up* or *conspiracy*, when Rusz said, "These aren't ghost cats, they leave sign," the obvious indication was that a handful of desk-bound policy makers in Lansing were just too lazy to get out and look. While in one breath he loudly decried the current situation as untenable, in the next his voice would soften as he lamented how slowly the wheels of government often seemed to turn.

"Never in the history of the DNR has anybody ever admitted they were wrong. Here we're talking about changing what the department has held up as policy for over fifty years. That's going to take some time.

"The bottom line here is that no one taking an honest look at all the physical and scientific evidence I've compiled could conclude anything other than the fact that we have wild cougars living here, what I believe is what remains of a population that was never completely wiped out."

With that he took a breath and downed the dregs of his coffee. I could see him chewing on another thought, the words percolating behind his stern-looking baby blues.

"For me, this whole cougar issue epitomizes everything that's wrong with wildlife management today, and it's about time the public sees it. We have a handful of biologists-turned-administrators here who are clearly putting politics and their careers ahead of curiosity and common sense."

Rusz paused, watching my scribbling pen.

"Sometimes I think this is bigger than the cougar . . . Sometimes I think this whole eastern cougar controversy might be the thing that exposes the bureaucracy and politics that's destroying real wildlife management."

Rusz took a sidelong glance at Mark, who sat smearing a crusty corner of toast through the egg yolk pooling on his plate.

"You wanted to know what the real mystery of the Michigan cougar is. Well, Mark here summed it up the first day of our field study up there at Seul Choix," Rusz said. "Didn't ya? We were standing over that first cougar kill, remember?"

Mark nodded dutifully and smiled.

"The mystery," Rusz said, "is why it's taken a hundred years for somebody to get out there and look."

•••

After breakfast we hopped in Rusz's black-and-gray Chevy and barreled north out of town. Dirty clothes and boxes of manila folders stuffed with papers were strewn about the inside of Rusz's pickup. An empty Coke can rolled out onto the pavement when I opened the passenger door.

It had taken longer to hollow out a space for Mark behind the front seat than to drive the couple-odd miles to speak with Shelia Grogan, a local attorney's wife and maternity nurse, who was one of the twenty or so callers Rusz said he heard from daily claiming a run-in with the elusive puma.

The Grogans lived down one of a hundred little dead-end roads cutting through a cookie-cutter development of bilevel homes, each little lot a perfect green square, hacked out of a forest of tall red pines planted in neat rows. The truck crawled down the shiny new blacktop, past driveways cluttered with Volvos, tricycles, and skateboards. Every home had a basketball hoop. Rusz's eyes darted between mailbox numbers and an address scrawled on a scrap of paper he studied over the steering wheel. I didn't remember any of these homes being here the year before, and instead of looking for the right house I found myself staring utterly agog and trying to decide what was more gloomy: the sameness of it all or how suddenly these suburban dreamscapes manage to crop up these days.

"I was sitting on the deck talking on the phone to a friend," Shelia Grogan said, "when I heard a stick snap in the woods along the edge of the backyard."

Rusz nodded gravely as Grogan walked us around the side of the house.

"It was dark," she explained. "I went back inside for the flashlight thinking it was either a deer or I was going to scare the crap out of someone."

But when Grogan hit the light, shining it out on the lawn, "there was this mountain lion a couple of feet away crouched at the base of that tree." Grogan said she was shocked, but oddly unafraid, at the sight of the animal.

"It just sat there watching me," she said. "It seemed sort of curious." Grogan remembered the face-off lasting for several seconds, maybe a minute, before she came to her senses and went back inside for the video camera.

"It was bigger than the neighbor's golden retriever," Grogan said, leveling her hand waist-high on the tree where the creature sat to indicate the height of its head. "It was brown and when it got up, it kind of sauntered off into the woods and that's when I saw the tail."

Grogan described the tail as long, cupping her hands in a saucer-sized circle to indicate how thick, and having "dark rings" around it. On account of the darkness, the video camera didn't pick up anything.

"Friends I told said I probably saw a bobcat or a raccoon." The DNR officer who returned Grogan's call assured her that there were no pumas in Michigan.

"People thought I was insane," she said. To satisfy her own curiosity, Grogan went to the Traverse City Zoo, where she saw live lynx and bobcats.

"They were all too small," she said. And then she came to the puma's cage. Except for the dark rings missing around the tail, there was no doubt in her mind.

"It was mountain lion. No doubt," she said. "I eventually mentioned it at our neighborhood homeowners' meeting and found out four other people had seen the animal, too."

"Mind if we look around," Rusz said. He had been listening quietly, taking notes. Mark had already gone off the way of Grogan's puma, off into the tree line looking for sign. Rusz and I followed, leaving Grogan on the deck. Stepping into the woods, I looked up and saw gray clouds forming over the tall December pines. I heard chickadees calling. A titmouse. A nuthatch made a dipsy flight away down the hillside toward a tiny cedar swamp.

Shelia Grogan had told her story plainly, sounding believable enough, but finally out of earshot I mentioned to Rusz that her encounter seemed like a little bit of nothing to me.

"You'd make a good DNR biologist," said Rusz with a frown. "One sighting doesn't mean that much even if it's the real deal. I focus on patterns and pools of evidence."

In this instance, Rusz deemed Grogan's story credible enough to record, but added that if a puma had passed through here the trail was undoubtedly cold.

"So what do we do now," I asked.

Rusz ignored the question and stood scanning the bottom where we could make out flashes of Mark, his off-white sweatshirt bobbing in through the underbrush toward us.

"Kid's an animal," he said, beaming. "If there's a cougar around here that boy'll find it."

Rusz told me that Mark had wanted to follow in his footsteps and become a biologist until all this controversy over pumas started.

"He doesn't understand any of it," Rusz said, adding that in a couple of months Mark was going to graduate and maybe become a gym teacher instead.

We continued along the top of the ridge following an old deer trail, evident by fresh tracks and the piles of glistening round pellets. Somewhere off in the distance a chainsaw droned. I smelled wood smoke in the air.

"So what do we do now," I asked again, sidling up beside Rusz, who suddenly stopped short, hands in his pockets, contemplating the toes of his tennis shoes for a moment before looking off into the middle distance with a eureka-like stare.

"I don't know about you but I got to get rid of some coffee." And with that he lumbered off fumbling with his zipper, looking for a suitable tree.

•••

For the rest of the afternoon we drove back roads, then off-road, bouncing along leafy two-tracks through public forestland. Rusz had pinpointed on the map an old railroad grade behind the Grogan property. A good place to search, but we never did find a way to it. Mark crawled out onto the hood and sat as the truck ground along, scanning for any suspicious droppings or animal tracks the way you might peer for coins glistening in the deep end of a swimming pool.

More than a third of Michigan is designated public, an estimated 3.2 million acres of forestland used for logging, mining oil and natural gas, and outdoor recreation that mainly revolves around hunting and fishing. If access by vehicle is any indication as to a country's degree of wildness, northern Michigan is no more wild than any other place in the East. With a little ambition and four-wheel drive, there's not a square acre in all this territory that on a sunny day cannot be accessed by either footpath or two-track road. Winter is something different.

On any other Sunday in December, the leafy two-tracks we drove would be all be impassable on account of thigh-deep snow, the biggest tracts of northern forests all but unreachable without snowmobile, snowshoes, or cross-country skis. The country on one hand seemed as split, bulldozed, and divided as any other, yet out here, despite the roads, there was still a quality of bigness to it. Here we were a couple miles from my house, a place I lived for half of my time in northern Michigan, touring through woods I'd never seen. And that made me wonder how much more is out there. It made me wonder how much of the woods others have seen, especially up here when a third of the year—one third of a life—is for most spent hunkered down by the woodstove, working, watching CNN, or waiting for the snows to pass. Another third we spend in darkness, asleep.

How much time is left then for mystery? How many of us are really out there looking for it?

Obvious by tire ruts and boot tracks on the road, a stampede of deer hunters had taken full advantage of the freakish winter warmth.

We found plenty of proof that the cliché of the hunter as a slob is sadly not often far off the mark. Vienna sausage tins. Orange corn chip bags. Empty cigarette packs. My heart sank even deeper when the first scat we found turned out to be human, a voluminous pile flagged by a flapping banner of Charmin snagged in the low branches of a juneberry bush.

And then we found the carcasses, what looked like a local dumping spot for the butchered remains of deer killed over the previous weeks. Hollow rib cages with leg bones attached. A chalky white scapula. A deer head, or rather most of one. The top of the skull was missing, where probably the antlers were. The rest of the bones were stripped of meat and had obviously been driven out here after butchering to be discarded along with a great many old tires, stained mattresses, and a handful of kicked-in televisions we also found littering the ditches.

Mark called us over to look at a dead coyote he'd found in a clearing. The animal lay stiff, its clean white teeth showing in a rictus smile, down in the middle of a grassy bowl of matted wheat-colored grass and rusty bracken fern. Standing over the corpse with his head down as if he were contemplating marking the territory with another leak, Rusz instead bent down and took up a stick, parting the sooty gray fur over the left shoulder where a bloody scab of matted fur marked the killing shot.

"Probably came from over there," he pronounced.

We saw the deer blind on the edge of the clearing a short distance away. A curtain of camouflage netting flapped loosely over a skeleton of rotting branches where we found the ground littered with Diet Coke cans smashed flat like huge silver coins and an overturned five-gallon bucket, a perfect stool for a hearty hunter to rest his fat ass.

We spent the next hour walking, inspecting every pile of bones, around which we found animal tracks laid down mostly by coyotes, the wiser ones that knew enough to stay hidden in the swamps and not come out to scavenge until night. The sign left in the dirt told that ravens had been working the bones, too.

When finally Rusz said he had seen enough of this place, it was not soon enough for me. I hadn't heard so much as a chickadee call. And the silent air, still and foreboding, smelled of rotting flesh, not of the clean coming rain anymore.

Next we drove west to a spot known locally as the Dead Stream Swamp. Back at the diner Rusz had pointed vaguely to the place on his topographical map, telling me of sightings he'd received over the past year that suggested it was a hot spot for puma activity.

While it was less than a half-hour drive away, I admitted knowing very little of the Dead Stream beyond the fact that people really didn't go there. Not into the swamp, anyway. I had canoed before back into the swamp through a long stagnant channel, what a fisherman might call "alligator water," that oozed out of the swamp and into the Platte, and found the brush so dense on the bank—the ground under it floating and spongy—that it was impossible to find a safe place to get out. The people who knew it best were my bobcat and coyote hunting friends, who often prowled the perimeter during the winter season with their hounds searching for fresh tracks. The swamp itself was a huge nasty snarl of roadless cedar swamp some two thousand acres square, just outside the nearby town of Honor, flanked to the south by Platte River and to the west by a series of lakes and the Sleeping Bear Dunes National Lakeshore.

Honor has its own gas station, a strip small, and a bar—the Sleeping Bear Lounge. The Platte River Inn and Country Store, which advertises ELEGANT JUNK, hand-painted in bold white letters on a red cinder-block wall. Bud's Auto Body Shop. Bud's Canoe Rental. Aside from a stooped-over old man pushing a walker, there was nobody on the sidewalk that day. No other cars on the narrow main street. We stopped at the Shell station to gas up and I ran into two fishermen at the counter buying jerky and beer. Both men had bellies like beachballs and one had the oddest-looking face I'd ever seen, flat like clay flattened with a swift whack of a cast-iron frying pan. Anyway, they had come all the way from Georgia after reading about the Platte in a popular fishing magazine.

"The river's full of 'em," Flat-face drawled. "But they ain't bitin' fer shit."

Hanging it up for the day, he then asked for directions to the best bar in Traverse City for catching the afternoon football game.

Steering back out onto the deserted main street, we drove past Bud's garage and a man in greasy coveralls heaving a black tire onto a pile of scrap metal, greasy old engine parts, and assorted automotive junk. I wondered idly if it was Bud.

Taking a left at Indian Hill Road, the Chevy squealed to a stop at the little bridge spanning the Platte. Every spring and early winter the Platte fills with lake-run brown trout and steelhead—basically huge rainbow trout— that surge upstream out of Lake Michigan to spawn. And the bridge where we stood was always a good place to see them. We parked the truck and right away saw fish below where the river gushed through a culvert pipe. Steelhead longer than my hand and forearm. Two finned in the slack water big and silver-sided, another one alongside a submerged log, and a fourth midstream hugging tight in the swirl behind a bowling-ball-sized stone.

"Look at that," Mark said. He was bent over at the waist, over the rail, transfixed along with the rest of us by the close proximity of enormous fish.

Moments later we were again driving along the southern edge of the Dead Stream Swamp, then turning around angled north on Indian Hill Road. The swamp side of the road was flanked periodically by dilapidated old trailers and ranch-style houses. American flags and signs nailed to trees warned BEWARE OF DOG, the dirty mutts on chains and pacing behind chicken wire fences.

We were looking for some kind of access road. But if there wasn't one of those Hatfield and McCoy style houses, then cedar trees, jackpines, clumps of alder whips, and red-diamond willows formed an impenetrable wall growing so tight against the road there was barely enough room to pull off. Driving north away from the river bottom, where the Dead Stream did open up into a mix of hardwoods and conifers, the land along the edge of the swamp was private and posted NO TRESPASSING.

We took an hour or so just driving the perimeter, Rusz constantly slowing the truck and handing me the map to confirm our position. He obviously knew more about the area than he'd initially let on. The map he handed me showed notations and tiny penciled-in dots to indicate what he told me were sightings called in to him over the last year.

Rusz had wanted to get out here and look for sign, but after driving in circles for going on an hour with no place to pull over we decided to break our own path. Mark bushwhacked off in one direction while Rusz and I found a game trail heading off in the other. Dense cedar overhead made it like walking through a portal, muffling the noise of a semi truck rumbling by, downshifting to make a turn.

"They tend to take the path of least resistance," he said, staring at the ground under his tennis shoes, explaining that pumas like roads. "They're lazy, like people. When hunting, they like it up high where they can get a good look around."

On either side of the trail, fallen cedars lay helter-skelter. It was cool and smelled of the blackness of earth. The farther we walked, the more deer and coyote prints we found, tracks so familiar to me that my eye considered the impressions hardly worth more than an obligatory glance.

Rusz had slipped into a curious silence. His pace slowed to a pensive crawl. He stopped to scrutinize every track that I had passed over, dramatically putting his finger down to touch some of the impressions.

"If there's one thing I've learned, it's that you never know when you're going to stumble into something," he muttered.

Somewhere out of sight a red squirrel chattered in alarm. I found where a tiny buck had polished his antlers on an alder whip. Wandering ahead of Rusz on the trail, I was startled by a big gray grouse that thundered up from the brush like a land mine, a steely blur banking hard across the trail. A pair of deer went out next, crashing away through the undergrowth, white tails flagging.

"Looks like a couple made it." Rusz was all of a sudden behind me, his eyes still fixed on the ground.

Rusz and I found two small piles of scat, each matted with deer hair and decidedly doggy. Coyote. Then farther down the road, we came upon a "smoker," as Rusz called the fresh ones, which looked liked something a cat might leave in a litter box. The dirt and leaves were clawed up in a pile around it. Bobcat.

"Yeah," he said, poking the turd with a stick. A puma's shit, he explained, was much bigger around, longer, and looked like Hershey's Kisses, or Tootsie Rolls, stacked end-to-end. I turned my gaze toward the woods, the way the deer had gone, and when I looked back Rusz was gone, or rather dropped down on all fours, like a Muslim facing Mecca, pressing his nose down close over the pile.

"What the—?"

"Oh yeah," he said after an audible sniff, "that's bobcat. It smells just like a cat. Want a whiff?"

I wrinkled my nose, shaking my head with an uncomfortable smile. Later I would read about scat carrying bacteria and airborne parasites, so I could explain my reservation as simple caution. The truth is, I simply wasn't ready to start sniffing shit.

"Aw, c'mon," he said. "Don't be a candy ass."

"Well, since you put it like that."

I knelt down next to him, screwed down my courage, and took in the full bouquet. Rusz was right. Smelled like a litter box. Rusz rolled his eyes but, satisfied, took up the turd in a Baggie, marking the location and date in his notebook.

A cold drizzle began to fall as we worked our way back along the trail toward the truck where Mark was waiting with two more bags of bobcat scat on the hood. The bobcat scat, Rusz explained, was for comparative DNA analysis—to further genetically rule out bobcat—as some critics were still insisting that the scats he was picking up and calling puma had actually come from some other feline. Rusz carried the samples back to the tailgate of the pickup where he opened a cooler, peered inside, then looked up at me asking matter-of-factly: "You wanna see what cougar scat looks like?"

Okay. Well, yeah. Sure.

The cooler was loaded with all manner of feces, bagged and labeled like evidence from a crime scene. Coyote. Bobcat. Wolf droppings from up in the UP. All bound for the Wyoming laboratory. Rusz pulled a sample seemingly at random, peeling the bag open like a drug dealer inspecting his stash. I could smell the pungency from where I stood, the musk heavy in the misty atmosphere. The bag was marked ROSCOMMON, a Lower Peninsula county not more than a hour east of where we stood. I asked him about it—"How'd you come across that one?"

He pretended not to hear. Rusz's blue eyes were transfixed, adrift, as his fingers manipulated the feces through the smeared and cloudy skin of the bag. Pinching the seal closed, he handed it over with a satisfied smile. "We'll know more when that puppy comes back from the lab."

The bag had a sodden heft, and the contents looked exactly the way Rusz said puma shit should . . . exactly the sort of leaving I would discover less than a mile from here in a few days.

Segmented. Black. Striped with hair, and dotted with off-white flecks of bone. It looked like crap all right. Maybe I was just tired, but I actually thought I'd be more thrilled to see the shit that was cracking the case. Or maybe the cynic in me was taking hold. Why was this man driving around with an Igloo full of doo-doo in his car? Rusz was a little quirky—watching him schnozzle cat crap confirmed it—but this seemed downright weird and certainly went to cast a pall of doubt over any joy I might have had finding the same sort of sign in the coming days. I handed the baggie back after a speedy appraisal and Rusz snatched it back with a sour face, seemingly perturbed, as if I had failed to display the proper level of enthusiasm. Stealing one last look for himself, he appeared for an instant lost in the possibilities. Then he snapped back and without another word dropped the mess into the cooler and slammed the lid shut.

A COMFORTABLE PLACE TO LIE DOWN

He who knows his own half acre knows the universe.

Patrick Kavanagh

The snow finally came in late December, just in time for Christmas. It piled up in the front yard—big wafting flakes like milky butterflies whirling on blasts of cold Arctic air—and collected up in the boughs of white pines, which bowed under the weight, the branches ever-so-gently arching to the ground. Picture-book clean. It was still snowing in the morning when Nancy, my wife, came smiling into the bedroom holding her belly with the most unexpected news. As we lay there holding one another, the wind outside ticked sleeting gusts against the house. My mind was in two places: one part wondering where a puma in this country might be holed up weathering the storm and the other in grimmer misgivings brought on by impending fatherhood.

I'm embarrassed to admit it but on both counts my old instincts told me to bolt. Nancy and I had talked about children. I wanted them someday, too. Now it was right there and I was thinking about ghosts. Torn. What did I know about being a good father? And why all of a sudden were pumas so damn important?

•••

After my meeting with Rusz, after following his little treasure map to what I fully expected the lab was going to tell him was puma scat, my interest in the case took on a significant and more personal turn. As I felt myself getting sucked in by the political intrigue and the very real possibility that somewhere out there pumas might actually be surviving, I started devouring any and everything having to do with the beast. I suddenly had to know more. For an almost constant flow of unfiltered eastern puma banter and puma related news, I started lurking on a handful of message boards dedicated to discussions about eastern pumas. More than educational, these places were also so entertaining that I soon found myself logging on with a frequency that bordered on the obsessed.

I began to recognize the names of a handful of familiar posters from all across the East: a financial analyst and a philosophy professor, a postman and a policeman, a handful of retired biologists, and occasionally a game warden or two. Some took time from their lunch hour to offer comments on all manner of topics related to pumas. Some posted with a frequency that made you wonder if they had any job at all.

There were admitted laymen from the South and pretentious self-styled puma experts from up in New England. Such a weird dichotomy of fanatics and cynics, people both hopeful and hopeless. I noted that the mystery of whether or not pumas actually lived in the East in some cases seemed to piss off as many as it inspired. And nothing seemed to fire more contentious debate better than mentioning the Michigan case.

Rusz was champion for the puma, they said.

No, no, Rusz was a fraud.

On a now defunct message board one anonymous poster accused MWC of being part of a vast conspiracy hatched by environmentalists who were systematically releasing pumas into the wild in the hope of repopulating the East. Other allegations warned that MWC was a bunch of eco-whining, anti-hunting troublemakers whose real agenda was to use the puma like the spotted owl to invoke the federal Endangered Species Act to block land access and curtail hunting—a five-hundred-plus-million-dollar-a-year industry in Michigan. I heard these criticisms right from the get-go when news of Rusz's work first broke. I even asked him about it.

"I am a hunter. Shot my first game before I was even twelve." Rusz had headed off this charge over breakfast, calling such rumors hysterical, desperate, and counterproductive: at best an unfortunate by-product of agency closed-mindedness, at worst a transparent bureaucratic ploy to impugn his credibility and avoid the issue. While he could never prove it, Rusz suspected that the DNR was behind the rumors. In other words, bureaucrats who can't argue the issues always try to discredit the source.

Bring him back around to the original question, Rusz said you need only look at the wolf to see that would never happen.

Wolves, he pointed out—not to mention the dozens of other birds, mammals, reptiles, and fish on the state's list of threatened and endangered animals—have been running wild in Michigan for decades, and it has never resulted in land being designated permanently off-limits to the public, let alone the state's one million licensed hunters.

And what about the pictures, the tracks, the DNA?

One supporter from Ohio who obviously believed everything he'd read in the papers about Rusz's remnant puma theory suggested that never before had "eastern conventional agency-think" been more fiercely challenged than up in Michigan.

He was talking, of course, about the pet theory. A quote from MDNR press secretary Brad Wurfel pretty much summed it up: "While we've never denied that there may be some individual cougars roaming the state's wild and perhaps not-so-wild areas, these are likely escaped or illegally released pets. We've never had any physical proof of a viable, resident cougar population."

Many longtime posters—believers from Rhode Island to Arkansas, plenty of whom could relate, having had run-ins with pumas summarily dismissed when they reported the sightings—had heard this same rationale parroted from the mouths of their own state biologists.

So were there wild pumas out there or not? When the question seemed so elementary, this suggested a paradox only a bureaucrat could understand, a convoluted rationale smacking of irksome governmental doublespeak and a perfect excuse for doing nothing. It was, as one disgruntled believer called it, "a comfortable place to lie down."

There were a handful of regular posters on these Internet message boards who actually seemed to enjoy the Gordian-knot quality of eastern puma debate. Real biologists, they took pleasure in reminding all the simpletons, were concerned with populations of animals, not the occasional individual caught on film or splattered on the road.

They certainly had a point. Even so, more than the folks who struck me as irrational in their moony-eyed belief, the ones for whom even a sketchy thirdhand sighting was something to log on and tell those in their cyber support group about, it was this other group—the irascible ones—who especially intrigued me. They were almost *too* cynical; as if somewhere along the line, tortured by false hope, these people had slipped from a healthy skepticism about pumas into downright negativity. I felt myself slipping into that mode from time to time, and it always bothered me. But it was easy to do, especially if you recognized what I saw as a shared longing of the soul with some of the nitwits who frequented these cyber sounding-boards. When you were there, you were one of them, even the arrogant, pretentious ones who tried to act like they were above it all.

After the initial shine wore off, it was mostly just the same old people offering opinions of others' opinions. Occasionally somebody new would stumble in with a sighting and get swatted down. And when things got slow, there was always the Michigan case to kick around. There was an angry edge in the way the cynics ranted. It was almost as if they were trying not to believe. It was as if the puma, the nature of the beast that at one point made the animal so alluring, had damaged them in some way simply because it refused to give in and be found. And it wasn't just the Michigan case. The way they almost seemed to take pleasure in squashing as meaningless the validity of every roadkill, every confirmed photograph and track . . . It really made me wonder why they even wasted their time in a place devoted to learning more about the eastern puma mystery.

All in all I got the impression that more than really getting out there and acting to solve the riddle of pumas in the East, there were a lot of people more interested in fecklessly talking on and on about it.

I've never been much of a talker.

•••

Thirty-one years old, but in many ways I'm still that little kid hiding out hermitlike in a swamp.

The doctors said my father's cancer, a brain tumor, was a fluke. This was a couple of years after the divorce. One day my mother, solemn and misty-eyed, unexpectedly picked me up at school and drove my younger brother and me to a place that was not our home. A couple of years later my dad was dead. After that, I used to get headaches and walk around thinking it was only a matter of time until I, too, would start acting goofy: forgetting the names of familiar flowers, running into walls, falling down.

If all that weren't enough, at my new school I used to get in fights all the time because of a funny last name and bit of a stutter. Bobby Big Butts, they used to call me. Or sometimes just B-b-baaAAH-by, getting stuck in the middle of the word like I always did. Mine was not a religious upbringing, not by any stretch, but I remember lying in bed at nights thinking that some-body up there must really, really not like me.

After my father's funeral, everything he owned sold at auction: our old house in the country with the vegetable garden; the red barn my father built to house the chickens and the hogs; the little fenced-in pasture where I remember we always kept a cow or two. Even my father's collection of deer antlers.

The property was just shy of an acre, but surrounded by cornfields on every side as far as I could see. I used to sit up in the neighbor's apple tree to get the best view out over the corn, down toward the woodsy hollow with the stream where I sometimes passed the time catching crayfish and water snakes. To the north loomed the Blue Mountain, rising up like a dark monolith from the fields, so near down the dirt lane that my father used to walk there to hunt deer in fall.

In our new home, an apartment in the suburbs outside of Harrisburg, my mother had a few boyfriends. I liked them all, even if in hindsight they seemed to pack up and move on right about the time I'd get used to them. That was the way of things. And while I never liked seeing them go, it did no good blubbering about it. So I hardened myself to it, to everyone. I could swallow damn near anything after I discovered the woods.

In my experience so far, putting faith in God and people was always a letdown. But the woods . . .

Never.

While other boys my age were dreaming of football fields and baseball diamonds, I started watching mountain-man movies. *Jeremiah Johnson. A Man Called Horse.* Pretty soon I wanted to run away and *be* a mountain man. I wanted to find a place where no one could find me, out there, where I could live by my wits, dress in furs, and eat moose meat in wintertime. I wanted to be tied to no one, my only friends the raven and the crow.

I wasn't a bad kid, just misdirected and a lot confused. My mother worked two jobs and, not surprisingly, we wound up having our differences. My brother . . . though we shared the same bedroom for years, we hardly ever talked. To stay out of trouble, I spent most of my time hiding out in a little swamp on the backside of that housing complex just past where the sidewalk ended where black locust trees, poison ivy, and thorny rabbitbrush made the place undesirable to every other kid in the neighborhood but me.

My swamp (I considered it mine because nobody else was using it) had a stream with crayfish in it and, just like home, plenty of deep-water pools where I used to pass hours catching minnows with a hand line and a hook baited with Wonder Bread. Fallfish, red darters, and chubs. Some of the fallfish were as big as trout, tasty when speared like a hot dog with a stick and roasted over a makeshift fire.

When I tired of fighting, I used to run straight from the bus stop to one specific tree in my woods, an enormous hollowed-out dead willow, so big inside its cavernous middle that I would crawl into the thing and literally disappear from the world for a while. I used to pretend I was part of that tree, part of the woods. A little savage like Sam in that book *My Side of the Mountain*, though I never could quite muster the courage to run away for good.

I could, and often did, patrol the perimeter of my swamp in a single afternoon, ripping up the surveyor's stakes whenever I found them and ducking into the brush to hide from frequently passing cars. The place was small but seemed so huge to me then, full of secrets and so alive. There were red-tailed hawks, groundhogs, squirrels, and rabbits. Pheasants and, occasionally, a woodcock—real game birds, like my father used to chase behind the old house. And then there were the silent animals hiding out here just like me. Red and gray foxes, raccoons, and deer—some of them were monster bucks as big as cows with antlers of the sort seen on magazine covers—but you rarely got more than a glimpse of them. Later, I would find myself thinking a lot about those big elusive deer while running around looking for pumas.

I dug under logs for salamanders and stalked the creekbanks looking for leopard frogs and animal tracks. I kept a journal of the tracks, what I recognized back then as the secret language of the animals I wanted to know better. I was, after all, fixing to someday run away to the real wilderness, but having no one around to teach me I had to learn to be a hunter and trapper on my own.

I think people who find themselves marooned, lost, or, like me, alone in a strange place wind up drawing their strength from routine and ritual they self-create. I not only constructed my own woodsy reality but indeed formed an entire philosophy, one grounded in the idea that if you wanted to learn about something and make it your own, you had to get down on your hands and knees, find a track, and follow the trail to where the thing slept.

I loved the land, and through its animals the land came alive. Maybe that's why I recognized so early that tracks were something to be deciphered and followed. I used to collect them in a sketchbook, tracing the impressions with a pencil as meticulously as one might if poised in front of a pyramid wall, or an ancient cave, transcribing by candlelight the painted symbols as if they were some lost language. Every trail in the snow or along a muddy creekbank held the potential for a lesson when blood compelled my spirit to follow. The raccoon's feet I drew as tiny hands. The footprints of deer wound like a string of tiny black hearts over the snowy page. My book was a journal of the silent wanderings of these animals, a kind of Rosetta stone, recorded in verse only another hunter might understand.

•••

Hard to say when I gave up on the dream. But it happened. Or maybe I didn't so much as give up on the notion of a life alone in the mountains as finally realize that what I also wanted was a home. Hanging out in woodlots, rooting under logs, and digging in the dirt taught me that the kind of wilderness a lot of people seek can be found all around when you bother to look. One particular experience made a profound impression. With the idea that I was going to move through the place in sections, systematically learning the names of everything in my swamp, I took a backpack load of guidebooks every day into my secret place, vowing only to move forward when I had identified everything within arm's reach. Everything from plants to insects, reptiles to rocks, birds to trees. After a week I could still chuck a stone into the center of my fire ring. I hadn't even made it to the creek.

So it made me wonder back in college when it seemed like everybody I knew had plans to leave the city and head west after graduation. Not for more school. Not for a job. Not for any other reason outside the notion that all those pretty mountains and all that open country might reveal something to them that they might never see by staying around home. Some of them would actually say out loud that they were looking for real wilderness. And I just wanted to shake them and holler, *For crying out loud, have you ever bothered to really get out there and have a look around?*

I wound up falling for a girl like I fell in love with the woods. No, even faster. Even better. She loved me right from the beginning in a way I never thought I could be loved, or deserved.

The woods filled my soul, but in hindsight I know when it was that I really felt whole. A veterinarian's daughter, Nancy was kind and independent, a good talker, smart, and pretty. She had big, lovely green eyes, and a chronic and contagious laugh. She had a more even-keeled appreciation for woods and animals. Not only did she see the good in people, cities, and towns—life that I watchfully avoided from behind a screen of shady trees—but she saw these things as necessary in a way that made me curious and ultimately more complete.

•••

When the puma came along for a time it stirred in me those childhood feelings of wonder. Rusz could be opinionated, nutty at times, and a little too red-faced in his certainty of his theories. But there was something about the guy I liked. What if he was on to something? What would it hurt to be a believer for a while? After all, what if the man had really figured how to track down the most elusive creature in the woods? I was willing, for a while at least, to give him the benefit of the doubt. Having always craved the kind of knowledge he claimed to possess, I finally saw a chance to find the dragon's keep for real, since in my mind to find the puma—the epitome of all that's animal—was to affirm what I've always suspected, which is that wilderness has always been out there, sometimes closer than we think.

It didn't quite work out that way. Throughout the month of December and on into the new year, Rusz had taken to calling me at least once a week. Still nobody but Rusz seemed all that interested in finding out just what was out there. Rusz still did most of the talking, and while I felt he wasn't telling me everything (by this point I had sent him a letter expressing an interest in doing a book on the hunt for pumas in the East), with each conversation he gave up a little more.

I remember one day—after a spate of local news stories featuring a few choice quotes from Rusz that prompted new online criticism—Rusz called clearly in a snit. He'd heard a little of what was on the Net, too.

"These people are mouthing off without knowing the whole story." This, I noted, was becoming a trend. Seemed like everybody who didn't agree with

Rusz was "ill informed." That or they didn't know the whole story. But I kept my mouth shut, only half listening, as he droned on. The point critics raised was that Rusz's experience researching large carnivores was nominal at best. (If Rusz was known at all outside of Michigan it was for his work studying waterfowl and birds.) In other words, what could he possibly know about pumas? Rusz, too, had never been affiliated with any group out there looking for proof of pumas in the East. So how was it that this wildcard could come onto the scene and in two years solve the greatest wildlife mystery of the last quarter century?

"From what I've seen those people online are all a bunch of kooks," he said. "The fact of the matter is that some of these nut jobs have been trying to prove cougars for decades and they're no closer now than when they started."

Rusz had no time for any of them. The way he saw it, most of the believers out there were so obsessed with the puma that they had elevated the creature to symbolize something more than what it was, which in his own words was "just a big dumb cat." He insisted anybody could find the proof, as he had, if they put in the time. Then he wondered: Maybe deep down some of them really didn't want to find the answer. Maybe for some of them keeping the mystery alive was the whole the point.

"Hopeless," he concluded, adding that from what he'd seen there was something deeply wrong with these people.

"A flaw," he called it. "A deep-seated flaw in their souls."

He let the words linger, as if the warning were meant specifically for me.

JOHNNY APPLESEED SAYS GO SCREW YOURSELF

There is no truth, only stories.

Simon Ortiz

The Kiowa poet N. Scott Momaday talking about the American West could have been referring to pumas in the east when he said, "it is a place that has to be seen to believed, and it may also have to be believed in order to be seen." I like the saying. And I like the sentiment. But belief when it comes to pumas can be a funny thing for the way it can close as many minds as it opens.

To borrow another line from that champion of the West, Edward Abbey: "What a storm of conflicting emotion!"

Along about the end of December I did a little article, a side job, for the outdoor page of *The New York Times*—what I thought was a fairly benign bit of reporting describing who Patrick Rusz and MWC were, the divergent views they held with state biologists about the status of pumas, and how Rusz was using scat analysis (science) to back up anecdotal reports in the hope of proving pumas roamed the North Woods. I got a small flood of reader response, mostly e-mails from people with stories of puma encounters along with an angry handful from doubters who, like this one from a man I'll call Thomas, deemed the whole a sham:

> Dear Dumb-Ass Writer: Show me one. Dead or alive show me one. You can't and you won't because there aren't any. Just like the loc ness [sic] monster, aliens, sascwatch [sic], flying saucers, they all leave footprints, scat, video tapes eye witness sightings, didn't they. Did they ever put one on display, show me one cougar that hasn't been shot or road kill, you can't because there aren't. Use some other scam to raise money.

Next came a call from a woman, a local, who asked if I'd come look at a footprint left by a puma that she'd seen "clear as day" lapping water from the creek behind her house. Over the phone, she sounded lucid enough. Well spoken. Sincere. I recognized the Honor address. So for fun, I stopped by the next morning for a look.

The muddy track was unmistakably, without question, the webbed hind foot of a beaver. A pretty big one; I gave her that.

Nearby I found more tracks and a pole-sized pair of freshly chewed aspen, the flesh-colored spikes sticking up through the snow. There were other tracks, boot tracks, too. Turned out a conservation officer had also answered her call the day before, and told her exactly the same thing.

The woman was incredulous.

"It snarled at me," she said quite unexpectedly.

"It snarled at you?" I didn't understand. The story she told me was that she had watched the cat through the bay window of her house a couple of hundred feet away up the hill.

"It kept us up all night." Her voice quavered. Her face became drawn. Nervously fingering behind an ear a curl of hair that had broken free from the beehive on her head, the woman stood like a bag lady up to her knees in snow and clutching the open flaps of a droopy thrift-store parka around her frail-looking frame.

"Snarled at who? You and your husband?" I asked.

"My husband . . . my husband is dead and gone," she said, turning in a huff. High-stepping uphill through the snowdrifts toward the house, clutching the collar of her coat around her throat and shouldering into what appeared a menacing headwind, she stumbled away, bent over as if she'd just been gut-shot.

•••

While the coming hunt for Osama bin Laden pushed the hunt for Michigan pumas to the back page, the sniping back and forth among the puma people online continued (*What, if anything, does all the evidence mean in Michigan? What lessons can be incorporated in the search for pumas elsewhere in the East?*) thanks to what seemed like a new local or regional story every week.

The formula for these articles was to lead off with a headline that pitted agency against advocate. "Cougars on the Prowl? DNR Says No Way." Open off with a run-of-the-mill puma sighting . . . "Millie Mayfield of Hayseed Holler was minding her own business shucking corn out behind the barn when she looked up across the pasture and came eye-to-eye with a ghost." Or something. Same story. Different byline. Jazz up the copy with a quote or two from Rusz. (It didn't slip past me, by the way, that on the one hand he claimed to hate all the press, yet on the other he never missed an opportunity to comment when faced with a reporter clutching a notebook and pen.) Then call the local DNR office and talk to whomever happened to pick up the phone.

Biologists and conservation officers stationed everywhere from the DNR's main office in Lansing to a dozen small-town regional outposts were continually being quoted in the papers, all taking issue with various aspects of Rusz's research. And with so many voices making wind in the controversy, it soon became terribly confusing trying to make sense of not only who was speaking for the state on the question of pumas, but also what the core of the debate was really about.

My leadoff question was pretty simple, I thought: What plans did the DNR have to find out more about the status of pumas living in Michigan?

"Whoa. Not so fast," said Ray Rustem. Rustem was head of the department's Natural Heritage Division and from his office in Lansing oversaw all programs related to nongame species, which in the case of pumas made him just about the nearest thing in the agency to a man in charge. I'd first contacted Rustem back in December, a conversation that from the word *puma* had turned into a brief and maddeningly convoluted exchange.

Rustem flatly denied that even so much as a puma track had ever been discovered in the state. This alone was pretty mystifying. Hadn't he been reading the papers?

Starting with the 1966 plaster cast taken by conservation officer Frank Opolka, I ran down a smattering of examples of tracks confirmed by both DNR and Forest Service employees that were highlighted in Rusz's by now much-talked-about sixty-odd-page report.

Rustem, the go-to guy, the man I'd seen most often quoted in news stories, admitted nonchalantly that he hadn't actually read over the litany of physical evidence compiled in *The Cougar in Michigan*.

Excuse me?

The week before I hit a similar wall with Pat Lederle, the endangered species coordinator working under Rustem, whom I spoke with after I couldn't get his boss on the phone. Lederle, too, was apparently in the dark.

"Where are the pictures? Where are the videos?" Lederle commented, as if there were none. "If cougars have been living in Michigan for the last century, why no instances of bear and bobcat hunters ever running one up a tree?"

When I asked about the reference to evidence of pumas breeding in the Upper Peninsula mentioned in David Evers's book on Michigan's endangered wildlife—a book compiled with DNR input and oversight in 1994—both men claimed to know nothing about it. I found their lack of interest not only perplexing, but also powerfully frustrating when it came to discussing other examples of the very evidence both men claimed they didn't even know existed, namely the unmistakable photos taken of pumas and, to a lesser degree, the footage Rusz had showed me of the cat in the Mesick video.

Midway through my stumbling conversation Rustem suddenly recanted: Yes, come to think of it, he had seen a copy of *The Cougar in Michigan* somewhere . . . he'd seen enough to conclude that Rusz's interpretation of the physical evidence and the Wyoming DNA report—the bedrock of the foundation's scientific case—had a couple of glaring flaws.

Now it was Rustem's turn to try to take charge of the interview. But I, too, had a copy of "Laboratory Examination Report, #01-23-W-CAT." It was part of the information packet Rusz sent me for fact-checking a couple of days after our first talk.

The report, dated October 10, 2001, concluded that, of the thirteen best scat samples tested—the best looking of those collected by Rusz and his volunteers in the Upper Peninsula—eight were determined to have come from "an animal in the Feline Family, most probably mountain lion."

Rustem, who obviously had a copy of the report right in front of him, found that phrase troubling.

"Most probably?" Did that mean these feline scats were from the rear end of a puma or just a bobcat with a gargantuan colon?

Rusz had already pointed out somewhere that it was anatomically impossible for a forty-pound bobcat to pass a foot-long turd as big around as a garden hose. And the Wyoming report apparently agreed, noting in the closing remarks that while "some overlap in DNA primer amplification exists between bobcat and domestic cat, physical size of all samples would rule out these animals." (After the report was released and to further rule out the chance that the scats were bobcat, a call to the lab confirmed Rusz's claim that Wyoming had run comparative DNA tests on roughly sixty known Michigan bobcat scat samples sent by Rusz.)

Always seemingly one step ahead of agency criticism, Rusz had also sent me copies of personal communications between the Wyoming lab and MWC, including a letter from Dee Dee Hawk—one of three forensic DNA examiners who'd signed off on the laboratory results—that attested specifically to the reliability of the lab's work. In these letters and e-mail memos, Hawk also noted that the preliminary tests on the Michigan scat samples were run against known puma DNA from Wyoming and showed "no remarkable differences from known mountain lions from Michigan or Wyoming."

Pumas sold in the pet trade usually have some exotic blood in their lineage, most commonly Central or South American. So did this mean the cats here in Michigan were identical to those in Wyoming, wild North American pumas?

I talked to Dee Dee Hawk to confirm some things Rusz had told me and—while careful to preface her comments by saying more testing needed to be done (she had an annoying propensity for overusing the word *prelim- inary*)—she sounded confident not only that the Michigan scats were from puma, but also that if the cats dropping the scat were exotic in origin, some hint of the genetic difference would have revealed itself by now.

This was a critical piece of the puzzle that fell neatly in line to support Rusz's remnant population theory. Good news. But as Rustem prophetically pointed out: "From what I understand, the testing isn't even complete yet."

Western pumas, he continued, are also readily available through wildlife auctions and on the black market.

Hold on now.

Was he trying to say that for the past one hundred years people had been sys- tematically dumping their unwanted pumas in every one of Rusz's study areas?

"I'm not saying that at all. What I am saying is that you or anyone could leave their office and be back in five minutes with cougar scat and no DNA test in the world could tell you exactly where it came from."

More than misreading data, what Rustem was insinuating here was that the good doctor might very well be manufacturing it.

It sounded like Lynx-Gate all over again.

•••

MDNR furbearer specialist Tim Reis pointed me to this other controversy being widely reported in the news early in 2001. Dubbed "Lynx-Gate" by the outdoor and environmental press, biologists had been caught trying to skew the results of a 1999 national survey to determine lynx distribution across the United States. Submitting hair samples from captive lynx intentionally mislabeled to indicate that they were collected in the Gifford Pinchot and Wenatchee National Forests in Washington—territory where lynx are rarely found—suggested that the biologists were in cahoots with the environmentalists. Establish a population of lynx where there were none and there would in theory be legal grounds to restrict land use under the auspices of the federal Endangered Species Act. No logging, no mining, and forest road closures to curtail human encroachment in sensitive areas.

Hardly a leap back to Michigan, offered Reis, who assured me that while hard numbers were impossible to attain, plenty of people in the state illegally owned exotic cats, including pumas, despite a 1989 law prohibiting unlicensed citizens from keeping or selling them. Wildlife parks, zoos, and a few private residents with a handful of old decrepit specimens "grandfathered in" under the old law do, in fact, keep pumas. Prior to his fieldwork, Rusz openly admitted that he and his volunteers had spent time with captive pumas, even entering their cages at a wildlife park near his home, to train themselves how to recognize puma tracks in mud, sand, and snow.

Skeptics naturally suspicious of Rusz wondered if he was hanging around the litter box, too, making the occasional withdrawal, then heading off into the woods like Johnny Appleseed with a sack full of puma shit over one shoulder and either planting specimens for volunteers to find or simply tossing a few zoo-puma scats in a package bound for the lab. The obvious payoff: In scientific circles discovering proof of pumas east of the Mississippi was akin to winning the lottery, literally, if you considered the likely windfall of new members and donations that MWC might conceivably collect through resulting media exposure.

Reis had no comment for me about that.

"What I'd like to know," Reis said, "is why all this so-called evidence has never been peer-reviewed."

• • •

The peer-review question is one Rusz had been dodging since our very first conversation, knowing full well that from a scientific standpoint it posed the greatest strain on his credibility. On one hand Rusz would tell you that he wanted the debate about the status of pumas based on science. Proposition G, part of the MDNR founding charters, states that the MDNR *must* use science to determine any management strategies.

So how could serious-minded biologists be drawn into a debate on what to do about pumas when the scientific data behind their supposed rediscovery was viewed by uniformed professionals as incomplete and riddled with fantastic claims argued *ad ignorantiam* or explained by ad hoc hypotheses?[5]

Peer review of evidence and the conclusions drawn from it serves as a sort of scientific quality control—a "gold standard" as one biologist put it—for any claims made in the name of science. As generally defined, peer review involves subjecting a scientist's work to the scrutiny of an impartial board of other scientists and experts in the field to ensure the reliability of, among other things, collection methods and laboratory protocol. Without it, one biologist I spoke to about Rusz's research likened the interpretation to puzzling over ink blots in a Rorschach test.

In other words, the conclusions you drew from the photos and hardened rocks of plaster, sightings and laboratory reports—whether due to a handful of nonbreeding FERCs or a remnant population of pumas teetering on the brink of extinction—depended largely on what you wanted to believe.

One side insisted Rusz was peddling just the kind of "junk science" they warn you about in journalism school. In an age when scientific claims are used to peddle everything from megavitamin therapy to hair-growing salves, ESP, alien abduction, and the soul-liberating cleansing power of over-the-counter colonics, a cottage industry of books has popped up to ward off not-so-obvious fraud. Titles like *Voodoo Science*, *Junk Science Judo*, *The Skeptical Environmentalist*, and *Why People Believe Weird Things*.

To paraphrase Robert Park, a physicist and author of *Voodoo Science*, junk science is defined by fantastic scientific claims that are pitched directly to the people through the media by special-interest groups or individuals, social or environmental activists, in an effort to sell bogus products or ideas, or to influence public opinion to force their own political agenda. Junk science, wrote Park, "typically consists of tortured theories of what *could be* so, with little supporting evidence to prove that it *is* so."

Junk science is often the by-product of a calculated and deliberate deception by charlatans to deceive, according to Robert Carroll and *The Skeptic's Dictionary*. It's different from "pathological science"—a term first coined by chemistry Nobel laureate Irving Langmuir and characterized by Carroll as occurring when well-meaning scientists with the best intentions are unwittingly subverted by self-deception. Or as Robert Park put it, the result when genuinely good and competent scientists unintentionally "manage to fool themselves [by misinterpreting] unremarkable events in a way that is so compelling that they are thereafter unable to free themselves from the conviction that they have made a great discovery.

"What may begin as honest error, however, has a way of evolving through almost imperceptible steps from self-delusion to fraud," continued Park, who outlined in his book a series of red flags that laypeople can use to protect themselves against being misled by bogus scientific and technological discoveries. Topping the list: a lack of peer review, and the publication in a scientific journal of any bold new conclusion (and means and methods by which it was drawn) that challenges conventional wisdom.

If you believed the laboratory reports, Rusz had apparently found puma scat in places where the cats had been seen for decades. Were these deposited by genuine pumas, denizens from the past that were still wild and reproducing? Everything else was just theory. And even a careful listener could have a hard time telling when Rusz began morphing hard physical evidence with his own scientific-sounding conjecture.

Rusz was able to keep ducking the peer-review question basically by insisting that while the volume of puma confirmations he'd gleaned from the DNA analysis of scat was remarkable and heretofore unprecedented in any state east of the Mississippi, the technique he and the Wyoming lab had utilized was anything but revolutionary. And he had a point. Critics would accuse the press of giving Rusz a free pass with the front page, allowing him to get away with skirting his scientific obligations with coverage that ultimately legitimized the illegitimate in the eyes of an impressionable public.[6]

But just hold on . . . These days DNA taken from scat, hair, and blood samples is a benign research technique used countless times by uniformed biologists to confirm the presence of animals, including pumas east of the Mississippi, without the scrutiny of peer-reviewing the steps behind the collection and processing of every sample. It's all right there in the news: Craftsbury, Vermont (puma scat, 1994) . . . Cape Elizabeth, Maine (puma hair, 1995) . . . Quabbin Reservoir, Massachusetts (puma scat, 1997) . . . St. Martin Parish, Louisiana (puma scat, 2002) . . . Kansas University West Campus in Lawrence (puma scat, 2003).

Jacklight a timber wolf on furbearer specialist Tim Reis's watch or pot one of Ray Rustem's bald eagles off a telephone pole and let it lie in a ditch, and DNA from the crime scene will probably make certain that the guilty swings. So why this double standard all of a sudden? Or is there even a standard?

Wildlife biology is like that. "It's a stepchild among sciences," wrote Edward Hoagland, "badly paid, not quite respected, still rather scattered in its thrust and mediocre in its standards, and still accessible to the layman, as the most fundamental, fascinating breakthroughs alternate with confirmation of what has always been common knowledge—akin to that stage of medical research that told us cigarettes were, yes, 'coffin nails,' and that frying foods in fat was bad for you."

For a supposed scientist, Rusz was definitely more than a little loosey-goosey with his theories. A little peer review would have done his credibility good. But at the same time I got the sense after talking to the MDNR's lead spokesmen in Lansing that in this case it was a red herring. In the meantime, there was still a story here. People have been seeing pumas for years in Michigan. A bona fide PhD comes along with some pretty compelling evidence suggesting that there might be more to the case, and MDNR spokesmen don't even have time to read the report? What is the obligation here? That was the underlying question in almost every article on the subject so far. And I had yet to read or hear myself a substantive agency response.

Hunting for answers, other reporters covering the story had moved up the political ladder to Mike DeCapitta, the endangered species specialist for the U.S. Fish and Wildlife Service based in Lansing. But DeCapitta also refused to discuss what to do about Rusz's contention that Michigan harbored a remnant population of pumas on the grounds that the science simply wasn't there to support the theory. DeCapitta told one outdoor writer covering the story for the *Michigan Outdoor News*: "Anyone can say or publish anything they want, call it anything they want. Doing so does not make it science."

And in an outburst that only went to affirm in the minds of cynics that this supposed scientist was not only unprofessional but quite possibly unhinged, Rusz responded that anyone who doubted the authenticity of his work simply because it wasn't published in a scientific journal could "go screw themselves."

PAWS FOR THE CAUSE

True hunting's over
No herds to follow
Without game, men feed on each other

Jane's Addiction, "Three Days"

By February the MWC board of directors was fed up with the puma controversy. I knew this because Dennis Fijalkowski, the conservancy's executive director and Rusz's boss, called my office unexpectedly on the morning of the eighth to commence dishing out a little of his frustration at the lack of public support.

"The board is breathin' down my neck—threatening to pull the plug on the entire project," he said. He then proceeded to tell me that he'd combed through the *New York Times* article I'd written.

"The conservancy's name was only mentioned two times," he spattered, "while Pat's name was mentioned sixteen times!"

Really? I hadn't noticed.

By Fijalkowski's measure, my little article hadn't helped out the cause one bit.

I wondered quietly to myself what cause he was referring . . . the puma's or his own?

• • •

Wildlife is big business in Michigan, perhaps more here than anywhere. A billion-dollar-a-year industry according to some figures, and from what research I'd done so far, I was finding out that there weren't many big deals going down at MDNR headquarters in Lansing that eluded the scrutiny of Dennis Fijalkowski.

I met Fijalkowski at a winter banquet put on at Boone's Long Lake Inn, a steak house outside Traverse City, by the local chapter of Whitetails Unlimited. Fijalkowski, a charter member of the group, wrangled a three-thousand-dollar donation from the club, the only grant MWC could muster for funding Rusz's fieldwork in the Upper Peninsula in 2001, and was scheduled to present a recap of what the conservancy had found.

"Friends call me 'The Fij,'" he said, pumping my hand.

The Fij told me he had a hand in forming some of the most important pro-hunting and wildlife advocacy groups in the state: the Michigan chapter of the National Wild Turkey Federation; the Michigan United Conservation Clubs (MUCC); and the Michigan chapter of the Wildlife Society, a consortium of professional wildlife biologists, researchers, and managers equivalent to the legal bar when it comes to the monitoring of professional ethics and standards. A self-described hunter-conservationist, he was also an outspoken critic of the DNR.

While setting up an MWC display in the lobby—a tableful of brochures, puma press clippings, and membership material—Fijalkowski (snappy looking in his wire-rimmed glasses, clean shirt, and tie) spoke proudly of his run-ins with the DNR.

It all started back to the early 1970s when, working for MUCC, Fijalkowski went on record taking issue with the department's effort to propagate elk in the Pigeon River country of northwest Michigan—the largest elk herd east of the Mississippi River, now regarded as one of the agency's greatest management successes—arguing that it squandered sportsmen's money and misdirected manpower away from more pressing game management concerns. That campaign ended up drawing little support.

In the early 1980s, when the MDNR wanted to artificially inflate Michigan's dwindling population of wild pheasants with a supposedly hardier Chinese strain, Fijalkowski turned his attention to pheasants. Now the front man for MWC, he went on a public offensive arguing that the MDNR's emphasis should not be on the quick fix of introducing a new species, but rather on a more long-term solution aimed at protecting existing habitat, which would in theory benefit the wild birds already here.

In the Sichuan pheasant, the MDNR saw a new game bird that might be able to adapt to Michigan's ever-more-suburbanized countryside and thus benefit small-game hunters, who were needed to pump up dwindling license sales. While biologist representatives were traveling back and forth to China working to secure the necessary breeding stock to get the game farms running, back home Fijalkowski was predicting that the state's plan would waste millions and ultimately fail.

Pete Squibb, the MDNR's upland bird specialist now retired after thirty-two years with the department, was put in charge of the Sichuan pheasant stocking program in 1984 and took the brunt of criticism from Fijalkowski, who—echoing a line I'd heard him use first in the lobby of Boone's Long Lake Inn while plunking down a stack of MWC membership applications—likened his very public squabbles with the MDNR to a fight of David versus Goliath.

"I run a little nonprofit with three full-time employees," he said. "They have over fifteen hundred employees and a two-hundred-and-fifty-million-dollar-a-year budget."

It came up in my conversation with Squibb, who sort of chuckled: "More like Dennis versus Department."

Squibb gave Fijalkowski credit for being strong-minded and a good leader.

"But he had an ego, and everybody in the department who ever had to work with him knew it. When the Sichuan pheasant came along, everybody suspected he was trying to drum up publicity for the sake of gaining notoriety and membership for this new organization he was heading."

Many of MWC's habitat restoration efforts had been done with funding and cooperation with hunting groups like Pheasants Forever and Ducks

Unlimited. The Sichuan stocking plan had the backing of Pheasants Forever, a pro-hunting group, which set Fijalkowski up to defending himself from accusations in the outdoor press that he and MWC were at heart an anti-hunting organization.

MWC's board members didn't have the stomach for all the negative press, Fijalkowski remembered, which resulted in orders that he back off talking to the media.

But twenty years after the first Sichuan pheasant was tossed off the stocking truck, it appears that everything Fijalkowski worried over came true. The Sichuan pheasant had an abysmal survival rate in the field. Raised in the warmth and relative safety of a pen, few if any birds ever survived long after opening day, let alone through a typical Michigan winter. Like colorful but dim-witted chickens turned out by the hundreds of thousands every fall, the ones not promptly potted by hunters fell easy prey to hawks, coyotes, owls, and foxes. Those that did mingle with their wild counterparts not only competed for food but also carried with them their own unique parasites and disease that biologists now know serve to poison the native gene pool.

Looking back at the demise of the Sichuan stocking program, Squibb would concede only that the birds simply did not do as well as the department had hoped.

"Eventually hunter support for the program dwindled," he said. "And the department thought the money could be better spent elsewhere."

Fijalkowski took a much more cynical view: "Twelve million dollars spent over ten years," he recalled, "for a bunch of birds that had the brains bred out of them and never stood a chance in hell at surviving in the wild on their own."

Back at the Whitetails Unlimited dinner, Fijalkowski and I ambled over to the bar and sat down. He bought me a bottle of something imported. Leaning in with a devilish smile, he continued . . .

His next great coup came in 1985 over an agency-proposed plan to expand the range of turkeys in Michigan down into the southern counties of the Lower Peninsula, where the birds had essentially been eradicated due to unregulated hunting around the turn of the twentieth century. Through his work with the National Wild Turkey Federation, Fijalkowski had worked years before with the MDNR in a few test cases of wild turkeys from other states being trapped and relocated to Michigan, where they enjoyed a successful release. Fijalkowski remembered these wild birds were taking hold, but not fast enough for the MDNR, which was being pressured by sportsmen's groups to move more quickly in opening a statewide hunting season.

"The whole turkey issue was just another case of [Fijalkowski] chasing ghosts," said John Urbain, the biologist in charge of the DNR's wild turkey program during that time. "He was just upset that the program was moving beyond him and that his early work with the turkey federation was being overlooked."

Dubbed "The Great Turkey Flap" by the outdoor press, Fijalkowski remembered, the MDNR wanted to redistribute birds from the north, which were largely descended from game farm stock released over the decades to provide sport for wealthy members of a huge northern network of private hunting clubs. But like the Sichuan pheasant, these northern turkeys had proven to be lousy breeders with survival instincts so poor they relied largely on supplemental feeding throughout the winter. As in the Sichuan pheasant program, Fijalkowski was against the plan and hired Patrick Rusz, then working as a freelance consultant, to compile what became a fifty-page document titled "Implications of Continued Transplanting of Turkeys of Game Farm Origin: The Michigan Case."

I got a similar story in bits and pieces though a series of phone calls with Rusz.

"The idea was pretty simple and straightforward," Rusz remembered with a touch of sarcasm. "Dennis and I had the crazy idea that the best way to propagate wild turkeys in Michigan was to start with a real wild turkey."

One of the things that stood in the agency's way was the cost, according to Rusz. Redistributing the game farm birds was cheaper. With manpower and transportation costs, the trapping and relocation of a truly wild turkey from another state averaged out to around five hundred dollars per bird in the mid-1980s. But simple economics in game management rarely makes biological sense. The data Rusz uncovered spoke to the shortsightedness of redistributing "game farm turkeys," arguing that for the long-term viability of the species the state should focus its efforts on trapping and transferring wild birds from neighboring states such as Pennsylvania, Minnesota, and Iowa that had seen burgeoning success trapping and relocating truly wild birds.

With the Sichuan pheasant fight still fresh in everyone's mind, outdoor news columnists had little problem painting MWC as chronic meddlers in the affairs of hunters and the department. Fijalkowski recalled how one columnist for the *Detroit Free Press* even called for his resignation, while others accused Rusz of being little more than a hired gun who had probably been compensated handsomely to trump up some pseudo-scientific document to support Fijalkowski's latest vendetta.

What went little reported was that Rusz's research was endorsed by the National Wild Turkey Federation's technical community. According to Rusz, NWTF's technical community consisted of one professional biologist charged with managing turkeys from each state in the U.S. harboring a wild turkey population. While I could never find anyone at the federation to confirm it, forty-six of forty-eight members voted in support of Rusz's findings, with only Michigan and Indiana abstaining. But by that time, Fijalkowski had backed off again. The issue was getting too hot for the board.

The upshot, what Rusz called a "crowning embarrassment for the department," was that the MDNR assigned its own biologists to research the question of how to best propagate wild turkeys in the state, a move that led to them eventually following almost every recommendation he had offered years earlier in the final pages of his report.

"We really burned them on that one," Fijalkowski recalled, throwing back a sip of beer.

Bringing the discussion back around to pumas, I asked Fijalkowski to give me one reason why the MDNR seemed so reluctant to acknowledge the puma in Michigan. The Fij flashed four fingers.

"I'll give you four reasons. Work avoidance . . . that's number one. Two . . . ego. They can't stand being trumped by some private conservancy breaking the biggest wildlife story of the century. Three . . . the federal-versus-state struggle over who controls resource management. That's probably a biggie. You admit there are cougars here, a federally endangered species, and all of a sudden the feds are going be here telling our state biologists how to run things. Four . . . I bet they'll probably tell you down Lansing that they have no money. And the sad thing is they're probably right."

A big man in blue jeans and cowboy boots moseyed over to the bar where Fijalkowski and I were talking. A dip of Shoal protruded from his lower lip. The back of his shirt featured an embroidered image of a wide-antlered buck. He leaned into The Fij, who nodded and looked at his watch. Time to go on. He stood and ordered me a second round.

"Ever think it might be more simple than that?" I asked. "I mean, just suppose for a second that the MDNR did come out and say there were wild pumas running around. They'd have every paranoid old lady and suburbanite with a cabin up north scared witless and calling in a mountain lion sighting every time a yellow Labrador retriever ran through their yard."

Fijalkowski glanced into the dining room, filled mostly with balding, serious-looking men hovering over tables piled with camouflage coveralls, binoculars, guns, and cartoonish-looking wildlife paintings.

"With DNR it's all about the money," he said, fanning off a few small bills to pay the tab. "It's one big good old boys' club down there in Lansing. Hunters are footing the bill and most of them don't even know it."

• • •

While hunters hate to hear it, the so-called blood sports are a biological tool used by wildlife managers to keep game populations healthy to sustain future hunting and fishing opportunity. In Michigan, this multibillion-dollar-a-year governmental infrastructure consists of policy managers, congressional liaisons, biologists, foresters, law enforcement professionals—every career imaginable, right on down to secretaries, mechanics, and office janitors—responsible for not only the conservation and propagation of game and fish but also endangered species; over three million acres of state forest; ninety-seven state parks that pull in more than twenty-three million visitors every year;

fisheries in the Great Lakes and interior waterways; forestry and fire control; land acquisition and disposition; oil and gas leasing; grant administration; and human resource management.

It's hardly an oversimplification to say that the money behind this organization comes primarily from hunters and fishermen, much of it through license sales. How much? Nobody in Lansing, not even the accountants, seemed to be able to give me an exact breakdown of the numbers. I asked a couple of dozen sources and the best answer I got, albeit off the record, came from a conservation officer friend of mine while sitting in the cab of his brand-new Dodge pickup bristling with antennas for all the state-of-the-art electronics equipment inside: "Eleven percent on a couple of billion a year. Do that math. That's one big-ass chunk of change."

By contrast, everything having to do with Michigan's endangered species must get by on an annual budget of roughly ten million a year, money that the DNR's Natural Heritage Division accumulates through the sale of conservation license plates (featuring the piping plover, Kirtland's warbler, or whatever the poster species du jour is that particular year) and moneys donated by taxpayers through a voluntary write-off on their tax forms.

The big money is in fish and game. And the State's big money getters are the Federal Aid in Wildlife Restoration Act (better known as the Pittman-Robertson Act, passed in 1937) and the Federal Aid in Sport Fish Restoration (or Dingell-Johnson Act, passed in 1950). Both established an excise tax on hunting and fishing equipment: everything from graphite Flippin' Stick rods to Mepps Musky Killer lures, Buckmasters compound bows, and Tink's #69 Doe-in-Rut deer pee. Odor-eliminating clothing and fish-finding electronics. Deer Crack mineral attractant ("Deer Crack Keeps 'em Coming Back"). The money items pulling down that 11 percent are Bass Tracker bass boats, deer rifles, goose guns, and even handguns (subject to a lower tax of 10 percent), most of which are sold to people who never actually hunt with them.

"It's a good idea that went wrong," according to Fijalkowski, "by essentially serving to undo progressive wildlife management."

Later in a phone interview, I got Fijalkowski to elaborate some more on what he'd alluded to back at the bar: "Federal anti-trust law was developed only to address monopolies in the private sector. Not the public domain. By law this federal excise money pumped into the department cannot be spent for anything else but wildlife and hunter education. And that's created the monopoly: a layered bureaucracy that controls a valuable public resource that's guaranteed its funding with essentially no public oversight."

In fact, the MDNR—whose mission statement on its Web site states that the department "is committed to the conservation, protection, management, use and enjoyment of the state's natural resources for current and future generations"—is monitored with regular progress reports by the Michigan Natural Resources Commission, "a seven-member public body whose members are appointed by the governor and subject to the advice and consent of the senate."

"The NRC—" Fijalkowski caught himself. "Don't kid yourself, these policy makers in Lansing are accountable to no one."

Fijalkowski described a job with the MDNR as a safe and cushy lifetime appointment working under a parade of governors and senators who come and go every couple of years. The latter have clearly defined terms limit and more mainstream priorities, the kind of headline-grabbing concerns that appeal to voters and translate into reelection.

"These people don't quibble in obscure areas of wildlife management where they have no care or understanding," he said. What Fijalkowski was saying was basically that while Michigan may have more than one million licensed hunters, the politicians leave the department pretty much alone in making sure its Budweiser-swilling constituency stays happy by bagging a buck every year.

As the old saying goes, "It's never pretty seeing how the sausage gets made."

The MDNR has done a stellar job when it comes to every species Michigan sportsmen love to catch and shoot. After all, more bucks *by* the DNR means more hunters and more bucks *for* the DNR. Michigan is a hunting and fishing paradise with a multitude of wild fish and game, millions of acres of forestland, and miles of river—more country than you or I or anyone could hope to explore in a lifetime. But at its core my woods and wildlife loving soul understands that it's essentially artificial, a sacrosanct wilderness—a false wilderness—strickly managed on the side of tastey game species hunters and fishermen like to chase around and eat.

•••

In 1914 unregulated hunting had knocked the white-tailed deer population down to an estimated forty-five thousand animals. In 2003 more deer than that—sixty-five thousand—were killed just on Michigan highways and suburban roads. The herd numbers well over a million animals—1.7 million at last count—with 750,000 camo-clad, gun- and bow-toting, gadget-hungry hunters in hot pursuit.

In 1918 the MDNR released seven wild elk in Pigeon River country near Wolverine. These were Rocky Mountain elk trapped and transported cross-country from Yellowstone National Park. By 1960 the herd had grown to two thousand animals. Today the herd of a more biologically manageable thousand head is supported by funds—hundreds of thousands of dollars every year—from the legion of hunters who pay annually for the opportunity to put their name into a lottery drawing for the once-in-a-lifetime shot at hunting one of the roughly one hundred elk the DNR allows to be shot recreationally each year.

In 1934, twenty years after the whitetail population bottomed out and still showed little sign of growing, Michigan biologists wondered if moose might fill the ecological niche left by deer. Over the next three years, sixty-nine moose were translocated to the UP from Isle Royale National Park in Lake Superior. With the end goal of creating "a self-sustaining population of 1,000 moose by the year 2000" (a precursor to instigating a hunting season), another sixty-one moose were transported from Ontario between 1985 and 1987. In a massive commitment of machinery, manpower, and muscle, moose were transported by flatbed truck then secured in harnesses dangling over the treetops from the bellies of helicopters, which dropped them one by one into the remotest reaches of the UP.

Admittedly, some of the MDNR's most successful reintroduction efforts involved nonhunting species such as ospreys, piping plovers, trumpeter swans, pine martens, and, after a little public relations bump with their back-country base, wolves.

In 1974 an attempt was made to relocate four wild Minnesota wolves into the UP's Marquette County. Guided by age-old hatred mixed with the general consensus among the locals that outsider environmentalists and Lansing bu-reaucrats were trying to shove the wolf down their collective throats, people fired back, literally. Angry radio men declared open season over the airwaves, a message picked up in every roadhouse tavern in the county, where bartenders put up jars filled with cash on the shelf, reward for anyone who might manage to put a bullet into one of the wolves. Before the year was out, two of the wolves were shot. Another was killed by a trapper. The last was hit by a car.

The MDNR got the message and, realizing it needed to soften anti-wolf sentiments in the target region first, redirected funds into public education and information. In the meantime the wolves kept coming, filtering in by themselves as populations grew in Minnesota and Canada. Biologists said nothing. Or more accurately, they told people who called to report wolf sightings that what they'd really seen was a big Upper Peninsula coyote. Fi-nally in the early 1990s, after twenty years of silent migration, the MDNR 'fessed up that a breeding pair of wolves had settled here. Time for federal re-search money to flow.

"There are more than 450 species on the Michigan List of Endangered, Threatened, Special Concern, and Extirpated Species," wrote Anne Woiwode in a Sierra Club endangered species update as true today as it was when first published in 1997. "The Michigan endangered species story is a bittersweet one of dramatic successes and disturbing neglect; of effective application and squandered opportunities."

Dennis Fijalkowski was not so diplomatic.

The loyalties of the department lie with hunters.

"But it's a flat-out waste," he said. "If you could ever get your hands on the numbers, you'd see a lot of money being wasted that could go toward helping other species of wildlife, like the puma, every bit as important to bringing balance back to the environment. Pumas would also benefit the hunter by enhancing the outdoor experience.

"Just the thought of sharing the woods with such a animal . . . A chance for our children to see a cougar in the wild! Wouldn't that be a thrill?"

But how can you be a hunter knowing that one recent California study showed that the cats kill a deer every couple of days and still be for pumas?

"The hunters I know want the puma back. It's part of our natural heritage. But instead of working to make the environment better, most of the money goes to paying salaries. The starting salary of the MDNR director is a hundred fifteen thousand dollars per year—fringe benefits, equipment . . .

"Just imagine what a massive operation it is running one of Michigan's fish hatcheries."

•••

In 1966 several million coho salmon fingerlings, hatchery-reared from eggs transferred overland from Oregon, were released into the Great Lakes in the hope of reviving the dying sportfishing industry. Nobody knew if salmon could survive in the lakes, let alone return to the rivers where they were released. By 1970, however, the minnows had grown into formidable slab-sided fish, and northern Michigan became the talk of the angling world. The catch that year amounted to some ten million pounds. Salmon mania took hold. And it was just the beginning.

Stocking chinook salmon was tried next. The average chinook grew even bigger, well over twenty-five pounds, the fighting equivalent of a cinder block with a jet motor attached. Fishermen began arriving from all over the country by the carload with their flimsy trout and bass fishing tackle. They found the beaches jammed with surf fishermen tending long rods rigged with bowling-ball-sized reels spooled with heavy-duty monofilament that looked like baling wire. Trolling up and down the coast was an armada of shiny new boats. Realizing the bank fisherman was seriously outgunned, these auto factory workers up for a weekend from Saginaw, Flint, and Detroit started buying. They bought everything. Rods, reels, boats, and motors. Paid cash money on the spot. Up here in the early 1970s, one old timer told me you could hop boat-to-boat across Frankfort Harbor and never get your feet wet. All thanks to the MDNR.

In 1973 the world's largest coho, weighing thirty-nine pounds, was collected at a state weir like the Platte River Hatchery just down the road from my house between Lake Ann and Honor. Throughout the state there are hatcheries farming trout and salmon in Grayling, Harrietta, Marquette, Wolf Lake, and Manistique. But the one on the Platte started it all.

For the past couple of months, I'd been keeping an eye on the property where I'd found the tracks and scat that Rusz was sure came from puma. If it really was a puma, I figured the animal should pass through again, so it became my habit to check the land for tracks after each new snow. Every time I checked the spot and failed to find a track, I felt that old frustration welling up. I really thought that eventually I'd find *something*. But the puma never seemed to lay down sign for me, unless Rusz was along or somehow involved. Every time I sped down Route 31 toward Honor, I passed the hatchery, and one day in March, remembering what Fijalkowski had said, I decided to stop in and have a look around.

Not another car in the parking lot, the hatchery complex—roughly a dozen mustard-colored brick buildings set against the gray winter sky—looked like a drab and dismal prison without the barbed-wire fences. The door to the interpretative center, a sort of mini museum dedicated to the history of Great Lakes salmon, I found unlocked. Nobody there, either. I had free run of the center, a mishmash of photographs and stuffed fish. Old fishing tackle. The story of salmon fishing in Michigan was told via a video that left me with the impression that before there were salmon swimming in the lake, the fishing out there pretty much sucked.

I'd come here before. The weir itself was a fun place to come in autumn with visitors from back east. A real mind-blowing spectacle, since it was the last stop for every salmon—those that didn't die along the way, that is— making the swim up the Platte to spawn. Here a cement wall spans the river, literally blocking tens of thousands of salmon from traveling any farther up-stream. Every autumn the salmon stack up here, blackening the water, shoulder-to-shoulder, nose-to-tail, packed so tight they literally push one another up onto the rocky banks, where they flop mightily (imagine the heavy slapping sound of a raw steak being whipped against a rock). It's a thrilling sight even if you're not an angler. When the run is on, the hatch-ery is sometimes crawling with tourists.

From here the salmon leap and surge themselves up through imitation rapids—human-made cement chutes and steps—into holding tanks, where once every week or so men in yellow rain slickers help the spawning process along. One at a time the fish are relieved of their slimy payload of either eggs or semen, euphemistically called "milk." The salmon itself then goes to the euthanasia tank, is speed frozen, and then either shipped overseas to the Asian food market or off to cat and dog food factories, while the milk and salmon eggs stay behind to be blended into some antiseptic mix that makes more salmon so the cycle can repeat itself again.

Walking outside into a stiff March wind, my thoughts drifted from Michigan salmon, to our brown and rainbow trout, Rocky Mountain elk and Sichuan pheasants, imported wild turkeys and moose. I wondered how much more interested in pumas we'd be if people could play one on a line, or pay a couple of bucks every year to throw their name in a lottery for a one-in-a-million shot at a chance to legally pop one.

It's only a matter of time until it happens here to the wolf. The law states that if the wolf population stays above three hundred in Michigan for more than five years, wolves are obviously no longer endangered. That means very soon the free venison buffet might be over. Word is, the DNR is already try-ing to figure out when would be the best time of year to hunt them, the max-imum number per year they could cull, and, literally, the multimillion-dollar question: How much do you think a person might pay to be one of the first in over a hundred years to hunt a Michigan wolf?

I followed the cement walkway around back to a large building where in-side there were ten long aqua-blue cement tanks filled with bubbling water and fish—millions of skittish salmon fry all no longer than a pinkie. I stood by the door and called out "hello" over the metallic din of the aerators but saw no movement from anyone among the metal pipes and oxygen tanks. A handwritten sign taped to the glass told me that inside these tanks were 4.6 MILLION CHINOOK FINGERLINGS AND 2.19 MILLION OF THE COHO VARIETY. All these fish and no one around to protect them. When I approached the nearest tank for a look, it was as if somebody'd thrown a handful of shot on the black water. Salmon fry dove en masse toward the bottom.

More salmon were in the tanks outside—1.6 MILLION COHO YEARLINGS according to the sign—where a dozen herring gulls lifted noisily upward, surprised, then fluttered down again to line the cement walls of the tanks where the yearling salmon (a bit bigger than the minnows inside) basked helpless in the water. To discourage the gulls, someone had taken pains to crisscross white string over the long cement ponds. But given the gulls' distended bellies, some of which looked like they had swallowed a baseball, it did little to stop the feast.

Gulls sat atop every metal light pole, laughing and crapping white splatters on the pavement below. The ones on the ground stood in line, lethargically preening. For half an hour I watched them effortlessly slipping under the lines, picking off the fish one after another, holding each little minnow for an instant in their beaks with the head and tail dangling like a mustache under the gulls' angry-looking eyes before hungrily gulping them down.

THE NEW PUMAS

These minorities cannot prevent the law—the constructed law—of man, nor the more ordered, flowing laws of nature, from occurring and proceeding. They can only forestall, and momentarily divert, these laws.

Rick Bass, *The New Wolves*

In March, word came to me through one of Rusz's weekly calls that the puma situation up in my neck of the woods might be bigger than anybody could have imagined.

"Sounds like the place is crawling with cats."

Was he joking? Sometimes with Rusz it was hard to tell.

"Put it this way: If I would have known what's been going on at Sleeping Bear I wouldn't have wasted time heading all the way to the UP."

And with that Rusz had another favor to ask me—to check out rumors that park rangers there knew more about pumas than they were letting on.

•••

Congress designated the Sleeping Bear Dunes a national lakeshore in 1970. A thirty-odd-mile strip of coastal woodlands set hard against Lake Michigan in the extreme northern corner of the Lower Peninsula a fifteen-minute drive west from my door, the park also encompasses two big islands—North and South Manitou—and sixty thousand rolling acres of lakes, streams, and hilly forests, a mix of aspen, oak, birch, and American beech. As you get closer to Lake Michigan the country turns into a vast moonscape of undulating sandy hills interspersed with cedar swamps and scenic oceanlike vistas looking west over Lake Michigan. At the center of the park is the biggest dune of them all, a place the Ojibwa called Sleeping Bear. It's a landscape alive with deer, coyotes, red foxes, beavers, otters, black bears, and bobcats. More than two hundred species of songbirds. It's also the country of a legend some might say analogous to why all of a sudden more and more pumas are being seen in parts east.

According to Indian legend, a mother black bear and her two cubs caught between Lake Michigan and a forest fire burning in the woods along the Wisconsin shore plunged into the lake to escape the flames. They swam east toward the rising sun across that seemingly endless sea. The lake was very deep and cold. On into the night the trio of bears swam as fierce winds blew tall waves that crashed over them. The next day, the mother bear saw a sliver of land, a bright and sandy shore where she collapsed, alone, her cubs drowned sometime during the night.

Up to the top of a great dune facing west, the mother bear sat facing the water, looking for any sign of her young. The mother remained there until spring turned to summer then fall, finally curling up on the top of the hill, where she fell into sleep and died. The Ojibwa say that the Great Spirit, feeling the bear's sadness and honoring her devotion in death, raised her cubs up from the bottom of the lake in the form of North and South Manitou Islands.

The two black bear cubs of legend may have drowned trying to swim across Lake Michigan, but in 1998 endurance swimmer Jim Dreyer—nicknamed "The Shark"—did not. I called Jim Dreyer with the intention of doing a story about him after reading about his "Quest for Gitche Gumee," a seventy-mile swim across Lake Superior from Grand Portage, Minnesota, to the beach at Hanock, Michigan, in the western Upper Peninsula.

Canadian Vicki Keith had been the first to swim across Superior, in 1988. In an incredible but little-known feat of endurance, Keith swam across all five Great Lakes, one right after the other, over a monthlong marathon session in 1988. For her Superior crossing, Keith found a narrower spot west of

Dreyer's route, a watery inlet twenty miles across from the shores of Orienta, Wisconsin, to Two Harbors, Minnesota.

After completing his Lake Michigan swim, Dreyer conquered Lake Huron (1999) then Lakes Erie and Ontario (2000). His goal was to best Keith's record for distance and enter the record books as the first swimmer to make a "direct crossing" of all five of the Great Lakes.

Stormy swells and high winds blew Dreyer twenty miles off-course during his first failed attempt in 2001. The next year he took to the water twice, again failing to complete the swim. Summer 2003 and another try landed Dreyer in the hospital nearly dead from hypothermia—so cold his blood and internal organs had actually begun to freeze—after three days and two nights soaking in Superior's forty-six-degree water.

His blood congealed almost to Jell-O, his right arm and both legs temporarily paralyzed, Dreyer was plucked by a rescue team just twenty-two miles short of the Michigan coastline. But he succeeded in setting a new Superior endurance record by swimming forty-eight miles, making it as far as Isle Royal National Park, the least visited place in the National Park System, known for wolves and moose that migrated to the island, experts believe, by crossing over much the same route as Dreyer took during the winter when the western edges of Superior are covered with ice.

•••

Thinking about the legend of Sleeping Bear and Jim Dreyer's seemingly impossible goal got me wondering about the very possible origin of pumas here in Michigan.

Why is it so hard to believe that pumas aren't simply migrating here, drifting east across the plains, perhaps slipping down through the hills, hollows, and dark northern forests of Canada?

"I don't know about the rest of the East," said Ranger Steve Yancho, "but I don't see how a cougar could have swum all the way from Wisconsin to here."

I was acquainted with Steve Yancho, a ranger and research coordinator at the park. We met in Lake Ann a number of years before, however people meet living in small towns. Yancho was slim, clean-shaven, quick to smile, and outdoorsy looking. He remembered me when I called, said to stop in at his office in Empire any time I was in town.

A couple of days later I took him up on the offer. Yancho sat across from me in his clean white office and confirmed that, yes, there were regular puma sightings by visitors and park employees that went back twenty years. He also offered that he, too, may have once seen a puma in the park. It was all just a blur, though. He couldn't be totally sure.

Before he could elaborate, the phone rang. Yancho muffled the receiver with a hand.

"I have to take this. Call me in a week," he said. "It'll take some digging, but I'll see what I can find."

•••

My thoughts over the next few days drifted from sleeping bears to wolves.

In 2001 a wolf fitted with a radio collar was shot in Missouri by a bowhunter who mistook the animal for a hungry coyote prowling around a sheep pasture. Biologists later traced the wolf back to Michigan's Upper Peninsula, a straight line more than four hundred miles north.

In 2002 another ninety-two-pound gray wolf again mistaken for a coyote was shot by an Illinois hunter. DNA confirmed that this wolf (the first killed in Illinois since the species was believed wiped out around 1900) had originated from a Great Lakes pack from either Minnesota, Wisconsin, or Michigan.

In 2003 still another adolescent North Country wolf stricken by wander-lust was found dead in an Indiana farmer's soybean field and tracked by his long-expired ear-tag transmitter back to a pack hundreds of miles away in Wisconsin's Black River Forest.

As I dug through old back-page press clippings it occurred to me that, un-like Jim Dreyer—whom I also happened to read had just announced that he planned to take on Lake Superior again as soon as his kidneys regained func-tion—big predators don't hold press conferences to announce travel plans or their arrival on distant shores.

From wolves to the ghosty eastern coyote. It wasn't so long ago that this predator, too, was a myth. Back in Pennsylvania, I remember the game commission for years clinging to the idea that increases in coyote sightings were simply rampant misidentifications of wild dogs. In the early 1980s, when more and more spring turkey hunters up before dawn and waiting for a bird to gobble were met instead by coyote yips and howls, the line was that the animals were "coydogs" (part coyote, part wild dog). Less than a decade later, coyotes were so widespread that occasionally a few were getting shot, which finally prompted official acknowledgment that coyotes were here.

Now the coyote is considered the greatest eastern infiltrator yet, a creature whose midnight yips and howls have become so common on the fringes of our largest cities and suburbs that on cool summer nights we scarcely notice their callings mixed in with the midnight wail of ambulance and police sirens.

Experts believe that like wolves and the eastern coyote, pumas—expanding their range thanks to increased protection in the West and a nationwide overabundance of white-tailed deer—are moving east, silently following the same migration trails and brushy river corridors. Down the Yellowstone, Platte, Missouri, Arkansas, and a hundred other gnarly banked tributaries racing down from the Rockies toward the Mississippi.

By recent news accounts outlining a litany of dead scattered around in places east of the Rockies where pumas aren't suppose to live, the cats appear to be coming. (Rusz pressed the theory that in Michigan, and probably elsewhere in the East, what we were seeing was not a puma "comeback" but rather these shadowy survivors being pushed out into the light by human encroachment and suburban sprawl into the last remaining pockets of wilderness that had always served as a refuge.)

In a recent article in *Outside* magazine Maurice Hornocker—a wildlife biologist and the first to begin seriously studying pumas in Idaho during the late 1960s—called it "the most amazing big-carnivore comeback in the history of the world." Amazing because, unlike wolves (all but gone by the 1920s) and grizzly bears (wiped out throughout most of the West by 1960), pumas—the one western predator never recognized as endangered—seem to be doing it pretty much on their own.

Hornocker is the preeminent voice in a group of experts who believe there are more pumas in the West now than when Europeans discovered North America. He also predicts that as western populations swell, the next generation of pumas—adolescents forced to seek out new territory and drawn east by the scent of prey—will probably hit the banks of the Mississippi by the end of the decade.

• • •

After two weeks gone by and a series of unreturned calls since my meeting with Yancho, I planned to pop in on him again. But then the phone rang.

"I'm really sorry. Meetings and paperwork, you know," said Yancho. "But here's the thing, I talked to my boss [Chief Ranger Roger Moder] and he doesn't think it's a good idea, you being a writer and all, to draw visitor attention to the cats possibly living in the park. You understand . . ."

Roger Moder never did return any of my calls. But Ranger Kym Mukavetz did.

Kym Mukavetz was tall and forty-something, an attractive woman, with short blondish hair and the slender build of a distance runner. Mukavetz, a twenty-year ranger with the park, was running late to the office one July morning in 1997, speeding south of park headquarters at Empire on M-22, when she caught a blur of movement out of the corner of her eye on the straight-arrow country road. Thinking it was a deer, she instinctively stomped on the brake.

The long tail registered first as a puma leapt from the woods onto the macadam twenty feet in front of her truck.

"It was just enormous," she said. "Grayish brown, like the color of a deer." The tail was long, so long it seemed to keep coming out of the woods after the animal, which in less time than it takes to tell, coiled itself on the double yellow line and then sprang again with a leap that cleared the opposite lane, landing it in the brush on the other side.

Mukavetz squealed to a stop, staring long after the cat, which was hurtling away across the a field toward Lake Michigan, dissolving like the Cheshire cat, phantomlike, in a dark line of trees.

On a snowy Saturday morning along about the end of March, I met with Mukavetz in her tiny, comfortably cluttered corner office at the Platte River Campground. Save for another man in uniform working the phone, Mukavetz was alone.

Sitting upright in her chair, behind a pile of maps and books and official-looking forms, Mukavetz nervously tugged at the chin of the black turtleneck as we chatted about the usual things that everybody who settles up north finds so appealing about the place: the weather; the slow pace of country living; the beautiful lakes and rivers; and the relatively short tourist season that in a typical year ends sometime after the first major snow in October, after the autumn leaf tours—"The Leaf Peepers," the locals call them—go home.

A career ranger, Mukavetz had transferred to Sleeping Bear after working a short stint in law enforcement at Great Smoky Mountains National Park. She described her job at Sleeping Bear as occasionally having to deal with unruly campers; reminding hikers and beachgoers to keep their dogs on a leash; writing tickets for illegally snowmobiling; and lots and lots of paperwork. The biggest excitement lately happened when Mukavetz answered a call about a supposed dead guy locked in his car at Old Indian Trail, a popular hiking and cross-country ski path.

"Turned out the guy was just sleeping one off," she said.

Mukavetz preferred talking about fly fishing, describing herself as "an enthusiastic amateur." She was living the fly fisherman's dream with a tiny place along the banks of the nearby Betsy River, one of half a dozen trout streams, like the Platte, within an hour's drive of where we sat.

When I asked Mukavetz about puma sightings she and other rangers had in the park, she held out a *one-minute* finger, left the office, and came back with a blown-up map of the park mounted on cardboard and bristling with a handful of pushpins. Each pin—only about a dozen in all—designated the location and date of a sighting.

A puma had been spotted there in May 1997, two months before her own encounter. Three months later, October 1997, another Sleeping Bear ranger spotted a puma crossing the road near the same spot where Mukavetz nearly collided with what she guessed was the same hundred-pound cat. In 2000 four puma sightings came in from park employees. Park curator Bill Herd was carpooling to work with another Sleeping Bear naturalist in February, when they rounded a bend and saw the cat crouched in the snow along a dense woodline of scrub cedar and alder whips. As the car slowed, the puma atomized into the brush. Herd pulled over for a look and found tracks that another naturalist later followed into the swamp, just south of the Platte River, before losing the trail in the undergrowth. (I interviewed Bill Herd later over the phone; he told me that over the years he believed he'd seen this animal two other times crossing the road near the same location.) Another park ranger, and again on Indian Hill Road near where I had picked up that strange scat for Rusz, a twenty-plus-year veteran named Larry Johnson who'd worked most of his career out West and had seen real pumas before, believed that he, too, had seen a "a tawny colored" puma, one he described as "gliding across the road, flowing so smooth it could have been on ball bearings."

But where were all the other sightings?

Yancho had told me reports in Sleeping Bear went back twenty years. So where were the other sighting reports?

Mukavetz just shrugged. Most sightings were word of mouth. Like the DNR, park rangers didn't really catalog reports of puma encounters, let alone have a protocol for advancing the most credible up the chain of command. If somebody in the office heard of one, maybe they might put a pin in her little map. Maybe they didn't.

"The word around here is that they're all escaped pets," she said.

Mukavetz saw one. Did she really believe that?

She crossed her hands on the desk, considering the question, her eyes puzzling over the map between us.

"Now I'm speaking to you personally. Not as a ranger," she said. Mukavetz confided that she had once heard a strange caterwauling at night while on patrol in the Smokies—the Great Smoky Mountains straddling the border between North Carolina and East Tennessee, another infamous haunt of eastern puma legend where local knowledge held that pumas had never been completely wiped out. Mukavetz admitted she had always been intrigued by the mystery.

I remembered reading how the Great Smoky Mountains had intrigued Robert Downing, too. During the USFWS study in the late 1970s, Downing noted that almost a quarter of the Smokies (nearly half a million acres) had never been logged. More than enough undisturbed territory to provide refuge for pumas held to be extinct in the area since the early 1900s.

Around the same time of Downing's study, Nicole Culbertson was also compiling her own status report of the puma in the Smokies. Her conclusion, based primarily on reliable sighting reports (twelve from 1908 to 1965 and thirty-one from 1966 to 1976):

> The number of lion sightings through the years suggest that the mountain lion may never have been actually extinct in the Great Smoky Mountains area. The lion may have been able to maintain itself in small numbers in the more inaccessible mountainous regions in or around the park. The present lion population could be derived in part from this small reservoir . . . it is believed that there were three to six mountain lions living in the park in 1975.

Mukavetz was unaware of Culbertson's work, but remembered it was common knowledge among the locals in the region that pumas had always been there.

"When I saw that animal leap across the road here," she said, "my first instinct was not to tell anybody."

"On account of what people might think?" I asked.

"Oh no," she said. "Nothing like that. I know what I saw. I was afraid if word got out people might come snooping around and shoot it or run it out of the area. I got to think about that cat, living out there, not hurting anybody. I was afraid to draw attention to it, you know. When people get involved with wildlife, unfortunately the animal always seems to come out the loser."

• • •

So how did the puma Mukavetz saw end up in the park? She wouldn't hazard to guess.

The nearest federally recognized breeding population of pumas in the United States—some 150-odd animals—live roughly a thousand miles to the west of Michigan in the Black Hills of South Dakota. Some believe this group accounts for the almost twenty-four separate puma confirmations that have come in recently from wildlife agencies in North Dakota. A Black Hills puma fitted with a radio collar was recently hit by a train 667 miles away in Oklahoma just south of the border of Kansas and 40 miles away from Arkansas City.

In Nebraska at least a dozen encounters have resulted in verified killed, videotaped, or, in rare cases, captured pumas, as in the recent Associated Press coverage of a wild puma that suddenly appeared wandering residential streets on the outskirts of Omaha. After a daylong chase involving a police helicopter, local television news crews, and Humane Society workers, this wandering young male was eventually brought down by a zookeeper's tranquilizer gun, but not before being blasted in the rump with a load of buckshot fired by a panicked patrolman who believed the doped-up cat was fixing to charge.

In August 2003 the *Democrat Arkansas Gazette* told of a deer hunter's remote camera capturing a puma on film. In Iowa, 2002, where one week after state officials verified to a reporter from *The Boston Globe* that as many as a dozen pumas may be living in the state, a 135-pound puma was hit near the west-central town of Harlan. A year later another was shot a couple of hundred miles away by a farmer as the cat prowled harmlessly along the edge of a field. *The Kansas City Star* announced that a gray squirrel was the last supper for a wild puma roadkilled in Missouri. The cat had all its claws and an injured paw (a missing pad) that investigators theorized was probably an old battle wound from a scrape with another puma, or possibly a bear.

Hundreds of sightings and recently a number of bodies have turned up in Minnesota. Starting in 1991, a 150–pound puma was treed by hound hunters and the animal, believed wild, was captured, packed up in a crate, and shipped on a one-way ticket to Colorado.

More recently, a fifty-four-pound female puma was shot late one night on the doorstep of a homeowner near Big Sandy Lake, Minnesota. Earlier that evening the man reported that his dog had been attacked, but not seriously injured, on the doorstep as the two were making their way into the house. Later that night watching television, the homeowner happened to gaze out the window next to the door and nearly fell off his La-Z-Boy when he got an eyeful of a puma murderously staring back at him through the glass.

The man composed himself, fetched his revolver—a .357—and cracked the door enough to slip the muzzle outside, dropping the cat in its tracks. The case got even more confusing when days later two puma kittens were found and captured by wildlife officials nearby. The mother's seemingly bizarre behavior suggested that the female was probably a FERC, though opposing arguments noted that it was equally plausible that she was a young wild mother of two looking for an easy meal of dog. We may never know. Minnesota has yet to release any DNA test results, which could shed some light on their origin; that is, of course, if anybody had taken the initiative to run the tests.

Similar confusion existed over the wildness of another Minnesota puma photographed by remote camera standing over the carcass of a deer kill outside the town of Savage, barely a dozen miles from Minneapolis. This was probably the same cat head-shot a couple of weeks later by police as it crouched on a popular walking path in Bloomington, a Twin Cities suburb. This puma, too, was dismissed as a FERC.

At least two dozen puma confirmations come straight from the files of Minnesota biologists, six of them carcasses turned up in the last three years. Yet spokesmen there are still scratching their collective heads wondering if pumas are breeding here or just passing through. If passing through, then to where? If they're following the migration paths first cut by wolves, skirting the shores of Lake Superior, their next stop should be northern Wisconsin and then the Upper Peninsula of Michigan.

But what about the origin of pumas seen in the Lower Peninsula of Michigan? The state of Michigan, by virtue of its unique geography, poses two confounding riddles in one. While the Upper Peninsula forms a perfect connective corridor for migrating pumas venturing here from the West, many believe we here in the Lower Peninsula are essentially cut off from east-moving transients since only in legend and back-page human interest stories do land-loving mammals make the swim across Lake Michigan.

Standing in the way of pumas moving here, so much water—arguably more formidable than a mountain range—makes for a real and insurmountable boundary, not some arbitrary human-made line on a surveyor's map delineating the politics from one state to another. To reach the Lower Peninsula of Michigan from the west, pumas would have to come around Lake Michigan and up from Chicago. Not likely, unless they're hitching a ride northbound in the back of somebody's car, which admittedly could very well be the case.

That or they'd have to trek nine hundred miles across the UP and slip across the ice in winter, only a mile, across the Straits of Mackinac. At any rate, the Mississippi River is the watery gulf guiding the politics of pumas for the rest of the East, a boundary maybe not as unconquerable as Lake Michigan but certainly one that makes even murkier the origins of pumas occasionally turning up here.

A puma killed by a train in Illinois. An eight-pound puma kitten struck and killed by a car in Kentucky. In 1967 a Pennsylvania deer hunter shot a puma with tainted exotic blood. In 1976 a farmer killed a male mountain lion in Pocahontas County, West Virginia, after it jumped the fence with one of his sheep. Two days later a pregnant female was captured nearby.[7]

By far one of the most interesting cases in the news involves pumas supposedly now running wild in Delaware, where wildlife officials there recently made the politically risky announcement that they have two, possibly three, cats living along the northern border with Pennsylvania.

A recent headline on the *Gannett News Service*, an online newspaper, dubbed Delaware the next "big capital" for pumas in the East. A state with more than 12,500 miles of roads, population 800,000, where an average of 338 people inhabit every square mile. Officials here believe these are probably the same band of pumas that account for sightings in the area that go back a decade on the outskirts of Newark—population 3,198—and Bear, where at last count 17,593 people were crammed into a concrete, highway-laced patchwork a scant 5.7 miles square.

While these Delaware cats are probably former captives, incredibly a body has never turned up. Sightings of pumas with kittens have been reported in the area, too, but nobody really knows for sure if these animals are breeding. But with this kind of rare acknowledgment, no more can anyone scoff that these pumas—accounting for only around twenty sightings per year—aren't for real. How are they are surviving? How in the middle of this sprawling humanity have they gone so long eluding car bumpers and bullets?

Delaware Society for the Prevention of Cruelty to Animals executive director John E. Caldwell told the *Gannett News* that because their domain is so urbanized these pumas will likely never be caught.

"It makes it almost impossible to hunt these cougars down with dogs," said Caldwell. "There's too many accesses and avenues of escape."

Back in Michigan, I heard echoes. If Rusz was correct and pumas were for real and breeding in small numbers, a hundred years of avoiding widespread detection meant the cats he'd found traces of must be hyperelusive, too. If pumas could have eluded capture and killing in a place as crawling with humans as Delaware, why not in northern Michigan? And if a trio of probable FERCs could do it, just think of what a truly wild puma—descendants of other wild pumas—might be able to pull off? Rusz believed pumas in Michigan had never truly been wiped out. But could a century's worth of evolution have so changed the habits of these crepuscular predators—our human altered landscape forcing a transformation so extreme (yet never with one solid example of human-caused mortality via the automobile or the gun in Michigan)—that the eastern ones only resembled in form the mythic man-eaters of the West? Rusz went so far as to say the old rules—the western model of detecting pumas—were of little help to those looking for pumas in the East because the tracking surfaces are different.

Wouldn't that be some news. How wonderful would it be if such a thing were actually proven true? My wilderness loving soul wanted to run with that.

The writer Scott Weidensaul might well have been talking about these new pumas when he wrote, "Faith, yearning, hope, and biology intersect repeatedly in the stories of these living ghosts, the more arresting the animal, the stronger grasp it has on us." Weidensaul was actually talking about the lost colony of grizzly bears believed by some to inhabit Colorado's San Juan Mountains and, specifically, the work of Doug Peacock and a handful of others who have for years tried to prove they exist.

> Brown bears (of which the interior grizzly of the Rockies is but one race) are big, bold animals with an almost mythic disregard for humans, an in-your-face creature in both a figurative and literal sense . . . But bears are also quite intelligent and adaptable, and some grizzly experts like Doug Peacock, who has spent years drifting through the San Juans looking for them, believe that the Colorado bears have survived by becoming the antithesis of the aggressive grizzly. The San Juan bears, Peacock and others argue, survived a century of ferocious artificial selection in which only the meekest, quietist, most secretive grizzlies made it. They became almost wholly nocturnal, immensely shy, and almost supernaturally wary around people, and they have learned to get by on a lot less land, sticking to small home ranges instead of wandering all over creation.

•••

After my meeting with Mukavetz, it was time to head home. Nancy and I had a doctor's appointment. We were both looking forward to the chance to finally hear the baby's beating heart.

Heading back again toward Honor, I decided to stop and check for tracks at the property near the Platte. Cinching up the bindings on my snowshoes, I headed off for a quick loop around the field, following the tree line past the usual number of deer and coyote tracks until I came upon a shallow trench in the snow made by a waddling porcupine.

The path led to a girdled sugar maple sapling, ringed with almond-colored chips of bark. Climbing up a tiny knob into the hardwoods, I eventually found the porky and three of its friends hanging out in the snarled dead branches of a haunted-looking tree. I saw them from a long way off silhouetted against the low, gray sky, like leafy clusters, what my eye first thought were squirrel nests.

A den tree. The porcupine shit was piled knee-high at the base of the old tree, outside a deep black gash in the trunk big enough for the animals to climb inside. Instead of climbing higher, the trio sat like prickly gargoyles, watching me. The snow revealed I was not the first visitor that morning. Ringing the tree were a number of coyote prints. I found, too, where a bobcat had come down off the knob, leapt onto a high stump, and lain in a ball as evident by the oblong impression, a bed, in the snow.

Later that night, lying in our own bed, Nancy and I took bets on the sex of the baby. She said girl. A woman's intuition. Something told me the opposite. Another couple of weeks and we would be able to tell for sure. But before I fell asleep I was again thinking about pumas, specifically what other mysteries would be revealed when in a few weeks the spring rains would finally come and melt away the snow.

THE IMPOSSIBLE BURDEN OF PROOF

I am not a seeker after truth . . . just evidence. I will draw my own conclusions.

Bernard Robertson-Dunn

In northern Michigan springtime never comes precisely when the calendar says it should. The winds typically shift southerly come May, bringing warm downpours and—after months of snowy, gray melancholy blankness and sensory-depriving cold—the good, almost forgotten smell of budding trees, blooming flowers, green grass, and soggy earth.

I left the house at dawn and drove south along a stretch of M-55 where the only snow left was the filthy hardpack piled by snowplows in the ditches where I counted half a dozen dead deer—old roadkills—a flattened rabbit, two opossums, a muskrat, and a moldering raccoon being picked over by a brace of hopping crows. Headed south, just outside Mesick the scenery changed from woodsy to pastoral. Dewy pastures. Cattle grazing. Red barns and stony gray silos. I spotted a coyote still in full winter coat loping along a jagged fencerow.

I was headed to meet Rusz, who had been planning the day's adventure for months: a search for puma bones. Back in November, a woodcutter clearing brush from a power line in the eastern UP's Chippewa County, near the town of Rudyard, had supposedly found a puma skull half buried in the ground. The rumor turned out to be true. As far as proof goes, a whole skull was something new and, I hoped, could make for better evidence than scat and tracks, which I was getting tired of Rusz telling me about since such evidence clearly never impressed the folks whose opinions really mattered.

Rusz tracked the skull down to Lansing, where it had been sitting on a shelf at the MDNR's Rose Lake Disease Laboratory. Biologists had consulted with zoology professors Barbara L. Lundrigan and Philip Myers, from the Michigan State University Museum, who concluded in a December 9, 2001, letter: "Given the animal's apparent age [two years], we were surprised at how unworn the animal's cheekteeth [sic] were. . . . This suggests to us (but certainly does not prove) that the animal may have been an escaped captive."

End of story as far as my contacts at the department were concerned. If Rusz wanted a piece of the skull for DNA testing, he could have it. As for actually heading out into the field to the spot the skull had been found, I couldn't find anybody in uniform willing to get their boots dirty on this one.

"So what," said Pat Lederle. "I don't see what any more investigation would prove." Certainly not breeding, which Lederle reiterated was the only real question that concerned his office.

This, in my mind at least, seemed to beg the question of how you could begin to know anything about anything if you weren't willing to go out and at least look.

I could have replayed the tape from our conversation six months ago in which Lederle, after allowing that *lone* (emphasis added) transients or former captive pumas probably are out there, bemoaned a lack of funding, understaffing, and no public support as the reasons professional biologists had little inclination for further determining their status in the state. As with wolves that had wandered into the UP on their own, the department was content to take a wait-and-see approach, believing that in the meantime pumas enjoyed a more-than-adequate prey base and millions of acres of forestland thanks to current management strategies.

Lederle talked about objectivity. But all I heard were excuses, and the more I listened the more I felt my own objectivity slipping, to say nothing of my dimming view of the science now being used by professionals—not just in Michigan but everywhere—to crack the riddle, which is to say very little.

"What more would the public have us do?" Lederle asked, adding that pumas seemed to be doing fine on their own if you were inclined to believe the media hype of the last six months. Everybody was all of a sudden seeing pumas, perhaps a direct by-product of the unrelenting stream of press releases from Dennis Fijalkowski and MWC that kept his organization and pumas in the news and by now only served to cement in the minds of cynics that MWC was somehow benefiting from the ongoing media exposure. Fijalkowski and Rusz insisted that MWC's puma campaign was running in the red. As a non-profit group, MWC's money matters were open to the public under law. Call a non-profit and request its "990 forms" and it must comply. The 990 is a line item accounting record that shows total amounts including monetary gifts, grants, contributions, expenses, liabilities . . . Everything from salaries to fund-raising costs. MWC had actually seen an overall drop in earnings (not unusual even for the most high-profile environmental and conservancy groups, which reported a similar drop in earnings in the post 9/11 economy) that continued well into 2002.

But back to pumas . . . How could Lederle be so flip? How could the agency really know if pumas were doing fine? How could they say for sure? There's never been so much as a basic habitat study done on behalf of pumas here, let alone a formal inquiry into their population status. What about a "wildlife acceptance" study, otherwise known as a "social carrying capacity" survey? They did it here in Michigan when the black bear population was showing signs of expanding south. And they did it for wolves, which are expected to slip over the ice any day now to set up franchises in the northern Lower Peninsula, if they haven't already. Since all the suitable habitat and feed in the world mean nothing if locals with guns can't stomach the idea of living in close proximity to predators that could potentially make trouble for them, such a simple poll seems a logical first step. And you wouldn't even have to leave the office to do it.

Feeling myself getting snippy, I let these questions slide.

Lederle was careful never to mention any names, but I took his last comment as a not-so-subtle jab at Rusz who had surprised and disappointed me by recently going on record voicing his opinion that, based primarily on clusters of anecdotal sighting reports (viewed as unreliable and scientifically worthless in determining puma population estimates by seemingly every wildlife biologist but him), there could be as many as eighty cats living in Michigan. Rusz's original guess had suddenly quadrupled, an even larger remnant population that he declared was evenly split between the Upper and Lower Peninsulas.

"For whatever reason, some people are trying to make a big deal out of cougars," said Lederle. "But I don't see it that way. We have over three hundred endangered and threatened species in the state. Why is the cougar all of a sudden so important?"

To this point in our conversation, I had done a pretty good job of keeping my pen moving and my mouth shut. But Lederle's rhetorical questions and laconic-sounding responses were really beginning to frost me. What Lederle was trying to say was that the laws governing endangered species don't play favorites, which is true.

But didn't it sound a little absurd, maybe even derelict, trying to equate Karner blue butterflies, piping plovers, least shrews, or, for that matter, any other of Michigan's endangered birds, mammals, plants, or insects with a huge, wide-ranging, apex predator like a puma? Didn't it seem just a little bit incongruous that the people in charge of overseeing the health and safety of Michigan's endangered species were suggesting they wanted to see a few dead pumas turn up before being compelled to act? And furthermore, if these were all once captive animals set loose on the countryside—pumas raised as pets and thereby inexperienced at hunting and conceivably unafraid of humans—weren't these the very animals the agency should be most concerned with tracking down?

Lederle brushed off these questions, poking again at Rusz's overzealous and glaringly unscientific stab at population estimate and how he came about it. I conceded that Lederle had a point. Before Lewis and Clark, the West was believed to be home to woolly mammoths, mastodons, and a lost tribe of white Indians. Likewise, in the 1800s many explorers who had visited Africa brought back tales that unicorns inhabited the uncharted savanna. People had supposedly seen them, but that didn't mean they were real.

"Take a step back for a minute and look at Florida," Lederle said. Florida, a state with roughly the same number of pumas Rusz and MWC were now theorizing we had here, averaged roughly two roadkill incidents every year—sixty-two at this writing—since the state started keeping records in 1972. (The Black Hills of South Dakota where an isolated population of 150 pumas now live reported fifteen roadkills just in 2003.) On the contrary, bodies weren't turning up in Michigan. Not in traps. Not run up trees. Not dead on the side of the road.[8]

Another point I'd been vexing over for months.

But where Lederle lost me was in his take on Michigan law, his insistence that the state was only obligated to prevent state-listed endangered species from being harassed or killed; it wasn't compelled to help them thrive.

Really?

I looked it up later and discovered that, in this instance, the language of state law couldn't be more clear. Much to the contrary, an endangered species in Michigan not only must be conserved and protected, but ultimately must be propagated and restored. The puma was one such animal.

It's right there in the Natural Resources and Environmental Protection Act 451 of 1994 (Sec. 36502):

> The department shall perform those acts necessary for the conservation, protection, restoration, and propagation of endangered and threatened species of fish, wildlife, and plants in cooperation with the federal government, pursuant to the endangered species act of 1973, Public Law 93-205, 87 Stat. 884 and with rules promulgated by the secretary of the interior under that act.

This language mirrors the mandate found in the federal Endangered Species Act. I also located a dusty document known as the "Eastern Cougar Recovery Plan" written by Robert Downing shortly after his failed hunt for pumas in the Southern Appalachians. Adopted by the USFWS in 1982 but never acted upon, Downing states:

> Recovery of the eastern cougar will have been satisfactorily accomplished when at least three self-sustaining populations have been found *or established* [emphasis added] in the U.S. Each population (which may consist of two or more separate but interbreeding nuclei) will be considered self-sustaining if it contains a minimum of 50 breeding adults, and if losses of these adults are being replaced through reproduction and/or immigration from nearby populations.

A laundry list of research directives follows, among them requirements that call for biologists to "find and delineate cougar populations"; "perform research, develop techniques, and train personnel for identifying positive sign of the presence of cougars"; and "perform systematic searches throughout the subspecies former range." In the event pumas are found, these animals are supposed to be studied for the sake of determining population dynamics, behavior, and subspecies identification provided that "no animals [should] be sacrificed for this purpose."

The not-so-obvious disconnect here is that the federal act only recognizes two subspecies of puma having once existed in the East: *Puma (Felis) concolor couguar* and *Puma (Felis) concolor coryi*, the so-called Florida panther. Technically, the sweeping power of the federal Endangered Species Act cannot be invoked for the study and propagation of released captives or western transients, which are not endangered subspecies as defined under current law.

By listing only *Felis concolor*—in principle any puma—as endangered, Michigan law is actually more liberal (it might be right to also call it more "convoluted") than the federal statute in defining what a puma is.[9] This critical change in nomenclature happened around the same time David Evers compiled his 1994 guide to Michigan's endangered animals mentioned earlier, a book project overseen and partially funded by the MDNR's Natural Heritage Division, in which Lederle's departmental predecessors seemed to believe evidence that suggested pumas were living, possibly breeding, in the same northern counties where Rusz and his team of volunteers had found puma scat.

Lederle wasn't the only one who insisted the state's hands were tied until better proof surfaced—scientific proof—of a viable puma population: a prerequisite for kick-starting formal inquiry that I couldn't find referenced anywhere in the state or federal law. (Neither could I find any reference as to how many pumas actually constituted a population worthy of study. How many needed to be found? Two? Ten? Twenty?) Nor was he alone in putting off my questions of investigative culpability by suggesting I contact the feds at the U.S. Fish and Wildlife Service, Lederle's way of marking the end of the conversation.

I got the call from Rusz about heading up to the UP before I had a chance to call Mike DeCapitta, the USFWS's point man in Michigan. But by now, paging back through my notebook and my growing file of laboratory reports, MWC press releases, and newspaper stories—nearly one a week since my first meeting with Rusz the previous fall, six months gone—I had no reason to think another long-distance phone call to Lansing might provide any divergent opinions as to the origin and breeding status of pumas that everybody on both sides seemed to agree, in some form, were here; no more than I believed that another photograph, plaster cast, puma scat, or wasted Sunday driving to the Upper Peninsula to hunt up a puma skeleton would get me any closer to answering the mystery of what was out there. When it came to what constituted evidence that pumas were real, the state seemed to have the ability to move the goalpost back to what suddenly struck me as an impossible burden of proof.

I had first become drawn to the mystery of the puma in Michigan because it sounded like a good old-fashioned, honest adventure. I'd imagined, wrongly it was turning out, that the search would totally be comprised of me bush-whacking out into some snarled, forgotten, and divinely inhospitable country. I wanted to be out there, compass needle spinning, breaking new trail. Not home wrestling through a morass of state and federal laws, laboratory reports and memos, and widely varying opinions and tortured vagaries about what constituted reasonable evidence of a wild, breeding puma population.

Lederle hadn't been the only biologist who expressed understandable frustration that every article highlighting the current controversy came with the running implication that folks like him weren't doing their job. Others I spoke to voiced genuine concern that the ongoing controversy was under-mining public trust in the department. Most blamed the media for inaccurately portraying the agency's position on the status of pumas in Michigan, suggesting that journalists looking for an easy angle perpetuated discourse and acrimony for the sake of splashy headlines.

This charge bothered me a lot. It bothered me because it flatly wasn't true. Under the law the department appeared to have an obligation here. Laws are put in place to ensure that we don't turn away from a problem just because it happens to be difficult. On the one hand I felt the biologists I spoke to were at heart all men of goodwill, good people with real day-to-day concerns who were frankly just tired of having to pick up the phone and be hassled by an-noying writers like me. As one Pennsylvania game warden I corresponded with put it, "Wetland habitat loss, deer management, the threats of bovine tu-berculosis and chronic wasting disease, West Nile virus, invasive species . . . could any reasonable person say the puma is more important than these im-mediate concerns?"

But instead of speaking plainly and just coming out and saying that at the moment they really didn't care all that much about pumas, biologists parceled words with the reporters and played a game of semantics. From a public relations standpoint, much of the trouble with newspaper people dogging the case no doubt stemmed from the DNR's own spokespeople who came off sounding as if they were flatly incapable of simply *pretending* to be interested when talking about pumas. Couldn't they even muster *a little* enthusiasm at the news pumas might be out there? This apparent ambivalence, combined with their convoluted statements, was exactly what kept people like me interested in that side of the story.

Paging back through my notes and news accounts, I found Ray Rustem, lead man in managing Michigan's endangered species programs, delivering the pet theory mantra so many times in public that it was beginning to read like the punch line for a tired old joke.

Time and again Rustem and others claimed that before the department made a move they wanted more proof. What was maddening was that nobody there seemed interested in doing any of the legwork themselves.

Call in a report that you suspect your neighbor is poaching deer and a CO will be rapping at your front door by the end of the day for the rest of the story. On the other hand, call in a sighting of a puma strolling through the backyard and in many cases individuals told me that days passed before anybody returned the call, if they phone at all.

But in the department's defense, I understood the frustration of dealing with citizens who couldn't tell the difference between a beaver and a puma. Around the time Rusz first called me with the rumor about the Chippewa County skull, I chased down another lead about puma bones that turned out to be the rotten remains of a German shorthaired pointer. I know this not only on account of the tufts of chocolate-colored hair still clinging to the bones, but also because of the leather collar I found lying quite obviously nearby in the melting April snow.

I called the phone number on the collar. The dog's owner lived a couple of miles away. Dexter had been "a hell of a grouse dog." He'd gone missing since last fall. Unfortunately, it appeared that Old Dex also may have had a nose for running deer, a trait not taken to kindly to by the locals up here and that, judging by the bullet hole in the skull, probably contributed to his demise.

Ray Rustem insisted that anytime there was more to a puma encounter than just a sighting, field biologists did a follow-up. He also told me that the state's team of wolf trappers working in the Upper Peninsula had been ordered to capture a puma, in the event they could find one.

During the MDNR's annual winter wolf tracking surveys, teams of biologists scoured more than two thousand miles of Upper Peninsula roads tabulating the number of wolf tracks. As a way to determine the population, the state had been performing these surveys annually since 1995. According to Rustem, during these track counts teams were always on the lookout for other sign indicating the presence of other rare species of Michigan wildlife, including pumas, although he insisted no puma tracks had ever been found.

"But even if we found tracks," Rustem said, "nobody could say for certain if it were made by a wild cougar or not." Ditto for a crystal-clear photograph, hair, a bona fide puma skull, or blood.

I heard all this before. In 1995, when an Iron County motorist in the Upper Peninsula called in to report a collision with a puma on a backcountry road, the local conservation officer responding to the scene found no sign of the puma last seen running off crippled through the brush. But he did reportedly find traces of blood and hair on the car's bumper.

I later verified the story with MDNR biologist Rich Earle, who happened to be stationed in nearby Traverse City. Over the phone, Earle told of comparing the hair sample with one he had personally taken from a puma kept at the city zoo. A microscopic analysis was enough to satisfy Earle of the match; nevertheless, he chalked the whole thing up to just another unfortunate incident with an escaped pet and tossed the samples in the trash.

Earle had actually chuckled when I pointed out the irony here, the impossible burden of proof:

Pushing the whole pet theory one step further to its next nutty extreme, with that kind of thinking you could live-trap or accidentally plow into a genetically pure North American mother puma and a couple of cubs and the pet theorists would chalk it up to another sad result of what happens when misguided pet owners fool around in the black market pet trade.

Was Rusz's remnant population theory any more far-fetched and implausible than the department clinging to this Occamistic notion that a century's worth of sightings, along with every hunk of plaster, every video, photograph, strand of hair, shard of bone, or swab of blood—and now even DNA—could (when not lost or tossed in the trash) simply be explained away as evidence courtesy of former captive animals?

Occam's razor, otherwise known as the "principle of simplicity," is a fundamental principle of logic attributed to the mediaeval English philosopher and Franciscan monk William of Ockham (circa 1285–1349). Underlying all modern scientific modeling and theory building, Occam's razor cautions that when deciding among scientific theories and explanations, "one should always choose the simplest explanation of a phenomenon, the one that requires the fewest leaps of logic."

Aside from religious discussions where Occam's razor is commonly used by atheists arguing against the existence of God as an unnecessary hypothesis (as Robert Todd Carroll carried the logic in an article for the online version of *The Skeptic's Dictionary*, "We can explain everything without assuming the extra metaphysical baggage of a Divine Being"), it's also a point puma skeptics like to make on the Internet.

"But Occam's razor is not about proposing explanations for a phenomenon; it's about explaining them," said Chad Arment, author of *Cryptozoology: Science and Speculation*:

> It [Occam's razor] is not a magical incantation that immediately clarifies complex situations, and is certainly not a substitute for experimentation and observation. The Razor is used to suggest where an investigation could start, when there are multiple possibilities which each lead to the same effect. We start there not because simplest explanations are the most viable, but because they are easier to prove false (and thus such explanations must be testable). Merely crying Occam's razor without actually proposing to test the simplest theory is an inadequate argument. Claiming a theory is more viable just because it is simplest shows a deep misunderstanding of the principle. Parsimony may be more

elegant in science, and there certainly are cases where [explanation of] phenomenon are very simple, but it is not by itself a measure of truth.

Knowing I'd be passing through the neighborhood, I built time into my schedule that morning to drop in on Tom Willis. I had some beaver pelts for him, five in all from a brief foray into trapping back before the puma began taking up all my free time, and two skunks that I'd removed from their den under my shed after tracking them there in the snow the day after they'd sprayed the neighbor's dog.

Whenever I go to visit Tom, usually once every spring after the end of the trapping season, I'm reminded of the fact that two hundred years ago men of his occupation were some of the richest in the North. John Jacob Astor—this nation's first multimillionaire—made his fortune in furs after opening the American Fur Company on Mackinaw Island in the early 1800s. Now one of *the* main buyers in all of northern Michigan lives in the woodsy outskirts of Mesick in a tilting trailer situated at the end of a washed-out lane where he keeps a bearish-looking black Newfoundland and a pack of the meanest, crustiest-looking springer spaniels I've ever seen. I turned off the main road, took a hard left past a busted mailbox and signs that read WE BUY DEER HIDES and VOTE LIBERTARIAN, and the dogs plodded from the woods like canine zombies, barking hoarsely and circling the truck. I pulled in alongside Tom's rig, a two-tone Ford Bronco, and parked in front of the skinning shed, a barn-like outbuilding surrounded on that day by fifty-gallon drums, heaps of cardboard boxes, an old ten-speed bike frame, and two rusty lawn mowers. The mowers were worthy of particular note given that there's never to my knowledge been one square inch of green grass anywhere on the grounds.

I stepped out of the truck into the pack, heavily huffing and sniffing at my shins. Tom was underneath the rear end of the Bronco, lying on his back in the mud on a sheet of plywood. Fisting a small sledgehammer in one hand, he gazed up into the undercarriage with a look of utter bewilderment on his ruddy, whiskered face.

"Hole in the damn gas tank," he said, answering my question by way of saying hello. "Damn thing's rusted to all hell." He puzzled at the problem a beat longer until finally his eyes lit upon the crucial spot perfect for a handful of swift, metallic whacks with the hammer.

Tom is a smallish man, fiftyish and spry, with bony stooped shoulders and big, workman's hands. Technically he's a buying agent for North American Fur Auctions, an international fur trading conglomerate that traces its origins back to the Hudson's Bay Company of 1670. To grossly simplify the business, representatives for garment manufacturers from Asia, America, Canada, Europe, and Russia regularly convene throughout the year at NAFA auctions to haggle and bid over lots of wild and farm-raised fur used for trimming gloves and making hats and coats. According to the NAFA, an estimated 2.3 million mink and fifty thousand farm-raised fox come from the United States every year, along with tens of thousands of free-ranging beaver, raccoon, otter, coyote, muskrat, mink, and fox furs, all handled eventually by men like Tom.

Tom's the northern Michigan middleman between the international buyers and the trappers and houndsmen, most of whom, like me, don't do it for the money anymore. My father trapped back in Pennsylvania in the late 1970s when red fox were fetching close to a hundred dollars each. A good-sized raccoon might go for fifty. Even opossums and skunks had enough value to make it worth the effort of skinning them. I used to work for a guy my age who, in high school, was already well on his way to becoming a millionaire after starting a landscaping business with a shovel, a rake, and a mower bought with money he'd saved trapping fox and raccoon.

Why trap when most of polite society regards the practice barbaric? Even other hunters, apparently sucked in by the current climate of New Age nitwitticism, view trapping as politically extraneous baggage and trappers themselves as an expendable minority in the struggle against anti-hunters. I should mention that those in my private circle who quietly regard my interest in trapping as suggestive of some deep-seated character flaw are always the first to call for consult when beset by undesirable critters. I'll live-trap when it makes sense. Most times it doesn't and, to be honest, I don't know anyone who's been awakened at 3:00 AM by a flying squirrel clunking around in the attic—or, like my neighbor, come home from an evening out and been sprayed by a skunk—who cares one whit how the animal is made to disappear.

One thing's for sure, I'd rather be outside hunting or fishing or trapping than cooped up behind a computer screen trying to explain why. I hunt and trap and fish because on the one hand the natural world is fascinating to me, so much so that I desire to play a part in its inner workings, to play my blood role as predator. Other times I think that it's simply a way to connect with the memory of my father, who died so long ago I can barely remember his face anymore. Or maybe it's on account of my never quite giving up on those mountain-man dreams, the idea that I and my family will always have food and furs to keep warm should one day the markets crash and the barbarians come again to trample the gates of Rome.

So to understand the game is to understand myself. How does this relate to pumas, my predatory betters? Maybe in selfishly seeking out the puma in the hope of finding it I'm upping the ante like the hunter over sixty who one day finds himself bored shooting ducks and deer and books a trip to Africa to stand in the path of a charging Cape buffalo and hear at night the lion's coughing roar. Am I driven to find the puma simply to prove my supremacy over it? And what about Rusz? He could never give more than a surface answer to this question. Was he trying not only to prove he was smarter than the puma but also everybody else out there, toiling away, looking thus far in vain? Was he out there trying to validate something, a career and reputation perhaps? And what about me? I keep going back to this childhood notion I have of wilderness . . . as if finding real proof of the puma would validate old hopes that out there somewhere was a perfect place, I just had to find it.

•••

These days I skin my catch, storing the raw furs in the freezer until spring in clear plastic bags, and leave to Tom the delicate work of fleshing, stretching, and drying the pelts for sale. Cradling the box containing my meager year's catch, Tom, kneeing open the door, led me through the passway into the barn.

"Got some more work for ya," he said. At first glance, the woman inside looked more Indian than Anglo. A bloody apron laced around her slender frame, cigarette clenched in her teeth. She was Tom's girlfriend, Marty, and she smiled under her tinted frames. A muskrat dangled from a hind foot on a metal clap nailed into the post in front of her, while around her feet were maybe a dozen more. With the knife hand she took a drag on the cigarette.

"I'll have these ready in a bit. Then I gotta get to those 'coon," she said, followed by a nod of recognition to me.

Like farmers of a sort, Tom and Marty are good, hardworking people. They are country, real country. A friend I brought here once commented that the skinning barn where Tom and Marty work had the charm of a slaughterhouse. But I have always loved the raw earthiness of it. On that day, as on most, hanging from the ceiling in neat, evenly spaced rows were hundreds of pelts—red and gray foxes, coyotes, otters, muskrats, scores of raccoons. The air inside smells like wet wool, an outdoorsy aroma with traces of river mud and cattails and damp autumn leaves. It's the smell I remember most, the heavy aroma of fur and animal fat, primarily raccoon fat, which Tom prefers burning over wood in his converted oil drum stove.

"It's free and really throws the heat," he said, gripping the handle of a coal shovel leaning up against the wall and, by way of example, set about scraping up the leavings under a nearby fleshing beam. "One year back when the raccoon were thick, I skinned, fleshed, and hung up to dry at least a hundred every day for six solid weeks. I burned a hole clean through the wall of the stove."

By law, every fur that comes to Tom must be recorded and tagged to identify the owner. Tom told me he has more than two thousand customers—trappers and houndsmen—from his territory in the northern Lower Peninsula.

After slamming shut the hatch door to the stove, he led me over to his cluttered workbench under the only window in the place, a grimy square of glass, where he pushed back his stained Hawbakers ball cap and cleared a space of magazines—*Fur-Fish-Game* and *Trapper and Predator Caller*—and took down my trapper's license number. While he attended the books, I asked if he'd been following the reports of pumas in the news. He had.

"I've seen just about every furbearer in the state come through here, 'cept a wolf of course," he said.

"Ever hear of anyone catching a puma?" I asked.

"No. But I don't imagine I would." Tom ran an aboveboard operation, adding that the puma is not the kind of thing that anybody he associates with would ever admit to trapping or running up a tree.

"It'd be nothing but trouble," he said, "what with them being protected and all. I know people who say they see 'em, though." Tom fired up a cigarette and listened intently as I told him where I was headed that day. When I mentioned the pictures Rusz had showed me in the diner of the cat in the Mesick video, he looked at Marty, who was already working on another muskrat.

"Honey, didn't you see something about that on the news."

Marty remembered something about that, offering her opinion that the DNR knew very well that pumas were around. "They just keep the whole thing quiet on account of it hurting the tourism," she said.

Tom took a drag and blew a cloud of smoke. "Woods are a big place. No telling what's out there."

I asked what he thought about why, when it seems like a lot of people were seeing pumas, nobody seemed to be trapping or treeing them. Tom reasoned that it took a special kind of trap—a big trap—to catch and hold a puma. Coyote and bobcat are the biggest land-dwelling furbearers pursued by trappers in the North, and both, roughly thirty to forty pounds, are about a quarter of the size of an average adult puma, whose foot wouldn't even fit inside the jaws of a Victor No. 2 double-coil spring.

As to the question of running one up a tree:

"Any dog that runs bear will run a cougar," he said. "But a cat without any claws can't very well climb a tree."

I mentioned that not everybody who owns a puma has the animal declawed. Tom pondered this for a moment. To him, it defied reasonable thinking why anyone would want to own a puma in the first place, let alone allow the animal to keep its fangs and claws.

"People are strange," he said.

"Crazy!" Marty added. Bending at the waist, gripping the muskrat hide with two hands, she pulled down in one swift motion, removing the fur from the animal like someone taking off a sock. She tossed the fatty carcass on the floor.

As Tom and I moved toward the door, I asked him his take on why so many people seemed to believe in pumas.

"People need to believe in something," he said.

What if the DNR is right? What if they are all pets?

Tom didn't miss a beat here, either. "I don't think it'd much matter if the cat was wild or a pet. You see one in the woods and you'd probably shit your britches just the same."

With that he walked me to the door. Casting a sly glance at Marty, already carving the hide off her third muskrat, he spoke loud enough for her to hear, "Maybe if I start cracking the whip around here we'll get your pelts in this month's auction. The Russians are buying up beaver like mad right now. Price for a good blanket is up around forty bucks. Best it's been in years."

Back on the road, finding the way east toward Manton and turquoise sky dappled by pink and vanilla clouds, I also turned back to my thoughts. Rusz hinted that he had some good news for me about the scat I'd found over near the Dead Stream. Another confirmation from the Wyoming laboratory—more DNA evidence not only from there, but also two other Lower Peninsula counties, it would turn out. I had some more questions for the people at the Wyoming laboratory. I had questions about Rusz, who—like Midas—continued to have a curious and uncanny knack for turning piles of shit into evidentiary gold.

THE TWISTERFUGE

And many false prophets shall rise, and deceive many.

Matthew 24:11

Hard to pinpoint the exact moment I started losing faith that, if anybody was going to come along and prove to the skeptics that pumas were really here, Rusz was the one to do it. Happening gradually, one theory at a time, it was a hard thing to perceive. From November to that May morning's scheduled hunt for bones, we talked almost every week. A strange, sometimes forced dialogue. Then at others, we chatted like old buddies though I never really considered us pals. He knew I was thinking about doing a book. One day he told me, "You know, maybe I should write a book, too. I mean, how hard can it be." Plenty of conversations he lightened up to the point where we'd kid around and joke. "Oh my aching ass," was the way he sometimes said hello when I picked up the phone. "Did you see the latest?"

He had a strange way of pronouncing certain words, little Rusz-isms to which I dedicated a page in my notebook.

Something that didn't sit well with him was not "palabble." (*Palatable.*) Acts perpetrated in secret were not *clandestine*, they were "clan-dissteen."

Recluse was "ree-cloos."

Waffle was "way-fell."

He coined words like "twisterfuge," as in: "Those biologists in Lansing with all their twisterfuge have this thing so screwed up."

129

He was sort of squirrelly like that, but also calculated. I don't think he ever forgot that a pen was never far away from my hand. When he knew I was taking notes, he often reminded me of somebody interviewing for a job he knew he wasn't really qualified for. He would tell me about sightings and other search areas in the state he was exploring, piquing my interest but only so much. Even when pressed, he rarely gave up any personal details about himself. And most of the non-related puma stuff he did offer was . . . well, pat. I got the impression he just tossed stuff out there that, later on, he hoped might read well on paper.

Rusz professed to be a family man, yet even when prodded he rarely ever spoke to me of anything other than work. He claimed to hate the press, but as evident by all the newspaper articles, he never seemed to miss an opportunity to offer comment to a reporter on a deadline. From time to time he would remind me of his credentials, proof that he was a seriously accredited scientist, as if I had forgotten that a huge part of the controversy surrounding his research was that he had violated one of the most basic and traditional rules of scientific etiquette and protocol.

On one hand, I respected Rusz for having the courage to open his research to me—a writer. We had no formal arrangement. I think it all boiled down to his sheer, unflinching belief. Call him cocky or confident, Rusz sent me copies of almost every document, every fax and memo, everything that he deemed pertinent in substantiating his theories and conclusions about the state of pumas in Michigan. He let me in, and in doing so he had to know that on some level he was opening himself up to criticism. On some level I liked Rusz, which is maybe why it was so troubling to hear him constantly cutting the throat of his credibility by publicly mixing science with speculation. But what soured me the most had to be the pictures.

The more he was featured in the news, the more images people sent him. Rusz had a stack of fuzzy kitty pictures. Gray ones. Black ones. Brown and yellow ones. Aside from the infamous "Alcona County Cougar" from the September 1997 issue of the *Detroit Free Press* and another great one taken in 1993 across the county line in Oscoda County a couple of miles away, the rest weren't worth showing around to skeptics, if you ask me. Which he didn't.

If you have to introduce a picture with something like, "I know this might look like a house cat, but here's why it's not . . ." that's bad. Though I suggested as much to him a number of times, Rusz never understood the basic fact that photographs were worthless in convincing hardened puma skeptics unless you could just hand the photo over, stand back, and shut up. Combining in some cases computer enhancement, a magnifying glass, and Rusz's own brand of rigorous interpretation—some of which required mathematical formulas used to "may-sure" (a Rusz-ism for *measure*) and compare tail to body length ratio to make a puma determination—and, well . . .

He really had a couple of doozies, the kind of stuff that made me embarrassed for him in front of an audience. One favorite was of a big puffy gray cat in somebody's backyard that he had convinced himself was a young puma cub. And maybe it was. That's the point. Looking at it, the average person couldn't tell for sure. It was just a gray cat, in my opinion. Far worse were the pictures of the black ones.

Government and bounty hunters across the U.S. killed tens of thousands of pumas prior to the late 1960s without ever documenting a single case of a melanistic, or black, specimen. In Florida the biological stresses of rampant inbreeding were chronicled on a scale never before seen in what turned out to be a surviving remnant population of around fifty pumas. Florida is home to a rare population of black bobcats biologists think resulted from the same degree of inbreeding. Florida has produced black bobcats, but they've never seen a black puma.

Not only would Rusz try to convince you that the black blob in the picture sent to him from God knows whom was a puma, he would also argue it to ignorance (insist his viewpoint was true because there was no way to prove it false) that it was a never-before-seen black variety, too. All these groundbreaking claims were beginning to add up: Not only had he announced the discovery of, not one, but two lost colonies of pumas in the Upper and Lower Peninsulas in Michigan, he also believed that the state harbored a black variety of this never-before-seen creature, too. From time to time Rusz would express incredulousness at why serious puma experts doubted his evidence and why some out there were not taking him seriously.

Could it have something to do with everything he was asking people to believe?

At first I thought it strange that Rusz never once asked me directly what I thought about some of the photos. Then I was glad. I didn't want to have to tell him.

Later, instead of wanting to crawl under a chair whenever he brought out some of these kitty photos to show off, I started listening not to the way he talked or even to the cloudy interpretations he offered, but rather to *how much* he talked. He talked so much, so forcefully, and seemingly without taking a breath that the folks puzzling over the picture—if they wanted to challenge his observation or offer another opinion contrary to his own— didn't have a chance of getting in a comment even if they'd tried.

I also realized one day that maybe when talking about pumas, not only about the pictures, he didn't care what anybody else thought, unless they totally agreed with him. The longer the case dragged out, the cockier he seemed to get. Those who didn't take his word that every shred of evidence he produced was legit tended to be dubbed "stupid and ill informed," all of them poor suckers duped by what he called "the MDNR's campaign of deceit."

Or in other words: the twisterfuge.

●●●

Rolling past the ROSCOMMON COUNTY sign, I checked my watch. Cutting it close. Five minutes to nine.

For the last half hour the drive east passed from farm country to piney woods. Swamps. On account of the deer, you had to be careful driving through cedar swamps in the early morning. The sun, an orange yolk in the sky, illuminated the almond-colored coats of the deer standing in the dewy light next to the road. Two does, then another, and another. All of them

ALCONA CO. 5-17-02
M. RUSZ /P. RUSZ   1¼" DIAM.

ABOVE: An Alcona County motorist reportedly saw this puma cross the two-track in front of his pickup in 1997. He pulled up to the spot, saw the animal lying in the bracken ferns, and snapped this photo. Dubbed the 'Alcona County Cougar,' the photo first appeared in the *Detroit Free Press* where it was dismissed by some as an escaped pet, while others insisted the puma was fake, a full-body mount. The following summer, MDNR conservation officer Larry Robinson allegedly spotted a puma in the same area.

RIGHT TOP: In 2002, five years after the picture of the 'Alcona County Cougar' made the news and four years after the Oscoda County puma photo (taken roughly ten miles away), Rusz claimed to have found this puma scat just eight miles from the Alcona Cougar site. This evidence, combined with sighting reports from the area that went back to the 1930s, led Michigan Wildlife Conservancy to conclude that pumas were breeding in the area.

RIGHT BOTTOM: While on patrol in the Upper Peninsula, Frank Opolka, who later went on to become the deputy director of the Michigan Department of Natural Resources, witnessed a puma cross the road fifty feet in front of his patrol car one night in 1966. In his spotlight, he watched the animal walk across an open field. Opolka returned to the scene the next day, found a track, and made this plaster cast.

LEFT: This photo, taken by a bow hunter in 1993 in Oscoda County, was uncovered by local historian Nelson Yoder and first appeared on the cover of the May/June 2003 issue of *The Northern Journal*, a small northern Michigan "heritage" magazine.

BELOW: Patrick Rusz stood for this picture in 2003 in the spot where the 1993 Oscoda County puma photo was taken.

LEFT TOP: In the winter of 2001, a Mesick woman shot home video footage of a large, deer-colored feline walking through the woods at the edge of her backyard. According to the Michigan Wildlife Conservancy analysis of the video, which included a visit to the scene, the tree has a broken limb (the light splotch on the tree's main trunk) that Patrick Rusz reportedly used as a reference to gauge the cat's height at roughly 30 inches at the shoulder. Biologists and, later in 2004, a panel of advisor/experts with the Eastern Cougar Network challenged this assertion by identifying the creature as a large house cat.

RIGHT TOP: The Chippewa County skull.

RIGHT BOTTOM: In the first week of the 2003 Michigan firearms deer season in the Upper Peninsula, a father and son were perched in their tree stand in the woods of Mackinac County when they reportedly witnessed a puma walk almost under their stand. The puma never saw them and continued away along the same path the hunters had used, leaving this near-perfect paw print impression in one of their boot tracks.

LEFT BOTTOM: Another shot of the track in Mackinac County, with a rifle cartridge for scale.

ABOVE: In May of 2001, volunteers led by Dr. Patrick Rusz of the Michigan Wildlife Conservancy launched a field study into a 33-mile stretch of Lake Michigan beachfront known locally as Seul Choix Point, part of the Lake Superior State Forest in the Upper Peninsula's Schoolcraft and Mackinaw counties, where they reportedly discovered puma scat, tracks, and a handful of deer carcasses that showed signs consistent with puma kills.

RIGHT: Patrick Rusz examines evidence from a suspected puma deer kill on the beach at Seul Choix Point in May of 2001.

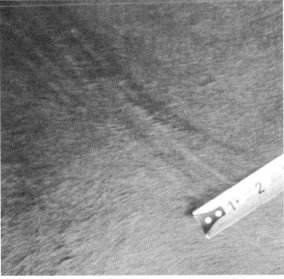

TOP: Rocky outcroppings, dense hardwoods, and vast cedar swamps are typical of the terrain running parallel to the beach at Seul Choix Point where Patrick Rusz theorized pumas were hiding out during the day. At night, his theory continued, they moved out to the treeline where they would ambush deer at the water's edge as the animals moved from the woods to drink.

BOTTOM: Claw marks on the back of a full-grown Belgian horse belonging to Tower resident Dale Willey. In the summer of 2001, the horse's stillborn foal had also disappeared days after a puma was allegedly seen stalking along the edge of the horse pasture. The body of the foal was later found outside the pasture, partially consumed. Willey believed the puma he'd seen was responsible. Fourteen days later, Willey found a large puma track—hard physical evidence that a puma was in the area—in soft dirt along the outside of the pasture fence.

RIGHT AND BELOW: The author discovered this track and this scat near the Platte River along the southeastern border of Sleeping Bear Dunes National Lakeshore in December of 2001. It's unclear what animal made this track; it is at least a week old and the photo is of poor quality. The scat was found a short distance away in the middle of a two-track road, partially covered with grass. Another three- to four-inch piece of the scat (not pictured) was damaged prior to discovery, run over and smashed almost flat in the tire rut.

BENZIE COUNTY SCAT
SAMPLE NO. 1

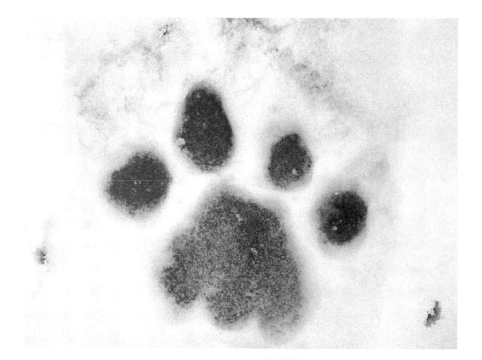

ABOVE: A puma track in snow. To teach himself how to recognize puma tracks in mud, dirt, sand, and snow, Patrick Rusz visited a wildlife park near his home that housed a pair of pumas. Note the most defining characteristics of a puma track: the prominent three-lobed heel pad and lead toe.

RIGHT TOP: Puma or dog? This image reveals how difficult it can be to identify a puma track. At first glance, this may appear to be a puma, based on the prominent three-lobed heel pad. However, dog paws look pretty similar, and are far more likely to show claws.

RIGHT BOTTOM: A dog track in beach sand.

Sleeping Bear Dunes

National Park Service
U.S. Department of the Interior

Sleeping Bear Dunes
National Lakeshore

You Are A Visitor In Cougar Habitat

There have been recent cougar sightings near this area. To see a cougar can be a thrilling experience. Cougars, however, deserve your respect! You are unlikely to see a cougar, but it is wise to know how to behave should you encounter one. Cougars are tawny-colored with black-tipped ears and tail. Adults are 5 - 8 feet long from nose to the end of a long tail.

If you encounter a cougar:
-Remain calm - DO NOT RUN.
-Pick up small children immediately.
-Stand up and spread your arms to make yourself look big.
-Maintain eye contact, back away slowly.
-If approached, wave your arms, shout, and throw sticks or rocks.
-If attacked, fight back aggressively.
-Do not approach a cougar.

Please consider these precautions when hiking in this area:
-Keep your dog on a leash.
-Keep children next to you when hiking.
-Travel in groups whenever possible.

Protect Wildlife By Protecting Yourself!

Please report any encounter to the National Park Service. Call: 231-326-5134.
The cougar is a state-listed endangered species fully protected by law.

ABOVE: Sleeping Bear Dunes National Lakeshore (SBDNL) officials posted these warning signs on all thirteen of its hiking/cross-country ski trails after a series of puma sightings made by (SBDNL) visitors, park rangers, and, most notably, the close range encounter reported by a park naturalist in the fall of 2003 on a popular hiking and cross-country ski path near the park's southernmost boundary.

standing chest-deep in brush and cedar green, a junglelike density that re-minded me of the pictures I'd seen of Florida palmetto.

I'd gone to bed the night before reading from Charles Fergus's *Swamp Screamer*, a natural history of the Florida "panther" and its modern struggle to survive. When we'd first met, Rusz had recommended the book as one of his favorites, along with David Maehr's *The Florida Panther: Life and Death of a Vanishing Carnivore* and Ken Alvarez's *Twilight of the Panther: Biology, Bureaucracy and Failure in an Endangered Species Program*.

Since Rusz constantly referred to parallels with the Florida case when ar-guing his theory that Michigan could very well harbor a remnant population of pumas, I considered the text necessary reading.

As in Michigan, pumas were believed vanished from Florida by 1900 de-spite persistent sightings and anecdotal encounters that in 1935 inspired a local hunter named David Newell to invite two Arizona houndsmen to chase pumas in Big Cypress Swamp.

In *Swamp Screamer*, Fergus writes how members of the Audubon Society were so appalled they wrote letters to Newell pleading that he not go through with the hunt. But at the time there was no law against it. (Florida would not ban hunting pumas until 1958.) Newell and his hunting party answered by killing eight pumas in five weeks, three of which were trailed and shot the first two mornings out and within a couple of miles of camp.

The number of dead certainly suggests either that pumas were more com-mon than people thought, or that the men meant business. Probably a little of both. Just imagine for moment what it must have been like camping out for more than a month in 1935 in the middle of the most grimy, godfor-saken, snake- and alligator-infested tracts of jungle swamp in the entire Lower Forty-Eight. Imagine every day rising at the crack of ass, loosing the hounds and heading off after them, slogging through stinking black-water muck and slapping at a cloud of malaria-carrying mosquitoes as you go.

While Fergus makes no mention of it, I can't help but think that maybe Newell had an ax to grind. To kill eight pumas anywhere in little over a month, let alone under what must have been the most miserable of conditions, you really have to be angry at them. Or maybe Newell was acting out of spite. Maybe he had seen a puma close up and been snickered at by some snotty game warden, told that what he really saw was a bobcat or yellow Labrador retriever. We'll never know.

What is known is that despite Goldman's *Puma (Felis) concolor coryi* being one of the first animals added to the endangered species list in 1967, pumas were officially extinct in Florida until a privately funded conservation group challenged conventional thinking in 1973. The World Wildlife Fund hired now legendary Texas houndsman Roy McBride to run down and tree a Florida panther if he could. Most believed the mission a fool's errand. The only pumas in Florida were the occasional FERCs getting hit on Route 84—otherwise known as Alligator Alley, built in 1967 and the major causeway cutting through the Everglades and Big Cypress Swamp. At least that was the official stance anyway.

In the 1940s the puma's primary food source—the white-tailed deer—was essentially exterminated statewide in a government-sponsored program to stop the spread of a tick that caused cattle fever. The swamplands of the Everglades were increasingly shrinking, drained and developed. Killing off the puma's primary food should have meant the end for any remnant population. And why weren't more hunters reporting sightings of them?

McBride promptly treed a female puma in South Florida, west of Lake Okeechobee. As recounted by Fergus in *Swamp Screamer*, she was a sickly looking specimen "nine or ten years old, skinny, tick infested, and with teeth worn down to nubs." Still the hunt made national news, an almost unbelievable coup, yet for the next ten years seemingly nothing more happened until Roy McBride returned with Chris Belden, a biologist working for the Florida Fish and Game Department, and treed another puma in the Fakahatchee Strand. They put a radio collar on it. That was 1983.

What researchers discovered over the next ten years was a predator on the way out. No more than fifty pumas were left in Florida. What some had once believed were physical characteristics that made the Florida puma a unique subspecies—notably a swirling cowlick of fur above their shoulders, a kink in the tail of many specimens, and a peculiar-looking flat face and "Roman nose" caused by what Goldman described as "nasals remarkably broad and high arched"—were actually physical deformities caused by almost a century of inbreeding. Researchers further discovered that many of the surviving males of the species were all but impotent. Some had only one descended testicle, while others were essentially sterile thanks to genetically mutated tailless or backward-swimming sperm. Radio-collar research began showing that the greatest cause of mortality among puma kittens was cannibalism by older, territorial males. As for adults, they seemed to have an unfortunate propensity for running in front of fast-moving cars. (At this writing, there have been sixty roadkilled pumas in Florida since the state began keeping track of the numbers in 1973.)

The situation was dire. While a great many took a Darwinian stance, arguing the sense of trying to save an animal so miserably mutated and obviously on the brink of extinction, turf battles were fought in Tallahassee among state and federal bureaucrat-biologists for control of the millions of dollars suddenly flowing into Florida's puma recovery effort. Voted the official state animal by grade school children in 1982, the Florida panther also became the poster animal for anti-hunters and environmentalists—pretty much anybody seeking to heap their political burdens on what was essentially the puma's broken back.

The reason Rusz gave repeatedly for not wanting to run a puma up a tree was that he wanted to avoid all this, what he called "the Florida circus."

"All collaring a cougar would show is the animal running around its territory anyway," he said. By collecting scat and, in the case of the Chippewa skull, bones, you could extract and compare DNA and tell everything you'd ever want to know about the animal: genetic relationships among specimens (breeding); origin (whether descended from South American or North American stock); separation of individuals; the sex of the puma in question. (By spring 2002 Rusz had for months been negotiating a research/cost agreement between MWC and a Michigan college, Central Michigan University, to take over scat testing from the Wyoming lab purportedly to perform these more advanced genetic tests.)

"Over fifty million dollars was spent in Florida before there was any real increase in the population," was the way Rusz summed up the Florida situation. His reading of the case showed that this Noah's Ark notion that—if you only provide suitable habitat—a species can recover and flourish after being knocked back into the shallow end of the gene pool simply doesn't work no matter how much money is dumped into protecting the land and providing an adequate base of prey.

To ramp up the native population, Florida biologists eventually had to resort to importing new blood—wild pumas from parts west. The controversial plan worked, but only after a legal battle against those who argued that importing a handful of Texas pumas would intentionally contaminate the native gene pool. There were also money concerns that a *Felis* (*Puma*) *concolor Stanleyana* and *Felis* (*Puma*) *concolor coryi* hybrid would be ineligible for protection with federal tax dollars under the Endangered Species Act.

But in 1990 genetic testing had revealed that some of the Florida pumas—notably those cats occurring in Big Cypress Swamp—were not a genetically pure strain of *Puma concolor coryi* anyway. DNA testing showed that somewhere along the line, captive South American pumas had crossbred with the natives and essentially from a legal standpoint corrupted their genes. It's now widely known that for almost a decade, starting in the mid-1950s, a small wildlife park known as Everglades Wonder Gardens had released up to seven pumas into the swamp—the now infamous "Piper Stock."[10]

This question of genetic purity's impact on state and federal puma protection reached a head in 1987 in the felony case of James Billie, a Seminole Indian who at first glance openly violated the Endangered Species Act by jacklighting a puma one night on the Big Cypress Swamp reservation. Before he was found out and arrested, Billie skinned the animal and reportedly ate some of it. But he eventually beat all the charges, not because under law his Native blood allowed him to kill any game on reservation property at any time of year, but rather because his defense team proved through modern tax-onomy techniques using DNA that Billie did not kill a pure strain of Florida panther, but rather a hybrid (probably a descendant from the Piper Stock) that was technically not protected under the law. This led to federal and state statutes adopting what is commonly referred to as "the similarity of appear-ance clause," which basically means that if it walks like a puma and looks like a puma, it enjoys full protection under the law.

What Rusz liked to point out about the Florida case is that the puma is capable of not only surviving but also eluding detection despite suburban en-croachment and a spiking human population. Also, the Florida case is show-ing that puma and humans can coexist. (There's never been a recorded attack on a person in Florida.)

Rusz was prone to use Florida as a case study when it benefited the argu-ment he was trying to make. But one issue he could never rectify to the sat-isfaction of the cynics is why—when in thirty years Florida has had almost as many pumas killed on the road as survive in the state today—Michigan has never had a single documented roadkill.

"I've been to Florida and talked to the people down there," Rusz told me once. "I've driven in a car around and through the entire range of the Florida panther in a little less than four hours. Here in Michigan we're talking about a handful of animals spread out over one of the biggest states in the nation. An area where especially in the north has far less traffic flow and, overall, far fewer roads."

A hard sell. And no one who really knew pumas was buying it.

Florida now has a population of pumas larger than the state's dwindling habitat can handle. The U.S. Fish and Wildlife Service is even looking for new homes in other states to accommodate the overflow. Arkansas was recently considered and found to have enough suitable habitat that pumas could es-tablish a healthy colony there. The only problem now is that the state fish and game agency doesn't want them.

I pulled into the parking lot of the Bob's Big Boy and tried to set aside all these vexing theories, unanswered questions, and reservations about what

I was getting deeper into. Further, as a case study, I had to wonder: How much does Florida matter when discussing how pumas might someday be welcomed in Michigan? Or more likely, does every state have to bumble its own way toward understanding and acceptance of the puma at its own pace?

Rusz and I had different ideas about the weight the Florida case carried in arguing for pumas here, just as we had divergent notions about what role science (namely the analyzing of scat samples in a laboratory) would play in the discovery. One thing Florida did show, one question that I was beginning to think needed to be asked first, occurred to me while I was sitting there waiting for Rusz.

Do we really want pumas here?

If we don't, all further discussion is moot. If we do, I believe one way or the other pumas will either be found or put back where they belong.

•••

After a greasy buffet breakfast of sausage and eggs, I left my rig parked under a light post in the back of the parking lot and climbed into the front seat of Rusz's new rig, a big dark blue Ford Expedition. As I settled into the seat, I mentioned how the puma business looked like it was going well. Rusz nodded. Said, "Ha!"

In the backseat were Mark and Larry, another relation to Rusz, this time by marriage. His wife's cousin, or something. Like Rusz's son, Larry wasn't much of a talker. Maybe my ever-present notebook, my constant scribbling, spooked him. He mentioned over breakfast that he believed he and his wife had seen a puma once in the UP while heading toward Brimley on Route 75.

"It was quite some distance away," he said. "But it was big and had cat-like movements . . ." That was it. The encounter trailed off into a realization that all of a sudden he was dying for a smoke. Rusz had briefed me that Larry was a retired Dow Corning worker, which left me with the impression he came along on these road trips for something to break up the time.

"I saw the thing," said Rusz, meaning the Chippewa skull. "I actually held it in my hands." He had taken pictures, too. Good pictures. It was puma skull all right. And in surprisingly good shape by the looks of it.

Rusz also filled me in on the latest from the Wyoming lab. The analysis of the latest round of scats were "amplifying"—that is, coming up puma—in at least three Lower Peninsula counties. Alcona, Roscommon, and Benzie. The Benzie scat was the one I had picked up near the Platte River, a couple-odd miles from the Sleeping Bear Dunes, back in December. Somehow I was not surprised.

Looking back, at this point, I would later wonder why I continued going on with this. Why go to the UP to try and find some moldering old puma bones when I had already talked to all the right people and pretty much gathered that not even a whole puma would change policy. For months I'd been vacillating between thinking Rusz was really onto something to thinking him a kook. Rusz was a lot of things, but was he charlatan? Did he pull the old switcher-a-roo with some of that scat before packing it off to the lab? Not all of it, but just some. These are things I often considered. And the mere fact that I was thinking about this as often as I considered the politics of pumas didn't bode well for my enthusiasm.

With four of us piled into Rusz's SUV the drive was particularly quiet heading north toward the Mackinac Bridge. With the bright sun edging well past ten o'clock high, we passed a series of billboard signs for The Mystery Spot and another tourist trap called Sea Shell City that promised a once-in-a-lifetime glimpse of a 500LB MAN-EATING CLAM. I mentioned wanting to see the clam and Rusz made a face. No go on The Mystery Spot, either.

We stopped for gas and jerky at Mackinaw City. While Larry smoked, I chatted with Mark about turkey hunting. Him and the old man had a few places lined up. They were already gobbling down around St. Charles.

Back on the road, the tall iron towers and sweeping steel cables of the Mackinac Bridge came into view. Rusz obliged the flashing road sign blinking CAUTION . . . CAUTION . . . CAUTION by easing off the gas and falling in

line behind a semi truck jostling top-heavy in a sudden blast of wind blowing off Lake Huron two hundred feet below.

"You hear about that woman who went over last year?" Rusz said, eyeing
the rearview mirror. "She was driving a Yugo or something. Wind just picked
up the car and over she went." He made a plunging arch with his free hand,
the other casually gripping the wheel at six o'clock.

I'd crossed the bridge dozens of times and found they were always good
for a few nervous anecdotes like this. Talk of history. Talk of death.

Two hundred years ago when British and French troops eyed one another
from spiky wooden forts overlooking the straits, the only way across the waters was by ship and, during winter, via cargo sleds muscled over the ice by
horses and men. Now streaking over roughly a mile of frigid water into the
land of the UP takes little more than five minutes.

I fiddled with the radio, finding an AM station with a happy historical
commentary of how the Mackinaw Bridge came to be, recording in my notes
both a slice of that history along with my own morbid recollections of other
suicides and accidental deaths.

*. . . since the late 1800s men dreamed of a bridge that might someday connect
Michigan's Upper and Lower Peninsulas . . . the Mighty Mac was officially opened
in 1957 . . . car lines stretched up to seventeen miles, waiting up to nineteen hours,
for ferries to take them one and a half miles across the perilous straits . . .*

"A plane once flew right into one of the suspender cables during a storm.
One of those commuter jobs. Killed three people."

*. . . rising five hundred and fifty-two feet—fifty-five stories—above the Straits
of Mackinac, the Mackinaw Bridge cost one hundred million dollars to construct
and today stands as one of the most astounding engineering marvels of the century and is the longest suspension bridge in the world . . .*

"Six suicides. People just pull over and jump. Can you imagine?"

*. . . forty-two thousand miles—enough steel wire to go around the earth one
and three-quarter times—were spun together to form the Mighty Mac's two main
cables . . . 1998 saw the one millionth car crossing . . .*

Nobody was listening so I went back to my notes. *Hopes and dreams*. I wrote these words in my notebook without knowing why. Unlike Rusz, I was feeling awfully pessimistic about our chances of finding anything that day. Again I wondered: What would puma bones matter even if by some stroke of luck we managed to find them?

I thought about my wife and the baby on the way. A boy. Midway across the bridge I looked out the passenger's window, considering watery oblivion through the taut steel cables and spied a white boat the size of a Matchbox car bobbing in the waves far below.

I didn't know it at the time, but a couple of months later, in August, the news would report another jumper, a woman, leaping from this very spot into Lake Huron with her six-month-old baby in her arms.

Hindsight. But at that moment there were only birds. Down below soared a hundred white gulls and we were above them, me wondering what it might feel like to plunge headlong through the middle of them.

• • •

The stop in Rudyard was supposed to take all of a few minutes. But Mike Zuidema was running late. We cruised down the main street of that sleepy little town, an empty row between feed and auto parts stores, and pulled into the dirt parking lot of Pure Country Family Restaurant, situated at the far end of town. There we spilled out of the Ford, stretching. Larry fired up a smoke while the rest of us headed inside to wait.

The only diners in the place were an elderly couple sitting in the corner on the same side of a table wearing puffy Jeff Gordon NASCAR coats. Copper cutouts of horses adorned the plain white walls. Metal auditorium-style chairs and blue plastic table covers. Rusz led the way to a table by the window where we could watch the street outside. A cook in a white T-shirt eyed us from the kitchen through a small window punched out of the wall. A waitress appeared through the swinging door with a coffeepot and menus.

Rusz had told me earlier that when he'd first come to the UP searching for pumas, he'd ended up feeling kind of silly looking for evidence of an animal the locals already regarded as being out there. As if to prove the point, he asked Katie, blond and blue-eyed, if she'd heard any stories about pumas in the area. Fishing around in her apron for a pencil, she looked up matter-of-factly and told us she had recently seen one herself "down by Ed and Joyce's place.

"It was nighttime out," she said. "I was driving home and came up on these glowing green eyes down in the ditch. I slowed down and it just crossed the road in front of the car."

"How far away?" Rusz asked, looking at me with an *I-told-you-so* smile breaking his face.

"Oh, about here to Henry." She pointed with the coffeepot in the direction of the NASCAR couple. Henry raised his cup and smiled.

"The thing's head came to the hood of my car," Katie said. "What are you doing up here? Huntin' the thing down?"

Rusz dispatched Mark to the truck to fetch his manila folders filled with his puma things while he and I listened to Henry tell of a benign encounter a friend of his had with a puma while deer hunting the year before.

When Mark returned, Rusz sent him back out to the truck again for a map. He opened the folder and selected an article from the top, a recent article from the *Detroit Free Press*, and proudly poked at a picture of himself.

"Oh yeah. I read about you. You're that shit chaser," she bubbled, reclining a coffeepot on her hip. "I heard of you."

•••

Mike Zuidema struck me every bit as the clean-cut government man he used to be. He pulled up against the curb, exited his black S-10 pickup, and walked smartly into the restaurant while I watched through the glass.

White-haired, clean-shaven, and fit looking for his sixty-odd years, he had quick, bright eyes and a good healthy tan. Zuidema was one of the volunteers who supplied Rusz and MWC with scat they ran through the Wyoming laboratory the year before. Zuidema was an ex-DNR forester.

Clearly a straight-shooter, a spit-and-polish looking man. He shook my hand firmly then apologized for being late, explaining that the man who'd actually found the puma skull, an Indian with the last name of Farmer, didn't feel like coming out to meet us.

"He knew I had people coming up here," said Zuidema. "Guy told me he was out fishing all night and wanted to take a nap. He sounded hungover if you ask me."

Zuidema was supposed to call back in an hour. In the meantime, he'd taken sketchy directions to the skull spot over the phone. With that Rusz gathered up his portfolio and dealt a business card to Harry and the perky Katie, who hollered after us as we single-filed through the door:

"Hey, if I catch that cougar I'll save the crap for you."

•••

We headed out of town, Zuidema leading the way, none of us exactly sure where we were going. Twice we had to pull over to reconnoiter around Zuidema's napkin map pressed out on the hood. As we drove east past crucifix-like utility poles, the country had a gloomy open-prairie look about it. Houses set hauntingly in the middle of great green fields, each with an empty swing set in the backyard. A raven or a hawk soaring in the big sky would look down on our course and see the roads we followed laid out in an orderly grid work, a country cut into sectional squares. A stop sign would appear every mile or so. Crossroads without character. 9 Mile Road. 10 Mile Road. And so on. Stopping and starting again like that through this patchwork of low-lying swamps, fields, and woodlots, eventually Zuidema's brake lights shone, turn signal flashing. Another ubiquitous white ranch house. The sign out front read NORTHLAND TAXIDERMY.

I thought we might be stopping again, maybe this time to ask for directions. But, no, turned out this was the place. A little beyond the sign, we followed Zuidema down a service road leading into a stand of pines and rolled to a stop.

"Well, this shaping up to be another cluster fuck," Rusz said, slamming the gearshift into park. My sentiments exactly. Lately the cluster fuck was my

BEAST OF NEVER, CAT OF GOD

leitmotif. I hung back at the truck with Larry, reclined against the Ford having another smoke, while Rusz, Mark, and Zuidema had a powwow.

Were I not acting as chronicler of the trip, I would have suggested we all just get the hell out of there and go home. A skull uncovered behind a taxidermy shop. Go figure. The implication seemed glaringly obvious to me, and I was glad to finally hear Rusz say it.

"Somebody oughta go see if that guy's been doing any dumping back here," he said. By Zuidema's map the power line where the woodcutter found the skull was only a couple of hundred yards through the pines.

The taxidermist wasn't home. After the others had filed off through the pines, I cut a path through the woods and rapped on the front door of the house. No one answered at the shop, either, a darkened little outbuilding with a big window in front cluttered with mounted deer heads, glassy-eyed fish, and a dusty mallard duck contorted to appear as if casually preening on a slab of driftwood. I jotted down the phone number on the sign at the end of the drive then headed back to join up with the others.

A power line was there, a line of utility poles set in a brushy swath a hundred yards wide littered with downed timber and pine tops. I held up on the edge of the trees, taking stock of the disappointing scene. Larry and Mark appeared to be aimlessly searching under the eyes of a pair of horses watching from a nearby pasture while Rusz and Zuidema were talking to a stranger who had apparently come down from one of the two white houses in plain view of where I stood.

Within the hour we had a skirmish line formed, eyes to the ground looking for bones. The stranger reemerged from his house with his entire nuclear family in tow. Two little children and a wife who, after considering the pictures of the puma skull Rusz had been carrying around in his shirt pocket, cast suspicion on the next-door neighbor.

This led into a story about some neighbors who had supposedly seen a puma "sunning himself out in the horse pasture on top of a stack of hay bales." And then, at least in Rusz's mind, came the clincher:

The wife remembered how the horseman had a colt killed the year before and soon after shot a black bear that he'd caught snooping around.

"Know if he reported it?" asked Rusz.

"I don't want to speak ill of the man," she said. "But he's been in trouble with the law before."

"For what?" Rusz asked, his eyes widening. I could read in his face that already a theory was beginning to form.

"Oh, you know. Drunk driving and some other stuff. Union stuff. You know . . . He blew some things up."

Rusz looked at me wide-eyed, beaming. I knew where this was going. And sure enough . . . The puma, whose bones we hadn't yet even found, had in a flash gone from being the obvious litter of a taxidermist to being the recent target of a pyromaniac union thug protecting his livestock.

Rusz and Zuidema convened: Somebody should go talk with the neighbor. And with that, we were off. Rusz and me, along to watch and take notes. We trekked briskly back to his rig through the pines, stopping one more time at the taxidermist's house. Still nobody home. Then we climbed into the Ford and I listened as Rusz concocted a story.

●●●

We left the truck running in the driveway of The Horseman's house, keeping to the gravel walkway as we approached the front door. I caught a glimpse of the curtains parting in the big bay window; the next second a little, slim balding man dressed in blue jeans and a plaid, tight-fitting cowboy shirt stepped out on the front porch.

The Horseman clearly didn't buy for a second Rusz's story that we were college researchers looking into livestock predation. As Rusz bumbled through the lie, the man fired up a cigarette and leaned his elbows over the porch rail, eyeing Rusz like an owl as he spoke.

"Have you seen anything? Wolves, bears, or bobcats?" Rusz asked.

The Horseman considered, picking a fleck of tobacco off the end of his tongue.

"Seen some wolves around."

"How about any bears?"

Rusz had never shown me any propensity for finesse, and at the mention of "bear" The Horseman stiffened up like an animal surprised.

"Look," he said. "Whatta y'all want."

With our ham-handed bluff called, an awkward second passed. A genuine look of surprise came over Rusz's face, but he kept to the story. Researchers. Predators. The Horseman's glare turned on me and I managed to muster a dumb smile, remembering my motivation: humble graduate assistant here to help the good professor out.

"I shot a bear out back after one mangled up one of my colts," he finally said. "DNR came out here and gave me a permit."

"What about cougars? We've got some reports one was in the area."

The Horseman looked at Rusz like he had pumas coming out of his ears. The answer was no and he stood stone-faced, awaiting the next question that never came. Instead Rusz fumbled for a business card. He handed one over and The Horseman slid it into his breast pocket without looking at it. And with that the conversation came to an end.

Back in the truck, Rusz put it in reverse and asked, "So what do you think?"

I told him I thought the guy was telling the truth.

"Well, he seemed nervous to me."

Well, yeah. No doubt, he was a little nervous. How many times are you accosted at the front door of your home in the middle of the afternoon by two unknown somebodies asking a barrage of leading questions?

"Yeah, well, I'll bet you anything that guy shot our cougar and it either crawled off to die in the brush or he dragged the sombitch back to that power line and buried it."

And that, as they say, was that.

When we met back with Zuidema and the others, we found that the family and all the kids had given up and gone home, replaced by Rob Farmer, the woodcutter, who had finally arrived but was having a hard time recalling exactly where he'd picked up the skull.

"It was last fall, you know," he said. "Everything's greened up now and different."

First he took us one way, and then another, retelling the story as we wandered.

"It was layin' out on the ground," he remembered. "I thought it might be a deer skull and then I seen the eye socket and the jaw and then I picked it up and saw this big old fang sticking out and I was like *Oh shit what the hell's this.*"

Farmer decided on a general area at the end of the power line amid a pile of brush and slashing. We fanned out and started looking while Zuidema hung back, still talking to Farmer. Larry wandered off firing up another smoke, while Mark, off by himself, tacked back and forth. Meanwhile, instead of bones I found the pale catacomb head of a morel mushroom poking up through the leaves. Placing it in my pocket, I found myself drifting away looking for more. But all of a sudden Rusz hollered that he'd found something.

The jawbone was caked with black dirt and moss. Missing some teeth. Rusz turned it over in his hands then handed it to Zuidema, who unceremoniously called black bear. And without further deliberation and any more evidence than this, Rusz announced that this was quite obviously the lower jaw of the black bear The Horseman had shot. Clearly, he potted the thing and dumped it here.

Come again?

Farmer said this was the general area he found the puma skull (though he said repeatedly he wasn't exactly sure). The Horseman admitted shooting a black bear (typically wildlife shot under depredation permit is collected by the MDNR). And here was a piece of a black bear jaw (we were poking around a taxidermy shop). For Rusz, that pretty much summed up the connection.

I looked at the faces around me, and as more speculation of poaching spewed from Rusz with nobody interjecting a single contradictory word, I had finally had enough. I suddenly wanted to get away from here, from all of this. But just as suddenly I realized how far we were from home. So instead

I headed off again to see if the taxidermist had yet returned home, maybe use the phone.

•••

The sun was sinking with my mood, but the adventure wasn't quite over.

As Larry and Mark dozed in the backseat I cooled off, feigning interest in my notes while Rusz quietly contemplated the road. I chalked the day up to a total and confusing loss. The only good thing was we were making good time heading south, home. By the time we crossed over the bridge and made the exit for the Big Boy, my plan was to shake hands with everyone, wish Rusz good luck, and try not to ever speak to him again.

But heading up the exit ramp, Rusz sort of offhandedly mentioned how there was still light enough to maybe make one more stop.

"I got this little hot spot near the restaurant," he said. "You're welcome to check it out with us if you want."

He refreshed my memory along the way. The very first day we met I'd seen Baggies of puma crap in Rusz's cooler marked ROSCOMMON. Those scats, he said, had come from the place we were headed, a private property I'll call Happy Acres, roughly three hundred acres of hardwood forest and swamp. We pulled off the main road and onto one of dirt. Larry and Mark jostled awake.

Happy Acres was an unfenced hunting club of sorts—mostly for deer and turkey—where, according to Rusz, the caretakers of the place had been seeing pumas fairly regularly for some time.

"Pumas?" I asked.

"Yeah, it sounds like there might be at least two of them."

Rusz recounted the sighting of a small one and another, distinctly larger animal, much darker in color. The caretaker of the property had seen it more than once and described the animal as black.

"We found deer kills here and scat," he said, "but for some reason the first batch you saw went to Wyoming for testing and didn't amplify."

Rusz had been looking for more scat here ever since, adding that the care-takers at Happy Acres had only agreed to let him on the property if he agreed not to try to trap the animals or run them with dogs.

"They like the pumas being here," he said. "And they don't want the DNR snooping around."

Finally the wooden arch HAPPY ACRES sign came into view. We passed under it following the dirt lane through the secondary growth—pole-sized maples and aspens and a few knotty birch trees—to a complex of small cot-tages and mobile homes set among the trees. Rusz stopped at the main house but nobody was home.

Driving the dirt road back behind the main house, we passed food plots hacked out of the trees like golf greens. Rye. Alfalfa. In every one of those lush green clearings deer standing cattlelike—herds of them already in their red summer fur—abruptly raised their heads to watch as the truck jostled slowly past.

The sun was dropping down behind the trees when Rusz finally pulled to a stop. Stepping out of the truck, I could feel the evening air still and cool. Larry and Mark stayed in the truck as Rusz led me clawing our way up a tiny hill where under the boughs of a cedar he pointed out the remains of a deer kill they'd found the year before. Now a near-perfect skeleton.

"This deer was all intact last year when we found it," he said, hunkering down and gripping up a handful of rib bones.

"See this," he said. "The ribs are all neatly sheared."

And they were. Rusz had found a couple of these kills on the property, but he wanted to get out and start looking for scat. We drove back to the care-taker's house and the assembly of outbuildings, leaving the truck there and going the rest of the way on foot.

The four of us walked the road in a staggered line, Rusz in the lead, then Larry smoking, then Mark, then me dragging up the rear, for the first time in memory without my nose in a notebook. The road system behind what constituted the club was a tangle of unmarked dirt two-tracks leading to more green food plots. Every opening had a deer blind—a wooden shacklike building—situated on the downwind side. There were deer everywhere fleeing, soundlessly bounding away, their white flags waving. But most peculiar to me were the porcupines. As the light continued to go gray we saw more and more of them hobbling through the leaves, crossing the road, some passing within feet of us seemingly unaware.

Coming to the top of a little rise, the road split in three directions; we were discussing who would go each way when a porcupine ambled through. For a moment I thought he was going to walk right through the middle of our circle. He had that absentminded porcupine look, dawdling along up to us as if he had something very serious on his little mind, when at the last second he stopped suddenly, sniffing the air and then turning to flare his prickly backside. Unconcerned with the display, Rusz kept on talking and we split up. Larry was headed back down the road to the truck, while by Rusz's recollection of the layout of the place Mark, he, and I would take the long circle around.

The three of us poked along, finding nothing on the road but oodles of deer tracks. We were headed west, evident by the sky glowing orange, streaked by purple clouds, over the treetops. Skirting the edge of a black cedar swamp, we came up on two diverging roads. Rusz and Mark stopped to discuss splitting up while I stood off to the side looking at my watch.

The two roads bulged around a patch of fallen timber and dense secondary growth and would, I understood, eventually meet up with one another a couple of hundred yards ahead. After Mark made off, Rusz mentioned that he had found a puma scat at this crossroads a couple months before.

"It's been a good spot," he said, eyes fixed on the ground. I tried to sound interested but all I could think about was home. Moving off ahead, trying to hurry along what I knew would be an agonizingly slow crawl. The road ahead bent around a screen of brush, and I paused there waiting for Rusz to catch up.

In Zen, specifically as I understand it through reading books on the art of archery, practitioners often talk of the "exquisite state of unconcerned immersion," or "the right presence of mind," loosely defined as a moment of inner peace and clarity—when the heart of the archer and the mark become one—directly preceding the loosing of the arrow. Eugen Herrigel described it as "a state in which nothing definite is thought, planned, striven for, desired or expected, which aims in no particular direction and yet knows itself capable alike of the possible and the impossible . . . this state, which is at bottom purposeless and egoless, was called by the Master truly 'spiritual.'"

Some believe that all answers to life's greatest questions are found in this state of wont-less rapture. We Westerners call it an "Ah-Ha Moment"—red-eyed and frustrated by a problem, we give up and walk away, and in this release the answer suddenly hits us.

Of course, there's also the saying that the delusions or false visions that come in times of great stress are simply the mind's way of creating what it needs. But I wasn't looking for pumas anymore. In fact, what I needed and wanted more than anything at the moment was to see the truck.

I cast a sorry glance back to see Rusz dawdling over obvious coyote tracks again. Turning back to look down the trail with a heavy sigh, I caught a flash of movement, a large animal quartering away toward me, slinking through the brush.

It was coming from the direction Mark had gone, moving as if spooked by him, or us, headed toward the opening of the two-track where I stood. The first thought that occurred to me was that it was a deer, a big deer, low to the ground, almost crawling. I'd seen old, big-racked bucks while out hunting try sneaking away from advancing hunters in this fashion, but the shape and color here were all wrong. The way it moved, the proportions . . .

I stared with a mix of shock and attachment. What struck me most was how it moved, like liquid flowing noiselessly over the leaves, pouring around the deadfalls. The color, not black exactly, was like wet tree bark, a sodden and shady gray fading along its flanks down into the legs, deer-colored . . . like the color of a raw almond shell. It spilled out onto the trail, and I saw the profile—a tail.

A long-ass fucking tail.

From a side-on glimpse of the animal it appeared so low to the ground that it looked like a wave of earth rippling up and away down the two-track I was standing on. I wrote in my notes later how thick the front legs were. The paws—the huge-ass fucking paws—looked the size of pies. It slinked fast and fluid, more like a low crawl than a run, straight away with the end of the tail almost touching the ground, sweeping down from a wide, dark rump. I was impressed by how wide the animal appeared, how when it stepped out on the trail before turning away, its head was tiny, so small in proportion to its shoulders that it looked almost not to have a head. All this in the few seconds it took my mind to jump from deer, to big dog, to the miracle moment when I realized it was a puma. And then it was gone.

I turned to Rusz who was just ten yards behind, but with his nose stuck to the ground had missed the whole thing.

I said:

"Did I just see a dog?"

Rusz looked up from the dirt dumbly. His hands were in his pockets. He had seen nothing, but he saw my face. Looked right away down the trail he said, "Huh? What?"

"I think I just saw something."

The next few moments passed in a frenzied void. I did not feel surprised. Not thrilled. Certainly not fearful. I just wanted to see that fucking thing again.

I grabbed Rusz by the shirtsleeve, yanking him off his feet not backward but ahead, almost running to the top of that little rise. I wanted, no *needed*, another glimpse.

"What. What did you see?"

At the top of the hill I spilled it.

"The puma . . . a puma. Big as shit. Holy shit. It was right there."

The road split off again and, my notebook tucked away for once, I suddenly commandeered the inquiry by pushing Rusz down one road, me down another, maybe to pinch off the puma's escape and get one more glimpse.

I hurried down the road, looking into the brush, not seeing anything. Stopping finally. Breathing heavily, trying to collect my senses, and still, even having come so close, trying to understand what had just happened. How could I have just seen what I knew I saw? It must be a mistake. The cat was gone. But if it was really there, I thought, it must have left some tracks.

I hoofed it back, beating Rusz to the place where we'd split, and there in the soft sand were the tracks. A line of thirteen footsteps, every one startlingly vivid in detail. Rusz appeared and appraised the situation. I said nothing as he hunkered down, half collapsed on all four over one of the tracks, the woods now echoing—booming—with him calling for Mark.

Mark was quickly dispatched down the road headed toward the swamp, while Rusz and I stayed at the scene and began marking off the tracks. Three impressions were especially good. While Rusz fumbled in his pack for the tape measure, I recorded in my notebook his remarks:

> Heel pad: width 2½-inches and $1^{15}\!/_{16}$ inches high. Prominent indenture. Three lobes on the back of the heel pad. Total length of track $4\frac{1}{16}$ inches. Width 4 inches. Stride length: 26 inches.

Rusz asked me how tall the animal appeared. Only a stone's throw away, I guessed it came midway up my thigh, almost thirty-one inches.

We shoved tiny sticks into the sand to mark each of the tracks, then headed off toward the swamp, where we came upon Mark standing over a line of fifteen or so more. More than a couple as picture perfect as the ones Rusz and I had just measured. Mark never got a glimpse of the puma, but the sign suggested it had obviously come through here, heading into the swamp.

As we stood there staring down, saucer-eyed, the daylight was beginning to go gray. Rusz was on all fours, his face hovering over the tracks. So close.

I caught a glimpse of his hands, his palms flat on the ground, and seeing the fingertips digging helplessly into the sand for a second I turned away.

Suddenly at that moment I felt sorry for him. Sorry for Mark. For Larry, wherever he was. Sorry for everyone. Me. Especially those indignant, arrogant do-nothings down in Lansing. And oddly even for the puma.

As my buddy Wayne likes to say, "Well I be dipped in shit."

Looks like there actually were a few pumas running around here. Looks like my perfect place was a deer and porcupine-infested hunting camp called Happy Acres in Roscommon County Michigan. Not exactly what I had in mind.

"This is huge," Rusz said. "We have to get a picture."

The three of us straggled off to find Larry and get the camera back at the truck. Hoofing it back to the scene, racing against the gathering dark, Rusz took pictures and did his track tracing by flashlight. It was then my quiet sadness was creeping up on me again with the sudden realization that we had nothing. We had the puma then lost it again. Exposed to the elements, the tracks there in the sand would be gone in a day. The pictures: useless. Due to the low light and the camera flash, Rusz later found them devoid of much detail. The tracing of the track . . . So what? Anybody can draw a puma track. And my sighting . . . Rusz was giddy jockeying around the track with his camera—"This is absolutely incredible," he kept saying—as if forgetting this sort of thing hadn't been reported hundreds of times before.

•••

Driving back to the restaurant, Rusz was a chatterbox of new plans:

Maybe we could set up a remote camera and get a picture; maybe we could set up at night with a spotlight and a wounded rabbit call . . . no, something bigger in distress. A white-tailed fawn. What we needed was a deer decoy and a call to imitate the bleats of a lost fawn. A live chicken!

Even I got caught up in the spirit of things, exclaiming, "Anyone know where we could get a live goat?"

We could walk a goat out there in the middle of one of those food plots, put a dingling little bell on it, and poke the sucker with a stick. Make some noise. Then we'd sit back in the brush and wait. At the very least, somebody needed to get back here in the AM and look for a deer kill.

"The only reason a puma would have let us get that close was if it was on a fresh kill," said Rusz.

Everyone was so very happy. Not only did we find tracks, but this time the puma was actually standing in them. I put on a good face but alone, finally, driving home in the dark, I knew I had just seen a puma and that it meant nothing, perhaps even less than nothing, to almost everybody other than me. I knew then and now that what I saw would be challenged, was and should be challenged. That won't change what I saw.

Earlier in the day, for a moment when I had Mike Zuidema alone, I'd asked him a question. "Why do so many people seem to believe in the puma? Why do you believe in them?"

Zuidema cast me a sideways glance, eyes squinting, as if it was quite possibly the dumbest question he'd ever heard. He spoke softly, plainly, as if one might to a small child.

"Because I saw one," he said, as if that alone was enough. Suddenly I understood. That would have to be enough, because when you came right down to it belief was all there was.

Bad weather the next day and other commitments kept Rusz away from Happy Acres for a few days. Much as I wanted to go, I was not permitted on the grounds without him.

When he did return the deer kill he was looking for was not there. He had other news, though. Rusz had called the owner of Northland Taxidermy, Randy Desormeau.

"The guy was clearly lying," Rusz said. "Said he remembered somebody brought him a cougar to mount a couple of years ago. Said the thing was a pet and that the guy who brought it in wanted a full-body mount."

Rusz's recollection of Desormeau's story was that the taxidermist had skinned out the carcass and put the skull outside, and that dogs must have come along and carried it off.

"He was really agitated by my questions," said Rusz, adding that when he asked Desormeau point-blank if he had the paperwork to prove the cat was a pet, the taxidermist said he could probably look for it but that he'd charge a hundred dollars an hour to do it.

Rusz was stuck to his theory that the puma was wild. The Horseman and the taxidermist were obviously in cahoots.

"I'm done with this. This would take a criminal investigation to find out anything more, and that's not my job."

• • •

For months after I would keep quiet about the puma I saw. I told myself the reason was that, as a writer trying to get to the bottom of this, such an oc-currence posed a glaring conflict of interest. Were it not for the puma's tracks so clearly legible on the ground, I might never have admitted the encounter at all—not because I am doubtful of what it was, but rather simply to avoid what I have come to see as the burden that accompanies the knowing.

You feel like something has to be done.

H. L. Mencken said, "The world always makes the assumption that the exposure of an error is identical with the discovery of truth—that the error and the truth are simply opposite. They are nothing of the sort. What the world turns to, when it is cured of one error, is usually simply another error, and maybe one worse than the first one."

Rusz believed the puma I saw was one of two, a big dark male. He believed that cat descended from other pumas that had been living silently in those woods since . . . well, since forever. I offered only once that it was equally plau-sible that the cat was a FERC. Happy Acres was situated near Route 75, the main highway headed north from the big cities of Detroit, Saginaw, and Flint.

Happy Acres was right smack in the middle of the first big tract of wilder-ness a person heading up that way would see. Maybe somebody with an un-ruly and illegally procured puma kitten decided 200 pounds later that owning a cat that could kill you wasn't that fun anymore.

"I'm not sayin' that explains it. I'm just saying you should consider it," I remember saying to Rusz a couple days later over the phone.

"We found cougar sign last year and had sighting reports the year before. We find scat and other sign. We go in and you see a cougar. That indicates a resident cougar. Haven't you learned a thing?"

Rusz got so agitated I decided never to mention it again.

I asked Rusz to keep the sighting quiet, but it wouldn't be long until my sighting and name (erroneously described as a writer and MWC "researcher," which I wasn't) was posted as evidence on the conservancy's Web site. I got a few calls and e-mails about it, a couple from people whose names I recognized from the Internet and had been given my number by Rusz. More than one of them wanted to know how much MWC was paying me to help prop up Rusz's case.

In the meantime I had followed up on Rusz's rendition of the conversation with the taxidermist, Desormeau. Desormeau was curtly on guard after I explained who I was, and what I was trying to find out.

"Some other guy called here already. I didn't like his tone, like he was accusing me of something."

Had anyone from the DNR questioned him about the skull?

"No. I told the guy who called the cougar was a pet. The guy who brought it in lives over on Neebish Island." Neebish Island was in the eastern UP, in the St. Mary's River, between here and Canada.

Desormeau said after he'd hung up with Rusz, he had a good chuckle over the whole thing.

"Tell you what. I'll look around and try to find the guy's number, but in the meantime I'll tell you like I told the other guy: You can call the Neebish Island ferry service. It's not a big place. They'll know who it is."

According to Sasha's owner, the eleven-and-a-half-year-old female was a purebred western puma that he'd bought in 1988 from a breeder down in Trout Lake. Sasha was declawed at two and a half weeks. He described her as timid, like an overgrown house cat that used to sleep with him in the sun, curled up in the grass.

"Yes, I had permits from the DNR *and* the Department of Agriculture," he said. "At one time or another I've had emus, hawks, and ostriches at my place. But I really loved that cat."

We talked for an hour, and he told me how when Sasha would come into heat it would lure other pumas into the open from the woods. One day he heard a commotion coming from her pen, and looked outside to see a full-grown puma lying on the top of her cage. The man claimed he took home video of the cat before running it off. He said he'd make me a copy, which he never did send.

Desormeau's story checked out and confirmed, at least in my mind, what I already knew: The Chippewa County skull was most likely from a domestic puma.

Sasha, her owner recalled, had choked to death on a piece of turkey.

But driving home that May night in the darkness, I didn't know any of this yet. I was feeling letdown and introspective. Pushing the pedal to eighty, I really wanted to get back and see my wife. As I drove I listened to her voice on the phone, a message: "The baby is kicking. When are you coming home?"

I played the message again, driving faster, yet mindful for glowing eyes along the sides of the road. If you're paying attention, any deer with a death wish can usually be spotted long before it makes that fatal leap out onto the road. But instead of deer, I hung up with pumas on the brain, specifically what I might do if rounding a bend I should chance to see one standing on the centerline. At that moment, mentally mired in the futility of it all, I truly couldn't decide:

Would I step on the brake or slam my foot even harder on the gas?

AND THE CHICKENS
TURNED UP MISSING

You said I killed you—haunt me then! The murdered do haunt
their murderers. I believe—I know that ghosts have wandered
on earth.

Emily Brönte, *Wuthering Heights*

T
wo months later, September, the tail end of a long hot northern
Michigan summer, I was sitting there in the gathering dark, slapping at mosquitoes in a makeshift blind beside a stranger with a
rifle trained across the field toward the blackening tree line.

Waiting. We'd only met a couple of hours before. The man, I'll call him
Norman, told me he had seen a puma here, or thought he saw it. And
tonight, if the bastard showed, he was fixing to put a bullet in its brainpan.

A week had passed since one by one a neighbor's chickens had turned up
missing. Then another neighbor, Larry Strouss, had discovered the family
dog, a 120-pound Great Pyrenees, all bloodied after scrapping out behind
the barn with a creature that came out of the swamp. Nobody in the little
town of South Boardman knew quite what to think at first. Strouss figured
maybe the culprit was a pack of coyotes or wild dogs, a bobcat or a black
bear. But then one foggy morning in August, Strouss discovered claw marks,
four deep gashes down the back of his eighteen-hundred-pound Percheron

mule after a night spent out in the pasture. Strouss's son, Alan, said he got a fleeting glimpse of the attacker—a huge, long-tailed catlike animal—running away toward the distant tree line.

A couple of nights later down the lane at a property belonging to Bill and Linda George, apparently the same animal tangled with a full-grown quarter horse, leaving the same bloody claw marks high on the animal's back and what looked like tooth punctures on its neck. Confusing reports from the two farms mentioned both large and small feline tracks, the larger of which MDNR biologist Tim Webb told reporters came from a "large feral cat" that exceeded one hundred pounds. Penny Melchoir, another DNR biologist who had responded to the scene, later agreed: "Track evidence, sightings, and scars on the horses are proof that we are dealing with a very large feline, probably cougar . . ."

The day after I heard the report on the evening news, I made the drive east, only forty-odd miles, to the home of Bill George, a mobile home baking out in a dusty clearing in the hot August sun. An apparent chain smoker, George was a wiry-looking man with inky blotches—long-ago tattoos, probably military—on his forearms.

"The wife," he said, "she's scared to death." He pointed a cigarette back toward the trailer. "We've been keeping a loaded shotgun beside the door in case it comes back."

George led me around the perimeter of the pasture.

"See there where that post's knocked over cockeyed and the dirt's tore up?" George supposed the cat had crouched there in the brush, just outside the wire fence, waiting, until the horse wandered close enough for it to pounce. Nodding at the U-shaped horseshoe tracks in the dirt, George guessed the post must have been knocked sideways during the scuffle. He called sweetly to one of two horses—a white Appaloosa and a smaller brown paint—grazing in the middle of the enclosure. George told me both horses, not just the one, had tangled with something in the past week.

"I thought it was a bear till the warden looked at the tracks and said it was a mountain lion."

With the tractor, George dragged an old bedspring around the entire perimeter of the pasture, combing the ground, then checked it every morning for tracks. He showed me a few of what he thought might have been made by the puma, a fresh set of tracks made just last night. They were indiscernible in the dry dirt, a trail of saucer-shaped depressions coming up out of the woods, skirting the edge of the pasture, and heading right down the middle of the dusty lane leading out to the main road.

The DNR had given George a permit to kill the animal, and ever since he had been staying up nights keeping an eye on the pasture with the shotgun, waiting for the thing to come back. He told me offhandedly that a couple of neighbors were doing the same. One of them, Norman, I came upon getting out of his pickup with a rifle after I left Bill George, who promised he'd call if the puma came back.

I pulled to a stop and gave the stranger my standard bit about being a writer, mentioned how I had just talked to Bill George, and, pointing casually at the rifle, asked if Norman had seen any pumas around.

"You might see a dead one here pretty soon," he said.

"Really?"

Norman described a huge gray cat with a long tail "about as big around as a sleeve of Skoal cans." He slung the rifle over his shoulder and formed his hands into a circle. Jutting his chin toward the trees, he said, "And I know where he's crossing at night, too."

"So you're staking him out?" I asked. "Mind if I tag along."

I didn't really think he'd say yes but a minute later I was walking alongside the man, chatting as if we were old friends. Norman, it turned out, didn't have a permit like the one Bill George had shown me. So technically, his intentions were illegal. But, the way Norman saw it, he owned the land we were on, fifty acres or so, so he didn't need some "stupid little chit of paper." His words.

I asked what else he knew about pumas in the area, but it turned out to be very little.

"Lived here all my life," he said, "and this is the first one I ever heard of."

We came to a lawn chair situated in a clump of pines along the edge of a woodlot overlooking a green rye field. A hundred yards to the trees, which Norman said was mostly swamp. He had sat here the past couple of nights, "ever since that man got his chickens ate."

Norman had on a cheap red ball cap (plastic mesh back, through which I could see that he'd lost all but a few wisps of gray hair), green army coat, and a pair of those blue Dickies work pants that plumbers wear. He fell heavily into the chair. Then, from the breast pocket of the coat, he retrieved four brass cartridges, pressed them one by one into the magazine, and slid the bolt closed.

"I seen him come out of there and follow the tree line down across the road. Didn't think much of it at the time. Now the thing's messing with horses. Killing chickens fer Christ's sake."

Norman didn't have any deep thoughts to share about the puma. He didn't much care if the animal was wild or somebody's escaped pet . . . though he did mention that it sounded like "some downstater came up here and dumped the thing." (One of Norman's neighbors had told him that the cat was eating dog food left out on the porch, though when questioned the witness had never actually seen the animal.) As we sat there whispering, a wedge of geese came over, honking. They circled the field once then locked their wings and glided down to the corner of the field.

"That's pert' near where he comes out," Norman said.

I asked what he planned to do with the puma if he did kill it.

"'Magin I'd follow the three S's," he said.

"Three S's?"

"Yeah. Shoot. Shovel. Shut up."

•••

Other than my wife, I hadn't really told anyone about the puma I saw. From Nancy I got only a polite smile. I actually thought she might pat me on the head, give me a "That's nice, honey," and tell me to go run along. I don't think she ever quite understood what all the fuss was about. My wife typically exhibits an endless tolerance for the sometimes peculiar burdens of my profession. But I don't think she appreciated the bags of animal shit in our freezer[11] or how much of our time the story was consuming. The baby, a new life, was only weeks away. And where was I? Every other weekend gone. My head buried in books. I had been along on a few sorties with Rusz into the Sleeping Bear Dunes National Lakeshore that summer, following up sightings, running down leads that in more than a couple of cases resulted in possible tracks and a few peculiar-looking scats.

One afternoon I went alone to the Clinch Park Zoo in Traverse City to see the pumas they have there. Pinched between the little marina on the bay and the main highway through town, the place pretty much encapsulates everything people find so shameful about zoos. The pens are small, sterile, and depressing, like goldfish bowls. I learned by reading the signs that the animals at Clinch Park are all damaged in some way. Cripples and rejects. Broken-winged hawks. Three-legged turtles. Bison and elk donated by a local game farm. The sign on the black bear pen said that Tina, Oscar, and Darla were handed over to the zoo after being abandoned as cubs. The pumas, Sunny and Spike, were once illegally owned and came to the zoo in 1993. Sunny, the female, hobbled with a pronounced limp, which I learned from a passing zookeeper resulted after her owner tried to declaw her as a kitten with a pair of pliers.

I crouched outside the pen for a long while watching them. Sunny mostly dozed high on a ledge built out of the back wall and made to look like rock, while Spike stood staring into infinity near a tire hanging from a rope in the middle of the cage, his head ticking around spasmodically as if being menaced by a swam of invisible flies.

When I got home there was a message on the machine from an unusually gleeful-sounding Rusz.

"You're not going to believe this," he said. Mark had seen a puma now, too.

When I phoned him back Rusz spit out his version of events then handed the phone over to Mark, who went over the details again. It was in the park, Sleeping Bear, near the spot where Ranger Kym Mukavetz, and later another park employee, had seen a puma bound across the road in front of her truck back in 1997. I wasn't even aware that Mark had been in the area.

Up for the afternoon looking for puma scat, he told me he chanced a stop at Otter Creek—a popular tourist beach on Lake Michigan—where he found a trail, a little wooded walking path, running directly parallel to a marshy cedar swamp and Esch Road. After an hour or so finding nothing, he turned around, heading back toward the trailhead, when he heard a car coming, a carload of beachgoers, grinding down the road off behind a screen of trees. Mark happened to look up that way, and that's when he saw it, a puma hurtling down the hill through the trees quartering toward him. His description of the cat was textbook—the long tail, muscles rippling, the deerlike color—as it bounded through an open grove of red pines right across the footpath in the wide open no more than fifty paces away.

As I listened, I didn't know what to think. Had I fallen in the middle of some weird father–son dynamic? A bit of puma-spotting one-upsmanship? I didn't think it possible, but the whole thing with Rusz was getting more weird. The encounter was certainly both curious and fortuitous. Curious because there was no other corroborating evidence at the scene: The family in the car (Mark found them parked down by the beach) hadn't seen anything actually cross the road. Something—a blur—that they remembered, according to Mark's rendition of the conversation, had been sitting in the brush alongside the road and had darted away at the approach of their vehicle. There were no tracks under the pines (too many old needles carpeting the ground); no tracks where the puma leapt across the trail (the dirt there was packed too hard). Curious. I also say it was fortuitous in that arriving in another few weeks was Harley Shaw, the preeminent Southwest puma expert.

Shaw had been scheduled for months to come take a tour of Sleeping Bear Dunes and some other of Rusz's study areas. Since we'd met, Rusz had been dropping Shaw's name in conversation as the puma expert working with MWC to help positively identify some of the track photographs and suspected deer kills he and volunteers had uncovered at Seul Choix Point and elsewhere. I looked forward to meeting him.

Shaw's arrival was the one bright spot in a hard summer of negative press for Rusz and MWC. Relations with the Wyoming lab had become strained.

Rusz had complained to me often of being unable to get the final laboratory results from Wyoming transferred to Central Michigan University. All his newer scats, including the one I'd picked up along the parks boundary near the Platte and Sleeping Bear, were part of this latest round.

From the beginning, Rusz had been criticized for using an out-of-state lab to analyze puma scats he was supposedly finding in Michigan, a criticism always mentioned in the same breath as those quiet allegations that he was fabricating and planting evidence, which, given my sighting, I now doubted very much that he was.

Wyoming was supposed to turn over testing to Central Michigan University. That had always been the plan. CMU would pick up testing where Wyoming left off. Rusz maintained he had only gone with Wyoming first on account of its experience dealing with forensic evidence related to pumas and because, when he'd shopped around for the cheapest price to have the scat analysis done, the Wyoming lab agreed to do the work for essentially the cost of the processing chemicals.

When I talked with Dee Dee Hawk in fall 2001, the results of the tests she had performed so far were entirely consistent with puma. She confirmed what Rusz had told me, that the lab had compared DNA found in the scat not only to canids (wolf/coyote) and bobcats (based on sixty samples sent from Michigan), but also to known puma samples from Wyoming and one from a domestic puma owned by an Upper Peninsula woman who had received the pet as a gift.

When Hawk wrote in her initial report back in October that Rusz's supposed puma scats "were feline, most probably mountain lion," the declaration from MWC that they were definitely from puma was backed up not exactly by DNA, but rather by the physical size of the scats. Bobcats don't crap turds as big as what Rusz turned in, and every reasonable biologist knew it. After that first report was issued, Wyoming had run suspect puma samples against known bobcat scat from Michigan specifically to rule out the latter.

Taking the genetic testing a step further, Wyoming was working to shed light on the nagging question of breeding—as I learned from e-mail communications that Rusz had long been feeding me. Through further in-depth analysis on the scats, Hawk was trying to determine the presence of individual pumas in a couple of Rusz's study areas.

This appeared to be startling news. In one e-mail to Rusz, Hawk indicated that preliminary tests showed three different animals from Stonington Peninsula in the Upper Peninsula's Schoolcraft County, a revelation that would back up a spate of sightings in the area of a mother puma with cubs.

In an August 2002 e-mail, Hawk wrote that "upon reviewing genotypes, it would appear there is the possibility of two animals from the four ros common [sic] samples," a find that referred to the Happy Acres hunting property in Roscommon County where the caretakers and other locals had reported a smaller puma and another larger, darker (some said black) cat roaming the area.

Dee Dee Hawk came across quite confident in conversation and in her memos. But as the months wore on, public debate got more and more prickly and put the Wyoming laboratory in the middle between the MDNR and MWC. In news reports, Hawk began more and more to hedge her words. Finally, while Rusz and I were up in the UP that weekend in May looking for bones behind the taxidermy shop and hassling The Horseman for a crime he didn't commit, Hawk told Ron St. Germain, a reporter for the *Lansing State Journal*, "I'm not ready to stake a reputation that has taken me fifteen years to build that these were scats of cougars."

Huh?

This didn't quite jive with what she'd felt back in 2001. Neither did it correspond with her later communications with Rusz that suggested the presence of multiple animals in at least two of his study areas.

A lot would later be made online about who said what and when. Much of it stemmed from naysaying articles in a few Michigan outdoor rags—pulpy hook-and-bullet newspapers—written by contributors better known for how-to articles with titles like "Worm-Rigs That Work" and "Ten Best Ways to Hammer Hot-Weather Bucks." While totally ignoring the new round of scat samples—seven scats from seven northern Michigan counties verified as puma by CMU that biologist Brad Swanson was standing behind—they rewrote an old story as if they had single-handedly managed to trump the editorial scrutiny of every major newspaper in the state, most of which agreed local and federal officials should be doing more to discern the status of pumas in Michigan. But coming into the story late and relying on what was being said now as opposed to what was said back when the story broke and was actually news, they made worse an already bad credibility problem for Rusz and MWC.

I later questioned Dee Dee Hawk about her apparent backpedaling. She responded, via e-mail, that her initial conclusions were only "preliminary" and she was unable to confirm them with further testing mostly due to genetic contamination in a few of the samples.

But what about her letter to MWC attesting to the reliability of the laboratory's work? What about the memos indicating the scats were not only from puma, but also the presence of multiple animals in a few of Rusz's study areas?

Those early reports, she explained, were really not technically confirmations. Really? Why not?

What would amount to a paragraph of cover-your-ass mumbo-jumbo I translated into one clear and concise sentence to mean:

True confirmation of a DNA test came only after more genetic testing so that the initial DNA tests, once tested again, could be truly considered confirmations, provided the initial results stood up over time to all that testing.

My e-mails back and forth with Dee Dee Hawk on this issue read like a transcript of Bill Clinton's grand jury testimony or a scene from Monty Python's "argument clinic." I couldn't decide and, in the end, it didn't matter.

The bottom line was, by August, Rusz's case—which at one point he was calling "irrefutable"—was suddenly starting to show some major flaws. While not every scat sample sent to Wyoming was contaminated in testing, Hawk had obviously washed her hands of all the samples and would no longer vouch that any of the scats she had analyzed from Michigan were even feline, let alone from puma.

Once again, it came back to this question of peer review. Harley Shaw summed it up to me the best: "That's exactly why you don't go mouthing off to the media until you're absolutely positive of what you have."

His white beard neatly trimmed, happy creases around his eyes, Shaw looked gnomish and wise under his khaki-colored packer hat. After a quick lunch at the Platte River Inn in downtown Honor, Shaw followed me alone to my truck. Rusz was leading the way to our first stop, the scene of Mark's encounter at Otter Creek.

We followed behind Rusz's Ford, the July afternoon bright, with a cutting blue sky. Shaw asked about the puma I saw. Rusz had spilled it back at the restaurant after a lengthy dissertation about the possibility that black pumas existed here. After all, he reasoned, ten percent of the sightings of pumas in Michigan were of black animals.

Shaw had visibly recoiled in his chair, gripping his coffee cup with both hands.

"Or maybe ten percent of people can't tell the difference between dark brown and black. Ever think of that?" Shaw composed himself by offering the kindly advice that maybe for credibility's sake Rusz should think about "backing off the black puma thing.

"It's too much for skeptics to handle," he said, adding that maybe Rusz should refocus and try solving one mystery at a time.

Back in the truck, Shaw wanted to hear about my sighting directly from me. I gathered by the way he studied my face during the retelling that maybe he was trying to get a fix on the legitimacy of it. He didn't pass judgment, and I didn't think it really mattered anyway.

I asked if he had been enjoying his time in Michigan. And what did he think of Rusz's efforts to prove we had pumas here?

"From what I've seen the country could support them," he said. "And there's certainly enough deer." Shaw tapped a finger on his knee. His eyes were fixed on the road ahead and, suddenly, his voice took on a low confiding tone.

Something about Rusz unnerved him, he confessed, not the least of which was the trouble with the DNA evidence from Wyoming—the fact that it didn't exist anymore. Shaw shook his head when I mentioned it. Shaw was a scientist, a recognized puma expert, and a good-hearted, honest guy by reputation. While he didn't come out and say it, I got the impression that he'd helped Rusz out initially not knowing how big a mess MWC would get itself into.

"I'm getting too old for controversy," he said.

And then he would say no more.

Shaw didn't say much of anything at Otter Creek as Mark retold his tale. We got in the trucks again and followed Rusz to the extreme southern end of Sleeping Bear, over the Platte River and past the property where I'd found the scat, to Old Indian Trail, roughly five miles away, a hiking and cross-country ski path and a new place where Rusz had been saying he found puma tracks, perhaps from the same animal—or another—whose crap I found the autumn before. That was Rusz's theory anyway, which he hurriedly announced in the parking lot before charging off down the shady trail.

Lagging behind and looking into the trees distracted by various songbirds and woodpeckers, Shaw acted as if he was hardly listening anymore.

Rusz could have this effect on people. After a while they just tuned out. They looked at birds, stole glimpses at their watch. Rusz was like a loopy college professor sometimes. If nobody raised their hand to stop the dissertation, he just assumed the class was with him and moved on to the next thing. In fact, if I were a passerby on Old Indian Trail and was asked who was the real puma expert, I would have naturally pointed to the guy doing the most talking. And that wasn't Harley Shaw.

The letter Shaw sent Rusz a week later was brief, to the point, and just about the kindest way I've ever heard somebody tell a person to get lost. After meeting Rusz, Harley no longer wanted his name attached to any more of MWC's research. He didn't want anything to do with MWC. And he asked that MWC remove his name from any evidentiary documents on its Web site, which they never did.

Rusz read Shaw's letter to me over the phone, and I could tell he was cut deeply by it. His voice sounded ragged, tired.

"Fuck Wyoming."

In his mind, Dee Dee Hawk had simply cracked under the pressure. That or the DNR had spooked her. As for Harley Shaw, he'd thought the guy had more guts than that.

"I warned them this was going to be controversial," he said.

Dee Dee Hawk later told me in an e-mail that politics had nothing to do with the Wyoming forensic laboratory cutting its ties with Rusz and MWC. The work, she said, had simply become too costly and time consuming. There was also that pesky matter of genetic contamination with a couple of the samples. And besides, CMU could do a much more thorough analysis.

"You know, I'm beginning to wish I'd never found those carcasses on the beach," Rusz told me after telling me the news about Shaw.

"Sometimes I wish I never got involved in any of this."

I was tempted to say something, some consolatory words. But what? Where to begin? On the one hand I really thought Rusz had some good, solid evidence. But the longer this went on, the more it became wrapped up with so much personal and political wrangling that the puma had become the last thing on anyone's mind, even his. Before I could say a word, though, Rusz snapped out of the funk on his own.

"Hey, what are you doing next weekend?"

He'd received another sighting of a puma down around Old Indian Trail. Rusz wanted to know if I'd like to meet up with him and look for scat.

•••

I ended up heading to South Boardman instead, visiting with Bill George then spending the last few hours of daylight sitting on a vigil with Norman and waiting to pop a puma that I didn't believe would show. Was the animal an escaped captive looking for an easy meal, or—as Rusz theorized after witnesses claimed to have seen two pumas (a mother and her cub)—learning how to hunt?

I read plenty of reports of pumas attacking horses:

The *Grand Forks Herald* reported in November from Hazen, North Dakota, that a young puma had mauled three horses in two separate attacks on a farm near Lake Sakakawea. The worst injuries were to a fifteen-year-old quarter horse that was left blind in one eye.

In California the *San Jose Mercury News* told of a daylight puma attack on a horse that left scratches, bite marks, and internal bleeding caused by a couple of broken ribs.

Nobody knows exactly why a puma would try to attack an animal ten times its own size. Some experts theorize that young pumas, hardwired to kill deer, associate the shape of a horse with its preferred prey and only recognize their mistake when it's too late. Puma attacks on horses are rare and appear to almost never result in the death of the animal.

An eleven-hundred-pound horse owned by a Minnesota couple, near Ely, did die recently after a puma attack. After a string of sightings in the area— everything from a report of two pumas in a ditch off Route 21 watching traffic go by to cat screams heard in the woods near the Hinden property right next to busy Route 169—Jill Hinden went out one morning to the pasture to feed her horse when she found the animal standing over a pool of blood flowing from bite marks to its neck. The horse was treated for the wounds but later had to be put down due to "a rapidly advancing infection from the bites to its neck."

Back in Kalkaska County, Michigan, a story appeared in the *Traverse City Record Eagle* in September showing an MDNR photograph of a four-inch-wide impression in the dirt. While the COs were quoted in the article as saying that they believed a large cat of some sort was involved in the attacks, to anyone with even a rudimentary knowledge of tracks it was obvious that the footprint in the accompanying picture was that of a large dog, leading some to wonder whether a puma was even involved in the attacks there.

The pictures left Rusz dumbstruck.

"Have you seen the latest?"

Over the phone, I heard the crumple of newspaper and the slap of him backhanding the photograph.

"From this it looks like our biologists here can't even tell the difference between a cat and dog track!"

Rusz would later visit the scene after the DNR had left and found a real puma track on the dirt road around the pasture and with that Dennis Fijalkowski went on public attack, incredulous at the news of officers issuing permits to kill what was described on the permits as "one large feral cat, species unknown."

"Here we have proof from DNA and other evidence that cougars are still around one hundred years after they were thought to have been wiped out, and the first thing the DNR wants to do when it comes across a cougar sighting it can't ignore is kill it?"

The story dragged on into autumn with news that the DNR had also placed a bear-sized live trap near the Strouss farm. But in the end, no puma was ever captured or shot.

•••

Nancy stirred late one night during the second week of September, shaking me awake and whispering, "I think it's happening." The baby was coming.

She woke me from a recurring dream I'd been having for weeks where I was back in that field with Norman, or a man I first thought was him, holding a flashlight as he shoveled up plumes of dirt from a knee-deep hole along the wood line. A puma lay dead, head-shot beside the hole, bloody around the mouth, blackened blood in the valleys between the teeth. After finishing the dig, the man spiked the shovel in the dirt and, wiping his brow with an arm, turned and with both hands fisted the puma's rear paws. His full face illuminated by the light, I saw him, recognizing the man not as a stranger; in fact it was me.

THE HOUNDSMAN

The Indians said never to let out your fears in summer,
when all the spirits were alive and anxious to interfere in men's
affairs. Better to talk in winter when everything was frozen, especially spirits.

Joseph Heywood, *Ice Hunter*

The first thing Fred Stempky confessed was that he would happily
kill every coyote in Michigan if he and his team of Walker hounds
were given half a chance.

"I hate the sons a bitches," he said. "I kill them with a vengeance."

Stempky is a gainfully employed insurance salesman who owns his own
business, so lucky for the coyotes he only gets to kill them on weekends. Clad
in his multicolored sweater and pressed navy slacks, he was definitely dressed
like an insurance salesman. Middle-aged. A full head of dark hair. Clean-
shaven. He sort of reminded me of a workingman model for a Sears or
JCPenney catalog.

Stempky and I met at his office on the outskirts of Cheboygan, a little big
town on the extreme northern tip of the Lower Peninsula six-odd miles from
the Straits of Mackinac, after I heard about his little roadside conversion
from a puma skeptic to a believer.

I called him. We talked. And the next week I made the drive three hours
north. Stempky shook my hand eagerly before we piled into the cab of his

pickup. Past fast-food joints and gas stations. I settled in figuring we had some distance to drive to get into the woods.

"Hell, no," said Stempky. "We cut the track just outside town."

•••

When fall came again to northern Michigan, then winter—another deer season with a million hunters in the woods—the pumas seemed to vanish like they always did. There was no more news from Kalkaska. At least three thousand houndsmen in the state running black bears in September and nobody but one reported a run-in with a puma.

I dropped away from the story after Gabriel was born. Nancy and I holed up for weeks, just the two of us and the little one. I talked so infrequently to Rusz from September through December—when we did talk it was always the same story—that I remember him asking me one day, jarring me from the distraction of watching the baby asleep on a blanket in the middle of the floor: "Hey. Are you still in the hunt or what?"

To be honest, I told him, I wasn't really sure what we were hunting anymore. For that moment at least, I really felt I finally had everything I needed.

•••

Over the past year, I had run into a handful of houndsmen who said they had found puma tracks in the past. Some even claimed they had treed the animals. While proof of the latter never did materialize, in the case of the former I actually saw some of the photos allegedly taken in the Upper and Lower Peninsula that were unmistakably puma tracks.

But these instances were rare. I was personally acquainted with two of the best-known houndsman in the entire state, John Cryderman up in the eastern Upper Peninsula and Mel Guntzviller in the northern Lower. Guntzviller spent most of his life making a living as a trapper and houndsman out west. Both were consummate dogmen. They hunted not only in Michigan but also out west for both bears and pumas. Which is to say they not only understood the cats, but also had dogs that knew puma scent.

Cryderman worked as a guide during the fall, driving hundreds of miles of snowy roads every month discerning various tracks looking for bears and bobcats for his hunters to trail and shoot. Neither he nor Guntzviller had ever treed a puma in Michigan or, for that matter, seen so much as a track. Both men were of a mind that people claiming to see pumas were more likely seeing big bobcats.

Other houndsmen I spoke to were less kind. To sum it up: "There are no [insert choice expletive] pumas in Michigan and anybody who thinks otherwise is either a [expletive] bunny hugger with a [expletive] political agenda or a complete [expletive] idiot who's never spent time in the woods up here before."

If he had to choose, Fred Stempky told me he leaned toward the bunny-hugger theory—"These days there's always a bunny hugger out there crying about this or that"—until a call came over the radio one snowy morning in January.

Driving to the place where they'd found the track, Stempky remembered he had been out since dawn, driving back roads, a pair of Walker hounds riding in a box in the bed of his big Dodge, and craning his head out the window looking for a set of coyote (Stempky pronounced it *kia-yoot*) tracks with just the right degree of freshness.

There was chatter on the CB, other houndsmen out doing the same thing. I've been on these types of hunts before. Within the hound hunting subculture there are factions: 'coon hunters, bear men, bobcat specialists, and men like Stempky who rarely put the dogs down on anything else but *kia-yoots*. A bobcat man out driving around looking for tracks might get on the radio when he's cut a good-looking coyote trail, and vice versa.

"Most guys, they find something they're not interested in running, they let somebody else know."

That day Stempky had a "spotter" working for him, an older buddy who didn't hunt anymore but who knew his tracks and liked driving around to help out the younger guys.

"Around ten o'clock he gets on the radio and says 'I got this track . . . and . . . I don't know.'"

The swamp was a short drive away from Stempky's insurance office on Route 27, the main road north into Cheboygan. He remembered the snow was shin-deep that morning, a fresh layer of powder having fallen the night before. He remembered the tracks, big and round as a softball.

"They were big. And most definitely cat." The animal was headed south. Stempky considered the trail going into the swamp on the other side of the road, figuring that it had been made sometime during the night.

"From there I just started slicing up the area."

Like most of the North Country, the landscape is cut by a mishmash of two-track, secondary, and lazy country roads. Before putting hounds on the ground, a hunter will always circumvent woodlots and swamps in his truck to look for tracks coming out. It saves the dogs from having to run miles of cold trail. If he comes to a woodlot and there are no tracks leading out the other side, this indicates the animal is somewhere in that particular chunk of cover. Time to go back and unleash the hounds.

Stempky explained how a bobcat might occupy a four- to five-square-mile territory. A coyote, only about two square miles.

Even when he was standing over the track Fred Stempky told me he couldn't believe his eyes. A puma. He had no idea how far this particular track was going to take him.

"I started trailing with my father when I was five. Over forty years running hounds and I never seen anything like it."

The tracks lined out and Stempky started driving, one section after another. Mile after mile.

"I just wanted to see it for myself," he said, adding that as the hours slipped by he got on the radio looking for help. Pretty soon eight truckloads of his friends—all of them houndsmen and all of them skeptics—were running down what everybody was convinced was a big puma.

Stempky got on his snowmobile and followed the trail for four and a half miles. Six miles. The trail was headed right toward the highway, toward town.

"I got the feeling it had been here before," he said. "You follow a track that long and your eye really gets in tune with what the animal was doing. This wasn't just aimless wandering. A coyote or bobcat will walk a road whenever they get a chance. This thing knew exactly where the roads were and would either turn and perfectly parallel them or simply avoid them where he could."

The trail eased west, toward Route 27 and Mullet Lake, five miles across and at that time of year covered with a thick layer of ice. The cat followed the top of a ridgeline, staying mostly in the trees, according to Stempky, until it emerged from a grove of pines and crossed the road at a three-way stop sign, through the backyard of somebody's house, before ducking into a thick cedar swamp.

Stempky figured here's where he'd have the cat cornered.

"We run coyotes out of there all the time," he said. "Lots of rabbits. Good cover. I thought we had him."

But out on Route 27, the road that morning a steady stream of lunch-hour traffic, Stempky showed me where he cut the tracks again, headed out of the swamp and across the double-lane, down a brushy embankment through the backyards of a cluster of summer beach houses lining the western shore of Mullet Lake. Finally the trail slipped between an abandoned cottage and a pontoon boat parked in the yard before striking out onto the ice, where a stiff wind was gusting so hard it obliterated any sign.

For the rest of that season, February and on into March, Stempky and his friends kept an eye out for those tracks, hoping to catch the cat when it came through the area again. Far as they could tell, it never did.

I asked if he believed there were others pumas around and, if so, how had he'd missed them.

"I'm not convinced I haven't been blowing by those tracks for years." Stempky explained how he worked, scanning the roadside snow from the truck, looking for certain-sized tracks, a certain pattern to their placement. All this done on the move.

"A track doesn't look right, I keep going. Dog tracks. 'Coon. Everything else is just trash."

After my tour of the puma trail we drove back to the office, where Stempky parked and sat staring out through the windshield as if about to deliver a deep thought somehow relating to the traffic out on the road.

"The ground I used to hunt as a boy has shrunk to a quarter of what it used to be. People from downstate move up here and buy five acres and then post it no trespassing." He remembered how a handful of private property owners tired of hounds and hunters traipsing through their well-groomed yards almost succeeded a few years back in a ballot initiative to ban hound hunting. More and more land every year was off-limits to hunters and hounds where, who knows, maybe a creature as crafty as a puma could hide out.

"A buddy of mine ran a wolf this year. Wolves aren't supposed to be in the Lower Peninsula, either." Stempky had been hearing tales about wolves for years. He remembered the story of a Coast Guard helicopter pilot patrolling the straits who a couple of years back reported seeing a pair of wolves coming across the ice.

"That's only a couple of miles away."

Most of the houndsmen I spoke with said that they'd rather have pumas in Michigan than wolves, pumas being more reclusive and fearful of hounds while wolves are notorious for killing them. From 1976 to 1998 the Wisconsin DNR paid $55,574 in wolf depredation costs, an amazing 76 percent of which went to compensate houndsmen ($42,305). In Michigan, costs for wolf depredation are handled by the Department of Agriculture and cover only livestock.

"What do we need another predator for," said Stempky. "Anymore you can't find any rabbits to hunt. No grouse. Instead you got hawks and owls and coyotes running all over . . ." He shook his head grievously.

"Now mountain lions? Pretty soon there won't be any game left."

• • •

The puma Fred Stempky believed he trailed that bleak winter day was headed due east, across the ice of Mullet Lake, toward the Black River Valley north of Pigeon River country, part of the seven-hundred-thousand-acre Mackinaw State Forest, home to Michigan's elk herd, and the small town of Tower (only ten miles away "as the cougar flies," according to Stempky) where back in 2001 Dale Willey had reported one of his horses attacked by what he thought was the same puma seen lurking around the pasture a couple of days before.

Willey told me matter-of-factly that the puma only came around in summer, usually July and August, before disappearing again every fall. A neighbor of Willey's told me of repeated puma sightings, one encounter in broad daylight when one was seen stalking a calf out behind the barn. The neighbor ran outside and the puma flattened itself out in the grass, close enough that she could see its tail swishing back and forth. Keeping an eye on the cat, she looped a rope around the calf's neck, led it into the barn, and ran back inside to fetch a rifle, but when she returned the puma was gone.

Three hundred yards from Dale Willey's pasture, a thirteen-hundred-pound quarter horse owned by Bill Bower was mauled by something in the same manner that Willey's mare had been the summer before. Bower's horse also appeared claw-raked and bitten around the neck. Then almost a year to the day later, Tom Lupu—a friend of Bower's and owner of the property—went to check on his daughter's Shetland pony before heading off to work. Lupu found the six-hundred-pound animal lying dead: "Its throat was ripped up and the ear was gone."

That evening Lupu sat with a rifle watching the carcass and claimed that around ten o'clock he saw the puma emerge from the tree line and make its way to the carcass. Although it was almost completely dark at that hour, nonetheless Lupu said he could see the cat clearly through his rifle scope and judged the animal's weight at 150 pounds. Not wanting to wound the cat, Lupu waited for the best shot, measuring its approach until, at what according to Lupu was less than a hundred feet, the animal seized up as if sensing something was wrong, turned, and bolted away without Lupu ever firing a shot.

By the time I finally got in touch with the Lupus, the pony was already in the ground. Teresa, the wife, said her husband had been sitting out every night with the rifle but had not seen the puma again.

"Five days. I called the DNR on Friday, told them what happened, and it was Tuesday before anybody showed up," Lupu said, adding that by then the carcass was pretty ripe and covered with flies baking in the hot sun. The horse had a broken neck, with tooth marks. "But there was no way that warden was climbing down in that hole to confirm it."

Lupu confessed he was as tired of talking to reporters as he was dealing with the DNR. The biologist who responded to the call, Bryan Mastenbrook, later reported that a bear was responsible for the killing. Case closed. However, the evidence was hardly conclusive, based on what he told me later was a partial track and an old scat he found in the nearby woods.

SIGNS

There's a panther in Michigan
Don't that make your Halloween
There's a panther in Michigan
Although he's seldom seen

Michael Peter Smith, "Panther in Michigan"

Apart from questions about Patrick Rusz (*was he really legit or a whack-a-do?*) and the befuddling jumble of whys behind the official stance on the status of the animal here and throughout the East (*as a barometer for the health and diversity of our eastern forests, why wouldn't biologists want to see pumas here?*), whenever anybody learned I was working on a book about pumas in the East, the topic that seemed to dominate the conversation was puma attacks. And not just attacks in a general sense, but rather the very real concern that if a wild puma was indeed found to be anywhere within a one-hundred-mile radius of where we stood sipping cocktails, surely it was only a matter of time until the cat would leap out of the bushes and chomp on us.

Puma proponents offer a standard litany of responses to calm this ancient fear. First you're supposed to say that a person has a better chance of getting struck by lightning or attacked by the neighbor's dog than mauled by a puma. Bee stings, snakebites, and West Nile virus cause more deaths annually than pumas. "Today more people die from bad egg salad than cougar attacks," wrote novelist Elwood Reid, "but that doesn't diminish our fixation on the re-mote possibility of a silent hunter pouncing on our backs." If that doesn't convince them, there's always Florida. A century's worth of proof that pumas can live in close proximity to people without munching on them.

Not only are the odds of injury or death by puma infinitesimal, but offi-cial concerns of public safety as a reason for not wanting pumas here ring en-tirely hypocritical. Black bears have caused more harm to humans in North America. Stephen Herrero's book *Bear Attacks: Their Causes and Avoidance* found that twenty-three humans have been killed by black bears since 1900, with an average of twenty-five attacks each year from 1960 to 1980. Admit-tedly most of these occurred in the West and Canada, where black bears can typically be more aggressive than their bumbling dump-raiding eastern cousins. And with anywhere from seven to eight hundred thousand black bears in the United States, attacks are proportionately rarer than mauling by puma. But isn't the real devil in the potential for attack? Black bears are man-aged as game animals, which is one reason why there are so many of them. We've grown used to them, and with familiarity we don't see them as threat-ening anymore—not like pumas, anyway—but that doesn't make them any less capable of killing.

Moving up the chain of game animals that can kill us, we find the moose. But unlike the black bear, whose victims are almost always campers, hikers, and hunters, a moose can kill you even if you've never set foot in the woods in your life. I don't know anyone whose ever been mauled by a puma, but I know people who have been attacked by black bears and one who was nearly killed by a moose.

My wife's college roommate had her neck broken in one of the 250 or so moose–car crashes that happen in New Hampshire every year. Coming home from dinner one night, she and her husband rounded a bend in the road and plowed the legs out from under a fifteen-hundred-pounder. A moose looks black at night, and its gangly legs are so tall that the motorist rarely even sees the animal until it's too late. As is typical in these mishaps, the moose toppled over the hood and crushed the roof of the car.

The state of Maine has so many moose–car crashes that the DMV even advises drivers, if there's time before a crash, to aim for the animal's tail. Maine averages seven hundred moose–car accidents every year, with one out of four incidents resulting in serious injury or death to the driver and/or passengers, usually due to spinal injuries and broken necks. In Massachusetts thirty-three cars collided with moose in 2003. In Vermont the number of moose–car collisions jumped from 2 in 1982 to 164 in 2002. But by far the most dangerous ungulate out there is the moneymaking sacred cow of eastern game agencies: the white-tailed deer.

The government's auto safety council estimates that 154 people die every year from animal–vehicle crashes in the United States, and 90 percent of these are caused by white-tailed deer. The National Safety Council recorded 211 fatal deer–auto collisions in 1995, and more than twenty-nine thousand injuries. Admittedly, 1995 was an especially bad year. Most years the death count averages one hundred.

Even though a deer is more likely to kill or maim you, it's nearly impossible to convince the average person that the puma is the less dangerous of the two. Hard to get past the notion that the backyard shrub-eating whitetail we see is harmless prey whereas the night stalking puma we don't see can and will eat us any chance it gets.

People have a macabre interest in animal attacks. And when you narrow it all down to the biggest obstacle—greater than rivers and the wide-open plains—it is this unconquerable and irrational fear that will always be the primary obstacle in the way of pumas reclaiming portions of their former range.

The last instance of a fatal puma-on-human attack this side of the Mississippi happened in 1844 in Lycoming County, Pennsylvania. Making his way to a neighbor's for a midwinter house call, one Dr. Reinwald was traveling alone on foot through a snowy wood when he was tackled from behind, his bag of medical instruments sent flying, by a puma that presumably sheared clean through the doctor's spinal cord with a single bite to the neck.

Ah, believers along the puma fringe say, but what about the unresolved circumstances surrounding the death of Leigh Ann Cox in 2003?

On the evening of May 3 outside the town of Leslie, Arkansas, Cox was found by family members outdoors, facedown in the grass and partially scalped, her clothes in bloody tatters and nearly ripped off her back. While Kenny Davidson's wife fumbled with the phone dialing 911, the man by all accounts went temporarily insane. Suspecting one of their five dogs was responsible for the killing, Davidson took his .45 and shot two of the dogs as they cowered in a corner of the couple's bedroom before authorities and an ambulance arrived and talked him down.

Confusion surrounding Cox's death swirled immediately after an EMT on the scene commented that the wounds Leigh Ann suffered—among them what appeared to be a broken neck covered with toothy punctures—were evidence enough to suggest a feline attack. There had been sightings of a puma recently around Leslie. A woman walking out of her house one day claimed she ran right into a puma standing in her yard. The two stared at each other for ten seconds before the cat wheeled around and ran off. Another Leslie resident claimed that he and his family had seen two puma cubs playing in a tree.

The sightings went back years, a few of the most credible coming from Arkansas Game and Fish Commission biologists. In 1999, just south of Leslie in neighboring Madison County, a muddy roadside track was found by biologists coming out of a locust thicket where a resident had reported seeing a puma the day before. Just north of Leslie, in south-central Marion County, in January and February 2000, two separate puma encounters were reported by two different biologists. In the first a puma was seen attempting to cross a road near the spot where, a month later, a track was found in fresh snow and confirmed by department experts as coming from a puma. But the most convincing proof that at least one puma was lurking along the southern edge of the Ozark Mountains came just three months after the death of Leigh Ann Cox. On August 2003 in Perry County near the town of Thornburg, around eighty miles south of Leslie, a deer hunter captured a clear image of a puma with a motion-sensitive wildlife camera.

Back at the the Cox killing, Davidson examined the scene himself after authorities left and found, sure enough, impressions overlooked in the dirt around the spot where Leigh Ann fell that were later said to be those of a puma. Days later Davidson allegedly saw the puma lurking near the house, prompting reporters to speculate as to whether the animal might be coming back to feed on its kill.

In a bizarre chain of events, the case got even murkier when autopsy results were leaked to the press. Overnight Leigh Ann's death went officially from being the result of an animal attack to that of a "blunt force trauma leading to death from unknown causes."

Deputy Prosecutor Stephen James later told the *Van Buren County Democrat* that this simply was not true. The local sheriff's office, medical examiner, and officials from the Arkansas Game and Fish Commission insisted the injuries sustained by Leigh Ann were consistent with a dog attack, yet there was never any conclusive evidence to support this. None of the investigators had ever thought to examine the Davidson dogs to find any incriminating DNA. Leigh Ann's body was also cremated soon after she was found. The AGFC still considers the Cox killing an open case, and the mystery that pumas lurk in the woods around the town of Leslie lingers to this day.

•••

I didn't find the story about the death of Leigh Ann Cox in Kathy Etling's book *Cougar Attacks: Encounters of the Worst Kind.* Suffice it to say there were plenty of other gory encounters there to keep folks wincing and pie-eyed over Saturday-evening cocktails.

Opening the book at random, I found the story of Montana game warden Mike Quinn, who in July 1990 got a call about a puma stalking a horse near Bigfork. Over the phone, Quinn advised the landowner to fire a warning shot over the cat's head to frighten it away. But in an hour the phone rang again. The puma was back.

Quinn arrived on the scene with his .357 service revolver and a Remington 870 riot shotgun loaded with a couple rounds of Double 0 buck. The puma was nowhere to be seen, but Quinn decided to take a look around just to be sure.

"I had a funny feeling," remembered Quinn, who turned around just in time to spot the cat crouched low in the grass, creeping toward him, tail twitching back and forth, not thirty yards away. Quinn drew his peacemaker and fired a shot into the dirt near the animal; at the pistol's report the puma charged. Etling doesn't elaborate on what must have been going through the warden's head at that moment. Presumably *Oh shit* is not a stretch. But he kept his cool, pitching his revolver to the ground and firing the shotgun from the hip just as the puma launched in midair. The shot smashed into the animal's head and chest. Dead on impact, the cat's momentum carried it forward so that it actually brushed past the sidestepping warden before skidding into a heap on the ground.

Roughly twenty fatalities and an estimated seventy-five nonfatal attacks have been attributed to pumas in North America in the last one hundred years. Etling catalogs most if not all of them; at least enough that it isn't long before you see two constants emerge.

One, people attacked by pumas rarely see the cat before it bowls them over; two, the most favored human target is children under the age of sixteen (more than 64 percent according to a study Etling cites by Paul Beier). Neither statistic is hard to reason out. For the last three hundred thousand years—as long as it is believed pumas have been evolving in North America—they have survived by being stealthy enough to creep up on prey as jumpy as a white-tailed deer. They're incredibly good at it. Conversely, humans have no real sense of smell. Our hearing isn't very good. Outdoors, we tend to be patently oblivious to our surrounding and slow to recognize potential danger. And compared with a deer, we're anything but fleet of foot.

To paraphrase an observation made by Ernest Seton in *The Lives of Game Animals*, the puma is essentially a house cat multiplied by twenty. To a puma, then, a human child must be like a ball of yarn, squeaky toy, and annoying little fly bouncing off the window glass all in one. Picture the average kid: delectably plump and blissfully unaware . . . a spastic little creature whose mousy little voice, echoing through the forest on a nature walk, must to a hungry puma chime like a dinner bell.

Children have not only been attacked on wilderness trails and camp-grounds but also plucked out of their own backyards.

In Colorado, 1970, a puma attacked a little boy as he played in his garage in the small town of Lewis. In Montana, 1989, a puma killed five-year-old Jake Gardipe just forty feet behind his home in Evaro Hill. In 1990, near the town of Boulder, a father taking his four-year-old to an outdoor toilet was confronted by a puma that was reportedly so transfixed by the boy, it stuck around after the two retreated back into the house, where the father retrieved a rifle and shot the cat in the yard. In 1999, Washington State, four-year-old Jacob Walsh was jumped and mauled in his grandparents' backyard while playing with his five-year-old cousin near Barstow. Jacob's aunt came scream-ing into the yard to face the cat, which after "chewing" on the boy had dragged him partway into the woods. When Jacob's aunt appeared, she was horror-stricken by the image of the puma standing there coldly staring at her while holding the limp and blood-streaked body of Walsh by his throat. The cat dropped the boy and hightailed it into the hills. Amazingly, Jacob had only been knocked unconscious. He sustained a fractured collarbone, more than thirty puncture and tear wounds, and lost more than two pints of blood. The cat, a male and a perfectly healthy young killer, was hunted down the next day and killed.

Once while traveling in the UP, I was lured by billboard signs SEE THE COUGARS into GarLyn Zoo, a wildlife park west of the Mackinaw Bridge along Route 2. There I sat for a while watching two amazing animals, much more lithe and fit looking than the hobbling crippled fatties back in Traverse City. These cats were bowl-fed, too, but blockheaded and well-muscled creatures. The pen they occupied had real trees and rocks and greenery. And the one, a big, powerful-looking male, paced incessantly. When a child would approach the glass or dash by on the way to see the goats over at the petting portion of the zoo, he would jerk to a stop and devilishly perk up at the sight. Sometimes the cat would even shadow the child at a trot for the length of the cage. Or if the animal happened to see the kid coming from a long way off, he would gather himself in a crouch, tail twitching, with hawkish eyes widening and horribly intent. While the zookeeper told me he was as docile as a 200-pound tabby cat, it was still a spooky thing to witness, hinting that somewhere deeply embedded in the fiber of this feline, might still be a wild and murderous tinge.

I probably said this before, but it strikes me as one of the more captivating facets of this mystery . . . the very real possibility that maybe—more than likely as far as I'm concerned—some of the pumas out there in Michigan and perhaps elsewhere in the East are survived from once-captive stock. I read how a huge part of the early success of the Florida panther recovery plan relied on captive animals taken as kittens from the wild and raised into adulthood with minimal human interaction at a place called White Oak Plantation. As if car collisions and naturally occurring diseases weren't enough, biologists found that one of the main causes of puma cub mortality in Florida was the nasty habit of the ultraterritorial adult males of the species to routinely hunt down, kill, and eat puma cubs, even those they may have fathered. The point is, pumas raised in cages can be released to reclaim their wildness. It can be done.

•••

I wonder why those pumas that occasionally tear people to bloody ribbons out west—especially around southern California—are never thought to be hungry escaped pets of LA drug dealers or released by Hollywood eccentrics. I read dozens of newspaper accounts of attacks in California and elsewhere in the West, and I've never once seen this question asked.

At any rate, what are you supposed to do on the off-chance you encounter a puma? According to Etling, whatever you do don't run. Running away triggers a puma's "predatory chase response." That is a very bad thing. Going back to Seton's house cat analogy, it's a little like briskly scuffling past Socks in the middle of the night on your way to the bathroom in a pair of fuzzy slippers. Or trying to run away from a frisky kitty when your shoes are tantalizingly untied.

Don't approach a puma in the wild. Don't go anywhere near a puma if you see one accompanied by a brace of tumbling cubs. Just like the warning labels reminding you not to drink the Drano or stick your fingers down the garbage disposal, some of the advice out there on how to avoid an attack should be common sense.

Other precautions require a certain presence of mind, since bear and puma country often overlap. For example, unlike the case of a grizzly encounter, where you are advised never to look the bear in the eye, if you happen to lock eyes with a puma you are advised to keep staring since breaking eye contact first is the universal animal sign of submissiveness and could incite an attack. With bears you're supposed to back away slowly, but when confronted by a puma your best bet is to actually run *toward* the animal yelling and screaming and, Etling advises, even growling and snarling as if you are actually the one about to kick some ass.

Should you find yourself in the unfortunate predicament of being mauled by a bear, you're instructed to grit your teeth and play dead. But if you are suddenly jumped by a puma—remembering that most of the time their stealth precludes you time enough to compose your thoughts, let alone form an action plan—fight back.

I don't mean to be flip. But any rational person knows that you have about as much of a chance getting attacked by a puma in the East as getting beamed aboard a spaceship and implanted with an alien Bigfoot baby. Which is one of the reasons why I winced when Patrick Rusz told me about the glossy, four-color brochure MWC was putting together. This was not unusual by itself. Every amateur eastern puma group from the Eastern Cougar Foundation to the Eastern Puma Research Network had similar material it mailed to potential members.

But after years of listening to Rusz and Fijalkowski publicly and privately bemoan the woefully inefficient funds that hampered their research, *Living with Cougars in Michigan* left me wondering how much more research could have been funded by the thousands of dollars it obviously took to print and mail out more than fifty thousand of these brochures.

Rusz sent me a sample to look at. The opening page announced, "We have cougars in Michigan!" followed by steps people could take to reduce risk around their home. How to recognize puma sign. Tips on how you can help the puma in Michigan (Step 5: "Contribute to the [MWC's] Michigan Cougar Protection fund . . . donations are tax-deductible!"). The back panel featured a solicitation ("Please send me more information about cougars!") for those looking for additional information: Rusz's research paper from 2001, *The Cougar in Michigan*, and the field guide *Detecting Cougars in the Great Lakes Region*, both manuals on sale for fifteen dollars each plus four dollars shipping and handling.

A person could also sign up for something called the "Cougar Trackers" e-mail list, where I found the announcement that donations were now being accepted for a compensation program designed to reimburse Michigan landowners who claimed livestock predation caused by pumas. Rusz was now hosting "Cougar Tracking Seminars" and charging fifty dollars per person. I never did get an opportunity to attend. But I did make one of another series of lectures being put on by Fijalkowski.

•••

At the local college in Traverse City, I found Fijalkowski starting the lecture in front of a long table piled with MICHIGAN IS COUGAR COUNTRY T-shirts for sale. He had one on himself.

"How many people here have seen a cougar in Michigan?"

The room fell quiet. A few hands shot up.

Pretending to be so deep in my notes that I missed the question, I caught out of the corner of my eye a few more hands rising pensively in the air. More than half the room.

"And how many here took the time to call in the sighting and were told by the DNR person on the other end of the phone, 'No, that couldn't possibly be what you saw'?"

Practically every hand stayed in the air.

Fijalkowski shot a look at the floor and shook his head. "Incredible, isn't it?"

From there an uncomfortable hour-long slide show commenced. Moving from the natural history of pumas straight into the decades-long "campaign of deceit" promulgated by eastern states, including our own MDNR, Fijalkowski grew vocally more irritated.

"But thanks to our research," he said, flashing a picture on the screen of a black-and-white tabby poking its head out of a brown lunch sack, "the cat is finally out of the bag."

Everybody in the crowd, including me, was surprised to learn that Fijalkowski claimed he knew of at least three roadkilled pumas that had vanished after the conservation officers were called to the scene. One of the stories he told was of the puma supposedly hit in front of the Buckhorn Saloon outside Cadillac, a rumor I followed up on (he obviously didn't). I found, according to the responding police officer's report, that the motorist in question had actually peeled out of the Buckhorn and slammed into a tree.

"You can't trust those people," Fijalkowski said. He was referring to the DNR.

What were supposedly Michigan puma pictures, the usual array of grainy images and the two good photos from Alcona and Oscoda County, were mixed in with crystal-clear stock photos of western cats. After a while, the images became all one.

Fijalkowski fired back and forth between the Alcona and Oscoda pictures taken four years apart. He mentioned the sighting reports here going back to the 1930s, followed by the news that MWC fieldwork in the area had uncovered a scat testing positive for puma DNA in 2002 and, in a leap, offered his conclusion that the cats were obviously breeding here. So much science was mixing with speculation it was hard to keep up.

When the slide showing the Chippewa County skull appeared, I was not only aghast to see Fijalkowski using this as part of his "irrefutable case," but also shocked along with everyone else to find out that this was just one example of the "black market trade on puma parts." According to Fijalkowski, MWC had received numerous reports that led it to believe some Michigan farmers and ranchers were killing pumas that threatened their livestock. Backwoods rednecks were shooting pumas for sport and then selling their skulls and furs. This, he explained, was one reason why pumas were so elusive and hard to detect in Michigan. It also went to explain why their numbers were so low.

I looked at the faces of the audience, eyes fixed forward and rapt in wonder. With eyes casting a forlorn gaze upwardly at the image of puma on the screen, Fijalkowski then gave the pitch: "If the state's not going to protect these magnificent creatures, for the sake of our children we have to step up and save this animal on our own."

After a long applause, the lights came up and the presentation was almost over. There were a few houndsmen in the audience, nonbelievers, who raised their hands to question as ridiculous Fijalkowski's charge that pumas were being killed illegally. Where were the bodies?

"I just showed you the bodies. I showed you the skulls."

Fijalkowski was clearly unfazed. He opened his arms to the audience, palms facing up imploringly.

"Are you saying these people who bring us these stories are all liars! Are you saying the pictures and track evidence are all a hoax? We have DNA to confirm pumas are here. Are you questioning the DNA?"

The man shot back: "A couple thousand houndsmen are out there every winter. I'm out there. And we're not even finding tracks."

Fijalkowski chuckled. "I just showed everyone in this room pictures of the tracks. I showed you pictures of real pumas. I ask you again, are you challenging the DNA?"

"All I'm saying," the houndsman said, "is there's no breeding population of mountain lions out there. And DNA doesn't mean anything. Just ask O. J. Simpson."

Fijalkowski rolled his eyes to the heavens and spoke directly to the audience. "I don't know, folks. I tried."

With that, the believers converged on Fijalkowski and I took the opportunity to slip away without saying good-bye.

•••

Every time I told myself I was done with MWC and the puma, the cat had a way of making a dramatic front-page appearance that would start me on the trail again.

On September 28, 2003, Eleanor Comings, a volunteer naturalist at Sleeping Bear Dunes, was walking through the woods along Old Indian Trail when a puma suddenly emerged from the waist-tall ferns ("So close I could have pet its back," Comings later told me) and coldly considered her with a stare before continuing along a deer path into the brush. For going on two years, Rusz had tried to tell anyone who would listen that there was a puma leaving tracks and killing deer in the cedar swamps very near Old Indian Trail, near the Platte.

He'd brought me and Harley Shaw there. Shaw was not convinced and even I thought it was a stretch, even though it was less than five miles away from where I found the track and scat Wyoming temporarily confirmed (then later rescinded) as coming from puma. CMU had made up for the work lost in the Wyoming debacle, confirming seven puma scats Rusz had packaged up and delivered. Brad Swanson, the biologist in charge of testing the latest round of scat samples, told me flatly when I followed up the news: "I'm certain there are at least seven cougars roaming Michigan." The Benzie scat wasn't one of them because, according to Swanson, he couldn't get the DNA to amplify in tests.

Comings, a slight-looking fifty-something, was twenty minutes from the trailhead parking lot when she noticed how incessantly the squirrels were beginning to chatter. She kept her pace, casting a glance up to the treetops, and when she looked down there was the cat, tan, and six to seven feet from nose to the tip of its "very thick, very long" tail.

"It was broadside to me," she said, adding that the animal was so long it straddled the entire trail. Comings was afraid but stayed calm.

"It didn't seemed surprised at all to see me," she said, emphasizing again how big an animal it was. Comings noticed something else: dark tan, or black, spots around its tail and hindquarters—a characteristic of juvenile pumas up to two years old.

After blithely considering her for a second, the cat continued off the trail, into the ferns. Comings recalled how she immediately started walking again, pulling the radio out of the holster on her belt, and calling headquarters for help. The cat was following her.

"I stayed in the ferns and bushes," she said. "I was scared."

For the next twenty minutes, until the cat dissolved back into the woods near the trailhead, Comings saw glimpses of the animal just off to her right. And it was doing something else.

"I heard it chirping," she said, a detail that meshed nicely with her recollection of the cat's having spots. It also fit with the idea that the cat might be a young juvenile communicating with another puma Comings did not see. The books all say lost pumas sometimes chirp to locate other pumas, leading one naysaying reporter to glibly point out that maybe the animal really was lost and "looking for its owner." Rusz took a more stark view of the encounter, suggesting in one newspaper story that what Comings had really experienced was a "curiosity stalk" and probably was lucky to escape without being attacked.

Whatever the cat in Comings's vision was doing, it left no other tangible sign of its passing. Rangers placed motion-sensitive cameras in the area for a month and got nothing. A pair of deer hunters would later witness at close range a puma dragging a deer across the open beach from the shore of Lake Michigan into the trees. But the men waited two weeks to report the sighting, and when rangers went to investigate the scene, all they found under a jackpine were scattered bones.

A month later, October, when warning signs were placed at all of the thirteen hiking trails in the park, it looked at first like a small victory for Rusz and MWC. Two years prior, back when I'd first interviewed Kym Mukavetz, the method rangers were using to keep track of puma sightings consisted of a handful of pushpins and a map. After a couple of meetings with Rusz, a few of which I sat in on while he spilled out onto the table photographic evidence of tracks and deer kills in the park—even a picture of the shit I found on the lakeshore's eastern boundary—rangers finally came up with real report forms that could be filled out, cataloged, and investigated in the event of an encounter. The park was now investigating all credible encounters. And there was even talk that the puma that came within a few feet of Eleanor Comings should be hunted down and captured, a move supported by Rusz and MWC, arguing that the DNR's reluctance to do any research had now clearly moved the issue into the realm of public safety.

The DNR remained curiously silent throughout; understandably, since from their perspective the signs didn't change a thing. In one particularly jubilant "Cougar Tracker" memo after the signs went up, Fijalkowski remarked that the "National Park Service" had finally recognized there were pumas in Michigan. Actually, the National Park Service (which implies the main office in Washington, DC) didn't say anything of the sort. The signs didn't make any statement about population or breeding status. In fact, the warnings were carefully worded so as not to imply anything beyond the notion that sightings (many of which rangers at Sleeping Bear Dunes National Lakeshore deemed credible) suggested visitors were "entering cougar country."

When DNR spokesmen were called by reporters for comment, there came a regurgitated list of rhetorical questions I'd heard a dozen times before: "Where did the cougar come from? We don't know. Is this an eastern cougar? We don't know. What's the population status? We don't know."

The next time I talked to Rusz he sounded flummoxed by how quickly the Comings encounter had been turned into a nonevent.

"What about poor Eleanor Comings? The woman comes within three feet of a cougar that turns around and follows her and these people are playing political word games about what it all means. She could have been killed!"

Rusz paused for a beat, the sort of dramatic pause that with him I came to recognize as precluding some stinging observation or biting bit of sarcasm. He rarely disappointed me.

"I think it's gonna take somebody getting killed for these people to wake up. Jeez." And then he laughed. "I don't know, maybe a mauling might be good. I could probably get Dennis to offer the first victim a free T-shirt."

LOST IN THE PUMA LATITUDES

Science fails to recognize the single most
Potent element of human existence
Letting the reigns go to the unfolding
Is faith, faith, faith, faith

System of a Down, "Science"

"They're not going to be satisfied until somebody gets killed and then I'm going to sit back and say 'See I told you so.'"

The day had been a long one, so by cocktail hour Old Bill was revved up. Ten hours of PowerPoint presentations and pictures of cat tracks, behemoth-sized cat shit, and mangled deer carcasses with bloody puncture wounds to the back of the neck—and that was the good stuff. As for the rest, Bill couldn't decide what was worse: the pie charts and population graphics or being lectured to by a bunch of laser-pointer-wielding stiffs in suit jackets and ties.

"Biologists—ha! They don't know shit."

Looping a pudgy finger around the top of a longneck, Bill took an abrupt manly swig of Bud, set the bottle down noisily on the bar, and with his eyes turned upward toward the white flecks of disco light spinning on the bar ceiling cocked his head in a manner that suggested deep thought. He then began to count to himself, on those fingers, exactly like . . . well, exactly like a man going back over his fifty-some years trying to put a number on all the pussies he's seen.

"Twelve. Yeah. I've seen twelve."

In appearance Bill reminded me of a grouchy version of the Skipper from *Gilligan's Island* without the hair. The other man on the bar stool between us—a skinny, long-headed, cigarette-smoking Canadian named Stuart—bore a striking physical resemblance to Woody, that cartoon cowboy from the movie *Toy Story*. The bar we were sitting in was called—fittingly, I believe—The Wits End.

"I'm talking up close. I've seen them walking down the sidewalk in the middle of the night. A couple times I've had to get between them—big ones—stalking these little kids."

If anybody else at the bar happened to be eavesdropping, it probably came as a shocker to them as much as me to learn that Bill hailed not from Montana or Colorado but, of all the places, Rhode Island. And the "them" were cougars. Mountain lions. (It's important to clarify since sometimes in Bill's world the "them" referred to dill-weed know-it-all biologists; other times the "they" were the government and all those pantywaist politicians.) Stuart preferred calling the cats pumas or, more accurately given his accent, "pewmas," as in "Der's bin a lota talk a'boot dem pew-mas up Nort, too, eh?" According to Stuart, it was the same story in Ontario:

Pew-mas all over the damn place.

Though I sat there genuinely interested in hearing more, watching Bill's eyes go buggy, the way he constantly kept looking at the door, in the back of my mind I couldn't help think of the bon voyage message left by buddy Wayne: "Have a good time, live long and prosper, and don't forget to pack a tinfoil beanie and your Willy Brush."

For months I had been looking forward to the Eastern Cougar Conference. A gathering of professional biologists, puma experts, conservation officers, and amateur researchers (not all of them like Bill and Stuart) from as far away as the United Kingdom, the conference in Morgantown, West Virginia, was only the second ever of its kind. Bill attended the first, back in 1994, and by his measure this time around was a lot better.

"People are really excited," he said. "Thanks to what's been going on in Michigan, this thing's about to blow wide open." Bill took another deep swallow of beer, adding that as far as he was concerned, Patrick Rusz was "a hero for the cause."

•••

The day before Rusz and I had driven down from Michigan together, me in the shotgun seat reading the map, trying desperately, and failing, to steer the conversation away from the subject of pumas. Going on three years, but Rusz and I had little else in common. And it wasn't so much that I was tired of talking about pumas, I was just tired of talking about the subject with him.

I'd driven down to his house early in the morning, arriving in St. Charles, a dreary, flat, and farmy-looking community west of Saginaw. Rusz was all packed and waiting for me outside. He'd never invited me to his house before. And I never asked to come visit. The place was unremarkable, a modest dwelling situated on a long lane well off the main road. Scrub trees all around and a pond out back. Rusz was fidgety and awkward showing me around. He invited me inside, but only for a second, hardly enough time to take in the ambience of the place. A tiny, sterile-looking living room with a couple of beat-up chairs. Plain walls. A bookshelf filled with old, obscure volumes. CNN on the television perched atop a tiny entertainment center. Rusz disappeared down the hall to say good-bye to his wife, and I took the opportunity to drift over to the stereo. I only had time to read the titles of three—*The Best of The Guess Who*, *Bing Crosby Christmas*, and *Blood, Sweat, and Tears*—before he appeared again.

"You ready—let's go."

It started the minute we hit the road. The talking. Rusz never did mind the sound of his own voice. I had the feeling lately that he was using me as a sounding board. Back in the beginning, I had little trouble just listening to his theories. It was not my job yet to judge. I asked questions and he answered them. Mostly I just took notes and nodded periodically regardless of whether

I thought he was full of shit or not. My aim as a writer was to delve as best I could into his character as a means of finding the real heart of the story. But Rusz, I came to recognize, was one of those personalities who tend to interpret a listener's silence as tacit affirmation of his words. After years of preaching the same thing over and over again—pumas were here . . . pumas were breeding . . . he was the one who collected the proof—he spoke with the firm and droning conviction that comes from a man rarely challenged, as if the sheer repetition of his theories was the measure of their truth.

We made one stop along the Michigan state line to meet a woman, Carol Stokes, who had sent Rusz a grainy video she'd shot supposedly of two pumas walking along a distant tree line behind her house. By now I had accompanied him on at least a half-dozen of these fact-finding missions, rarely to uncover any real facts. They got to be uncomfortable affairs toward the end. The times I was along, if Rusz was told a puma was in the area—in this case two, which Rusz told me from his take on the video looked like a mother with a cub—he had an amazing track record at being able to find its track . . . or rather, something that he would tell me later could have *possibly* been a puma track.

The Stokes stop was no different. The house was situated on the edge of a massive, well-landscaped housing development. A lot of places people claimed to see pumas were like this, the last place in the world you'd expect a puma to be. Vinyl siding and macadam, factory smokestacks and power lines everywhere you looked. There was a little woodlot in the middle of it all, behind the Stokes backyard across a tilled-over cornfield hundreds of yards wide. Rusz said he recognized the tree line in the video.

Once we crossed the field, I wearily went through the motions of looking for tracks. Out in the sun, the dirt underfoot was hard as cement. You couldn't have dented it with a chisel.

I drifted off walking the wood line anyway while Rusz disappeared into the trees. Pretty soon came the call that I'd been expecting. He'd found tracks. And then came the uncomfortable part of walking up to him crouched down, looking very grave at the impression on the ground, and saying without breaking his stare on the ground: "Take a look at this."

I called dog track. I called dog track because experience in these matters told me that whenever you found a track that looked sort of like it came from puma, if you took the time to look around there were usually other tracks nearby that would tell you for sure that it wasn't. And these were almost always dog.

It was a big track. No obvious claws. Good and round. But even if we were hunting in puma country and this was the only track I had to go on, I wouldn't be putting hounds on the ground just yet. In this case there was a clear line of dog tracks in a little muddy seep—dog tracks all over, it turned out—and Rusz happen to come upon the one that admittedly looked enough like puma to give a reasonable person pause. But after I pointed out the other tracks, it was time for reasonable people to move on. Rusz kept lingering at the first, pondering it, still trying to get me to see the telltale three-lobed heel pad. Pointing out the lack of claws.

Back on the road, for the next seven sullen hours I kept my eyes ahead, trying not to look at him. The only thing I remember from the rest of the drive was a sick fluttering in my stomach. Somewhere in Ohio, I saw a red-tailed hawk in air flapping hard with a writhing snake dangling from its talons.

•••

Stepping out of the truck in the hotel parking lot, I suddenly remembered how much I despise East Coast humidity. The air was dank and heavy. I'd never spent so much time alone with Rusz and was suddenly looking forward to a shower, calling Nancy, and settling down alone for a spell in the quiet of my own room.

An hour later, I found a double shot of Scotch and a corner to occupy in a downstairs conference room. Jay Tischendorf, a Pennsylvania-to-Montana transplant, veterinarian, director of the American Ecological Research Institute in Great Falls, and the man who worked in Yellowstone National Park with Maurice Hornocker during the 1980s in the first organized study to find pumas there, walked up and immediately introduced himself.

Tischendorf seemed an affable and fit-looking fellow. An adviser for both the Eastern Cougar Foundation and the Eastern Cougar Network, Tischendorf was largely responsible for organizing this year's conference. I understood he had a keen interest in seeing pumas one day return to the East. We had talked on the phone and e-mailed occasionally over the preceding months and I liked him immediately, both for his calm and reasoned insight into the puma phenomenon and because he was one of the few puma people I'd met who never seemed to have a bad word to say about anybody.

I met Chris Bolgiano, author of *Mountain Lion* and vice president of Todd Lester's Eastern Cougar Foundation. Lester founded ECF after splintering off from the Eastern Puma Research Network. I really wanted to meet him and was more than a little disappointed when Bolgiano told me Lester, a deep underground coal miner by profession, had a sudden work conflict and would not be able to attend the show.

Lester, whose hobby before chasing rumors of pumas in the mountains of West Virginia was hunting and breeding champion 'coon hounds, had his life changed forever when he came face-to-face with a puma one day while out in the woods looking for a missing dog of his. I read articles about Lester and in almost every one he said by way of explaining his attraction to the mystery that, when that puma in the woods he encountered up and dissolved away, it took part of his soul along with it.

"Broke off and vanished," wrote Jay Kirk, a writer for *Harper's* who profiled Lester as part of a feature on eastern pumas that month (April 2004). "If it were your soul that had fled into the mountains, you too would spend every spare hour of your life hunting after it like Ahab gone mad."

If Rusz had ever been able to find it within himself to frame his desire like that, who knows . . . maybe he would have found more widespread sympathy, more tolerance for the often sloppy manner in which he presented his case. As it was, Rusz came across as heartlessly bent on vindication; victory, not discovery. Three years running around with Rusz and I'd never been able to coax such eloquence out of him. And it wasn't for lack of trying. Had he forgotten? Did he even know?

Roughly a decade after Lester's life-altering encounter, 1996, he found an independently verified puma track in Wyoming County, West Virgina, a discovery that helped solidify his standing as a dedicated and credible amateur researcher. Lester was the one who tried and failed in 2000 to petition the Department of the Interior for better protection of pumas in the East.

His latest attempt to prove the existence of pumas in the West Virginia mountains revolved around trying to get a picture of one via a remote camera study Lester was almost single-handedly conducting in the Monongahela National Forest. Breaking the country up into twenty-five-square-mile grids, Lester—in addition to his full-time job at the mines—busied himself for hundreds of daylight hours rotating twenty remote cameras. Month after month driving hundreds of miles, changing batteries, and checking film from April until September 2003.

According to the ECF autumn newsletter, the total photos taken from that time showed: 639 white-tailed deer; 192 black bears; 40 coyotes; 20 bobcats; 10 raccoons; 2 opossums; 2 grouse; 2 wild turkeys; 1 rabbit; and 1 "unknown," probably a deer. But no pumas.

The tenacity in men like Lester and Rusz was admirable, but I was curious to learn what the former hoped to achieve with a picture. Rusz had uncovered two unmistakable puma photos taken in Michigan, the 1993 and 1997 photos from Alcona and Oscoda Counties. For that matter, CMU had positively confirmed a puma scat Rusz had found here in 2002. But the MDNR had set a precedent: Pictures don't mean a thing. They don't prove origin or breeding. And the scat . . . well, legit or not Rusz's name was so controversial in anything having to do with pumas that no professionals on the outside could be sure where that came from or what to believe.

Even so, Lester is not alone in clinging to his hope that agencies will all of a sudden be inspired if someone, just once, could only get a clear picture of a puma.

So I was naturally curious: What did Todd Lester think would happen if he did manage to get the one-in-a-million photo he was after? If the Michigan case had shown the community of puma proponents nothing else, surely it illustrated how easily biologists can flatly ignore even the most compelling evidence when they're not inclined to do anything about it.

Bolgiano was a slight and learned-looking woman. She looked about as confrontational as a librarian. But when I made the comparison of Rusz's efforts to those of her president, Todd Lester, I saw behind her tinted frames those doelike eyes of hers narrow, searing a hole in my forehead. Her expression turned very grim.

"I think I can answer that," she said. "Unlike the conservancy, we've gone to great lengths not to alienate people around here."

Bolgiano explained that since state wildlife biologists would ultimately be in charge of managing pumas, it just made sense to work with them. By building inroads with agency biologists, keeping them abreast of their findings, and basically making nice, if the glorious day should ever come when Lester did come down from the mountaintop waving a picture of a puma in his hand, Bolgiano seemed to be suggesting that maybe, just maybe, the two conditions imperative before any taxpayer money can flow—origin and breeding—might not matter all of a sudden. According to Bolgiano, the biologists whom ECF had dealt with so far had been very supportive of their remote camera surveys.

Hope. Bolgiano was full of it.

"I'm sure everything's cordial right now," I said. "But I have to wonder if you'll get the same reception should you ever manage to find something."

It was a petulant thing to say in the face of her touching optimism, and Bolgiano couldn't have looked more stunned if I had at that moment dropped an anvil on her toe. I would have apologized if I wasn't so fed up. Fed up with all this nattering and false hope. Biologists weren't going to do anything to research pumas unless they were forced to.

I had suggested as much to Rusz on more than one occasion. If he believed so strongly that he had a solid evidentiary case, why didn't MWC just sue the MDNR for the dereliction of duty? Why didn't Fijalkowski shoot a memo out to all MWC's "Cougar Trackers" and get them involved in a coordinated letter-writing campaign to show the DNR that people really cared about the issue rather than drag the debate out for three years in the press?

Bolgiano had a question of her own.

"Why hasn't Rusz moved to have any of his theories and supporting evidence subjected to scientific peer review? It's such a simple thing that would go so far in helping his credibility."

She had a point. Until then it was just theories. For three years Rusz had told me he was working toward that goal and I was beginning to wonder if he'd ever do it. Bolgiano then wished me good luck, mustered a pursing smile, then, noticing a familiar face across the room, graciously excused herself without another word, leaving me standing alone against the wall rattling the ice in the bottom of an empty glass.

•••

I tried very hard not to offend anyone else the rest of the evening. The room slowly filled with all sorts of characters. I chatted with two conservation officers, two good old boys from North Carolina, and a hippie chick volunteer from the Defenders of Wildlife who was signing in conference-goers at a check-in table.

I met a delightful divorcée from Pennsylvania who sported a name tag that read COUGAR GROUPIE handwritten in black Sharpie under her name, BEV. Within a minute after she introduced herself, I learned that Bev lived alone in the country now that her husband, whom it sounded like she had been married to for almost as long as I've been alive, had for some reason either run off or left her.

"I'm a writer, too," she segued. "Or, well, I was before I retired. I wrote commercials. On a regular old typewriter. You probably don't use one of those."

She was into all wildlife, not just pumas. And the people here were interesting and fun. As she spoke Bev kept surveying the other faces in the room, a gesture I might've interpreted as rude were it not for the feeling I got that she was not the kind who took herself too seriously. The self-described "Cougar Groupie" seemed to know everybody. Bev pointed out Robert Downing to me.

"He's over there. Who's that man he's talking to?"

It was Rusz. From my vantage point it looked like Downing was the one getting a talking-to.

"Oh," she said. "I've heard about him. It certainly looks like they're having a good conversation."

Downing had long ago retired from the USFWS. Now an old man, he little resembled the bushy-looking woodsman I'd seen in black-and-white pictures stooping over a cat track in the Georgia mountains thirty years before. A white aura of stubble bristled on his bald, almost perfectly spherical head. His posture was upright and strong, and up close his eyes were dark and lively and sort of devilish looking, as if he still had a wild streak.

I sidled up beside him, thinking Rusz might take a breath and introduce me. Rusz had told me on the way down that he wanted to meet Downing, too, and now it looked to me as if he had the man good and proper.

It was the usual fare, a mini sermon punctuated by all the personal insights and logical leaps to which I and everybody else in the room had grown accustomed. I flashed back to a similar exhibition that had so put off Harley Shaw. But Downing seemed genuinely interested, so I left the two of them alone.

I went down to The Wits End for a change of scenery and a dark beer and winded up sitting by myself for the next hour watching ESPN. When I wandered back down the hall to the conference room, the party was already beginning to break up. Downing had gone. Rusz had Jay Tischendorf in a corner now.

The next time I saw Rusz he suddenly appeared behind me. He was headed out to get a bite to eat and wondering if I wanted to come along. I passed, telling him it had been a long drive. I was tired and planned on turning in soon. I asked him if he'd met anybody interesting, and he sort of half rolled his eyes.

"Yeah. I met a lot of people who don't know shit about finding cougars."

And with that he strutted off down the hall alone.

•••

Rusz was slated for two forty-five-minute lectures that first day: "Evidence of Cougars in Michigan: A Historical Summary" and "Methods for Detecting Pumas in the Great Lakes Region."

In no hurry to get downstairs, I dawdled around my room that morning watching another Iraqi standoff on CNN and perusing the summaries of conference subject matter on the docket for discussion that day. I called Nancy, more to see how the baby was doing than to chat. He was well over a year old.

"It's Daddy," Nancy told him. "Say hello to Daddy."

"Daa," he said.

"We miss you," Nancy said. "When are you coming home?"

"Another day. I miss you both, too."

Downstairs I grabbed a cold bagel and bucket-sized cup of black coffee. The conference had already started. Slipping into a seat way in the back, I counted nearly one hundred heads, including Rusz sitting up near the front behind Downing.

I was especially interested in a presentation by Eric Anderson, an ecology professor from the University of Wisconsin, and his lecture titled "Distribution of Cougar Sightings in Wisconsin 1994–2001." I had been intrigued by Wisconsin as it relates to the idea that pumas occasionally showing up in Michigan's UP might be transients that, like wolves, slipped around the headwaters of the Mississippi and entered from Minnesota.

The only hitch in that theory is that Wisconsin, despite a regular influx of sightings, has never had an actual specimen turn up. Northern Wisconsin forms a little hump of land separating the UP from Minnesota. If pumas are following the example of wolves, they would first have to pass overland through here.

Anderson was slender and bespectacled. He wore a heavy, dark goatee in contrast to a high forehead washed clean of any creases by the white glare of the overhead lights. When the lights went down, Anderson ran through a PowerPoint presentation about the history of pumas in Wisconsin starting with the last known specimen shot in 1908.

According to Anderson, pumas were once commonly found in the oak savanna environment and coulee country in the southern part of the state along the banks of the Wisconsin and Mississippi Rivers. This country was the source of at least twenty-six puma confirmations before pumas were believed wiped out—among them eleven actual bodies. After 1908, Wisconsin biologists have yet to find any tangible evidence to suggest that pumas survive there.

From 1994 to 2001, according to Anderson's analysis of "rare mammal observation cards" filed by citizens with the Wisconsin Department of Natural Resources (WDNR), there had been 404 sightings of pumas across the state. Lone animals and a few anecdotal reports of pumas with cubs. Only thirty-seven of these have been deemed "probable" by Wisconsin biologists. Of the rest, 308 were considered "possible" sightings, leaving 59 where circumstances and physical evidence at the scene led investigators to believe the encounter was a misidentification of some other form of wildlife.

The best sightings now seem to concentrate up in the heavily forested northern tier of the state, primarily in Prince Oneida and Lincoln Counties near the border of the UP. Not surprising, this is where the predominant number of Wisconsin's estimated 1.7 million deer reside.

I did find it surprising while reading a number of articles about the possibility that pumas live in Wisconsin that many locals believe the pumas they supposedly see are coming not from the west via Minnesota but the other way, from Michigan's Upper Peninsula. I wondered what the Michigan biologists back home would say to that. The WDNR regularly conducts winter wolf tracking surveys, as Michigan biologists do in the UP. In Wisconsin they cover more than four thousand miles of roads every winter, twice as much as in Michigan, yet reading those reports you discover they, too, have never had the occasion to stumble upon a puma track.

According to Anderson, the WDNR sounded at least a decade ahead of Michigan in keeping track of puma sightings, a major first step in actually doing something constructive for the animal neither state believes is really out there. This left Anderson hopeful, as well it should, since every indication is that pumas will eventually be coming into the state from somewhere adding to the few many think are already there.

"Do we give this thought ahead of time or scrabble to catch up?" Anderson asked rhetorically. "Here we have an opportunity to develop a management plan ahead of the curve and be ready for pumas when they return."

A baby-faced Clay Nielsen, a PhD from Southern Illinois University, the director of habitat research for the newest amateur puma group on the scene (the Eastern Cougar Network) and one of the men who conducted the necropsy on the wild puma killed by a train in Randolph County, Illinois, in 2002, Nielsen was far less optimistic about the chances of pumas ever migrating in any number into Illinois.

Pumas aren't even protected in Illinois. He was far more upbeat about the puma's chance of reestablishing a population in the states west of the Mississippi, a way to toss in a plug for ECN as one organization that was building relationships with wildlife agencies so that biologists could be better prepared and more knowledgeable should pumas return.

Rusz was up next, looking dapper in a deep blue shirt and pants. In front of this crowd he needed no introduction. But he got one anyway and I could see he was nervous, rocking and passing his notes from hand to hand. When the lights went down, though, he transitioned smoothly into a more reserved rendition of the Rusz I knew. I'd seen all the slides flashing on the wall behind him. I'd heard all the evidence before. And that's why I sat there feeling nervous for him, almost flinching at every new slide, praying it wouldn't be one of his fuzzy black feline photos that could induce one of his evangelical fits.

Most of the evidence he presented—the pictures of tracks, scat, and the two photos of bona fide pumas from Oscoda and Alcona Counties—wasn't new to many of the people sitting in that room. In fact, Rusz's case had changed very little in three years. He was still bursting with the same theories about remnant populations. Still enthralled by sightings. These were hard-core puma people in the room all of them aware of the controversy surrounding the Michigan case and the East in general. As evident by the Internet message boards where a lot of them hung out (I recognized some of the name tags they wore), more than a few thought Rusz a charlatan and a kook. When Rusz finally finished and called for the lights, I saw nothing in the faces that made me think the presentation had changed any of their minds.

That first day the conference proved a mixed bag of insight and entertainment, opinions of opinions, conjecture, and hints of government conspiracy.

The speakers were PhDs and DVMs, ecologists and biologists, and part-time puma sleuths. After Rusz gave his talk without any follow-up questions from the audience (bad sign), we were subjected to a torturously long-winded introduction for an Ohio man named Bill Reichling, an amateur field researcher for John Lutz's Eastern Puma Research Network.

I found out later that John Lutz had boycotted the conference out of a sort of protest against the other amateur puma groups that had helped put together the show. Rusz had had dealings in the past with both Bill Reichling and John Lutz. Lutz had even sent Rusz an e-mail prior to the conference warning that certain members of ECN and other "conspirators" had invited him to the conference only to mock and ridicule him. I knew John Lutz only from his posts on the Internet, where the general consensus on his motives and, indeed, his sanity was far from flattering.

Rusz occasionally corresponded with the man. I knew this not because Rusz had told me, but rather because Lutz broadcast it on the Internet, obviously taking a great measure of pride in telling everyone that he had just had a powwow with the man from Michigan who was sticking it to the DNR, who Lutz often referred to online as the "Department of Natural Retards."

The puma people are broken into factions, basically three groups in the United States, each with a very different take on how to best convince wildlife agencies that pumas deserve more consideration in the East. Lutz's supporters—almost exclusively members of his EPRN—were the sort who seemed to glom onto the puma mystery in addition to Bigfoot, Loch Ness, alien abduction, black helicopters, and spontaneous human combustion. While I may have my quibbles with what Todd Lester's ECF hoped to prove with a picture, at least his heart and the hearts of his members seemed to be in the right place.

Lutz's followers, the ones I'd met, seemed to use pumas as an object for their own political antipathy, a convenient medium for mucking up trouble. John Lutz had a little newsletter he put together for EPRN members. He maintained a puma reporting hotline. He was launching a Web site. He was virtually a daily presence in every Internet discussion board dedicated to pumas. Consequently, everybody in the puma world knew him even if they didn't hold his efforts in the highest regard.

Especially annoying to almost everyone who tried to take this eastern puma business seriously was Lutz's habit of coming onto Web discussion groups and announcing his possession of some exciting new bits of evidence. Lutz claimed to have it all. Videos. Photos. Funny thing was, he never actually got around to ever revealing any of it. Lutz was a great one for spreading Internet rumors of disappearing roadkilled pumas and black panthers. Regretfully, the people who brought him this evidence always wanted to remain anonymous, just like his highly influential team of deep-cover, on-the-inside informants who supposedly kept him abreast of all the outlandish lengths government agencies regularly went to in what was a concerted multiagency conspiracy effort to hide the existence of pumas in the East.

To a man, all the EPRN members I chanced to meet face-to-face believed in the same conspiracy. Bill Reichling was by far the most harmless looking of the lot. Dressed comfortably in workingman's denim, gray-haired and stout, he looked like somebody's grandfather, and probably was. Reichling told us how his fascination with the puma had started out, like most, with a glimpse. Heading off into the Ohio woods one day to shoot targets with his younger son, he saw one. Or thought he did. Whatever he saw, it was enough to send Reichling off on a little father–son adventure that has lasted sixteen years.

Reichling told of learning how to track from local Shawnee Indians. Father and son spent weekends following up sightings together, finding the sign where nobody else could.

With no real laws governing the sale of everything from African hyenas to Asiatic binturongs, Ohio is the nation's hotbed for exotic pet sales. There's a pet auction there virtually every week where puma kittens and full-grown adults can be bought for eight hundred dollars—or most times less. This adds to the estimated fifteen thousand exotic big cats some reports guesstimate to be in private hands nationwide. Yet the pumas Reichling believed he was chasing around were all wild deer killers. Like Rusz, Reichling believed he could link a sketchy history of anecdotal puma sighting with an array of

211

physical evidence to support the notion that Ohio, like Michigan, had a remnant population of pumas.

Reichling had the same propensity for logical leaps as Rusz. He showed a slide of a couple of scratch marks on a tree. Claw marks, he called them. Reichling told the audience that this and a couple of sightings in the area were enough to convince him that this tree was actually the territorial boundary of a big male puma he'd been chasing. Reichling was very serious about this. He showed slide after slide of what he contended were puma-killed deer, while exposing some wild theory about being able to determine cat-killed carcasses from those taken down and scavenged by coyotes simply by observing the little white hair "pluckings" he found around the bodies.

Coyotes and dogs, Reichling explained, tended to pull the hair off their prey in chunks, usually taking with it a bit of flesh, too. But pumas—he had read somewhere—used their side teeth to *shear* the hair from the deer before ripping a volleyball-sized hole in the chest cavity, ducking their heads inside, and pulling out the guts.

Voilà!

While it was good to find tracks and other physical evidence at the scene, Reichling claimed to be experienced enough in these matters that by looking at the size and configuration of the "hair hank" alone he could determine whether a puma had made a particular kill.

As with Rusz, it wasn't all nonsense. I had observed pumas, wolves, and coyotes feeding on roadkilled deer at the Traverse City zoo. They actually do have different means of hair removal, much as Reichling explained. That's where facts ended and the fantasy began.

Mixed into his slide show, along with pictures of plaster casts so obviously from a dog that it literally made my head snap back, were some real casts of puma tracks and a handful of deer kills that had all the textbook markings of a puma kill.

Reichling, like Rusz, had clearly found puma scat. He had one unique set of puma track pictures taken in a freshly asphalted parking lot. The long line of dusty tracks looked as if they had been lifted from a guidebook, which is to say there was no question.

All good stuff. The problem was that Reichling, again like Rusz, had apparently lost the ability to filter good from bad.

"I'm just an old farm boy," Reichling said to sum up, "but if it walks like a cougar, kills like a cougar, and answers the call of nature like a cougar, then it must be a cougar."

I'd heard that line before. Reichling declared that he would not stop his crusade until Ohio recognized and made an effort to study the wild pumas he believed were out there. Whether pumas really lived wild in Ohio or not, I also got the impression from some of the things Reichling said that maybe— and I'm just guessing here—maybe just as important as the little bits of genuine evidence he happened to come across once in a great while was simply the chase itself, a hunt no doubt all the more precious to an aging man still able to run around the countryside chasing down dragons with his boy.

•••

While some key players were missing, I found all the puma factions in some way represented in Morgantown. By the end of the first day, three of the four original founders of the Eastern Cougar Network had even assembled. And I mean that literally. Mark Dowling, Bob Wilson, and Ken Miller seemed to go everywhere together.

Miller was a high-tech entrepreneur and ECN's Web master. Wilson was a high school science teacher. And Dowling was a money man, a banker by profession. The only one of the original founders missing was Jim Close, an air pollution specialist with the New York Department of Environmental Protection. Close quit ECN shortly after their Web site launch in 2002. According to Close, Dowling had altered a quote of Close's because it hadn't been "cleared" with him first, yet still posted the news story as if it were the original text.

ECN has billed itself as an "objective research organization that collects data and reports news." It's currently the best online source for links to newspaper accounts about the pumas that are nowadays showing up more and more, far-ther and farther east of the Rockies. ECN follows up most of these reports and, in cases where the evidence suits, transfers puma confirmations to its online "Big Picture" map.

Taking the view of eastern wildlife agencies that citizen sightings (too often fleeting misidentifications of other more common animals) cannot be relied upon as a true confirmation of a puma, ECN gives a colorful blue dot only to those pumas verified by a body (dead or captured alive); clear pic-tures or video that can be certified by date, time, and place by the original photographer; or DNA evidence from scat or hair, analyzed and identified by professional biologists.

Another lower level of confirmation, indicating very strong evidence of a "probable cougar," gets a red dot and, according to ECN, requires track ev-idence verified by a professional, kills or attacks on game or livestock done by pumas showing their telltale technique, or a clear sighting made by a uni-formed state or federal wildlife official.

On its Web site, ECN claims not to be an advocacy group, that it is only "interested in documenting evidence of wild, free-roaming cougars and as a result, animals of a known captive origin are not included as confirmations or probables." ECN does this with the help of a network of wildlife agency officials, independent experts, and biologists who essentially put their col-lective seal of approval on physical and scientific evidence, which includes helping to verify the origins of any puma that happens to turn up dead any-where east of the Rockies and those known populations in west Texas, the Black Hills, and south Florida.

Connecting the dots on the computer screen, ECN's documenting meth-ods seem very tidy—very scientific. But to overhear some of the whispered conversation in that West Virginia hotel conference room, what ECN calls a credible and objective approach most others denounce as being in cahoots with the same government agencies and their biologists, who have so far been anything but proactive when it comes to real research and protection of pumas east of the Rockies.

Unlike the Eastern Cougar Foundation and John Lutz's Eastern Puma Research Network, ECN doesn't have any rank-and-file members, so such concerns fall on deaf ears. Instead, it assembled a long list of advisers—biologists and western puma experts—and by piggybacking along on their credentials ECN had for the past two years worked the media to set itself up as the go-to source and "final word" on anything having to do with eastern pumas.

Dowling had contacted me shortly after reading one of the magazine articles I wrote about Rusz and the Michigan case. We kept up a regular dialogue via phone and e-mail for months. Dowling, whom departing founder Jim Close told me was the person who really ran ECN, had long refused to recognize as legitimate any of the Michigan evidence uncovered by Rusz: the seven scat samples verified by CMU; the track evidence and observations made by MDNR and Forest Service employees; the sighting made by rangers and naturalists at Sleeping Bear; unmistakable pictures taken in Oscoda and Alcona Counties in 1993 and 1997. All of it on the grounds that Rusz had clearly lost his scientific objectivity.

Consequently, Dowling and I had some good debates about what constituted objectivity in the realm of eastern pumas. While he got no argument from me that Rusz had made some major scientific missteps along the way, I didn't think you needed to be a scientist to see the perfect image of a puma in a photograph (i.e., the Alcona and Oscoda County photos) and put a damn dot on a silly little map.

Three years into this, I wasn't looking for the puma anymore. I'd looked and found it. Everybody on both sides said that, yes, there were probably pumas in Michigan. Whether you came from the camp that saw them as FERCs or viewed them as scattered survivors from the past, what did it matter? For once the law of the land (the "similarity of appearance clause") and our hearts agree: It doesn't matter, not a whit.

Pumas now need advocacy, not more groups running around talk, talk, talking about more objectivity. We have enough real scientists for that. So my question to Dowling was always the same:

What was ECN really doing for pumas in the East if it wasn't an advocate for them?

In our debates, Dowling never seemed to understand that you could be an advocate for something and still maintain your credibility. I got to know Dowling as extremely knowledgeable about almost everything having to do with pumas east of the Rockies. But as much as Patrick Rusz had a reputation for blind belief in all things puma, Dowling struck me as the type who pushed objectivity not only to the point of being downright negative, but also to a black and pessimistic place that made him prone to tearing down the efforts of those really out there acting to solve the mystery—even if they sometimes made mistakes.

Easy as it was to pick and find fault with people like John Lutz, Patrick Rusz, Todd Lester, Bill Reichling, and a dozen other amateur researchers out there, the fact remains: These people were really doing something.

Judging by the fact that his e-mails had suddenly stopped, I gathered that Dowling didn't agree with my shared observation that there might indeed be a conflict of interest at ECN when the people they were beholden to for the sake of maintaining their scientific credibility were some of the very same individuals and agencies that had never shown any real interest in pumas.

That night at The Wits End after the first day of conferencing was done, my new friend Bill from Rhode Island, a follower in the footsteps of Lutz, put it in harsher terms.

"They're a bunch of suck-ups," Bill said of ECN. "Middle-aged lost-in-life wannabe biologists. Ha!"

Even so, I liked Dowling. We'd talked briefly earlier in the evening and agreed to meet up later and bury the hatchet with beer. I was waiting for him to finish up with his ECN powwow, but it dragged on for hours. They came into the bar, the three of them moving in a pack, sat in the corner with grave expressions as they talked.

Stuart and Bill moved on to a drunken debate about the easiest way to tell a puma track from that of a dog. It involved a straight edge and lines drawn at an intersect through the outside toe pads of the track. And I couldn't follow any of it. They asked the bartender for a pen and began furiously scribbling likenesses of tracks on bar napkins.

I took the opportunity to step outside and call my wife, only to realize how late it was and, not wanting to wake the boy, decided better of it.

When I returned to have that promised nightcap with Dowling, I saw that he and the ECN crew had already slipped away. So I ordered another beer and listened as Stuart told me about tracking pew-mas in Ontario.

"I'm so good at it I can predict where they're going to turn up next. Yeah. The ministry guys hate me. When I come around they're like 'Aw, c'mon, eh, not that guy again.'"

I asked Stuart why he did it. What was he hoping to prove?

"Prove?" He blew a long plume of smoke and, for a moment, looked sort of confused by the query.

"I don't know, really. Nothing. I mean, what else is a guy going to do with his time, eh?"

At this point in the story, the answer did not strike me as being as odd as it might have three years before. In fact, I went to bed that night thinking maybe that's all there was. Maybe Stuart, crocked on his barstool, had just given me the most honest answer I'd heard so far.

What else is there?

I could think of a few things, a life, waiting for me back home.

•••

Facedown on my pillow in a damp circle of drool, I woke ready to get the day over with, Friday. I wanted nothing more at that moment than to be done with pumas and people and politics and just go home to hold my wife and baby in my arms.

For the rest of the day, I felt that old sadness coming back, that bitter feeling of the utter pointlessness of it all. Between speakers I lingered out in the hall where the overheard chatter centered on woeful discussions about increased human population growth in the East, suburban sprawl, and game and forest management; the puma was talked about as if it were some sort of elusive cure-all. Everywhere I turned was debate. Pumas are already out there, they just need to be found. Others said no, they're not. At least not real pumas anyway. After another day of listening to talk about the mystery of eastern pumas from every possible angle, I was reminded of an old saying that anybody who sets out to discover the animal is doomed to fail. Pumas will be found when they are ready and, I would add, when we are finally worthy enough to receive them, which three years following this strange saga and one weekend in Morgantown suggested that for now we are not.

I didn't want to hear another word about eastern pumas. And I definitely didn't feel like driving seven hours home talking more about it with Rusz. But, of course, that's the only thing Rusz and I had in common. He started harping on it the minute the rubber met the road.

"Did you learn anything back there?"

I confessed not learning so much as confirming what I already suspected was true.

"Well, I didn't. What a waste."

I listened to him jabber on about how misunderstood he was, how much a waste of time it seemed now to have driven all the way out here just to listen to a blabbering bunch of know-nothings when all he really wanted to do was be out there looking for pumas. He had the pictures. He had the tracks. He had held their shit in his hand. He had proven there were pumas in Michigan.

"You saw one. You tell me they aren't out there. How has everything gotten so mixed up and confused? How am I the bad guy?"

The night before, I had snapped at him. I don't remember exactly what I had said, but I do remember growling at him to stop.

"Please, for once would you just shut up!"

To say that he didn't know how we had gotten here, I told Rusz flatly, he had to be either lying or stupid. I'm pretty sure I told him that for a PhD, for a guy who calls himself a scientist, sometimes he didn't strike me as very bright.

I was not angry with Rusz so much as disappointed. Disappointed in the way things had gone. Disappointed in him for not doing the work the way it was supposed to be done and being so confoundingly unable to ever admit a mistake. Disappointed in him and also in the people so blind as to not see on their own what was there. Back home in my office, there were three years of press clippings and conversation notes that gave me every reason to believe that he and MWC may have actually done harm to furthering eastern puma research. And not just in Michigan.

I didn't care anymore what motivated Rusz. I didn't care that he was sometimes less than scrupulous with the facts. I didn't care about his pictures of fuzzy house cats, pet puma skulls, and handfuls of shit. Nobody else seemed to care. None of it mattered. Nothing mattered at all.

We didn't talk for a long time. I sat and stared out the window, falling asleep counting crows. I slept peacefully and for hours, all the way to Michigan, opening my eyes only when I felt the truck slow as it poured down the highway exit ramp.

I woke feeling good again, as if I had just opened my eyes from the longest sleep to find this thing was about to be over. It was dark as pitch out, the digitized numbers on the radio clock glowing 2:00 AM. I still had another three hours of driving to get home. Home. A few miles away from Rusz's house I asked him for the first time where he was from.

"Not far. I grew up only about six miles from here."

I started to tell him a story about growing up in Pennsylvania, a long, long way from here, but I could see he wasn't really listening. He was concentrating on something off to the west, out in the darkness beyond the glow of the headlights. A field.

He nodded as we headed past.

"Out there," he said. "Couple hunters said they saw a cougar back against those trees a couple years ago."

He planned to look into it. Maybe go looking for its tracks.

"I got a feeling," he said. "I got a feeling there might be something out there."

EPILOGUE

This is a book of nonfiction, but it might better be described as a "commentary." While I think the hundreds of news article written about the Michigan controversy in the past couple years more than adequately substantiate my observations on key evidentiary facets of the case, it should be stressed that what's recorded here is what I experienced, heard, and felt during my relatively small and unimportant role in the search. My proximity to the story and its key players made a lot of what's here difficult to write. But in the end I sought accuracy in reporting every messy reality as I saw and heard it unfold, even when sometimes I didn't like or disagreed with what I was seeing and hearing. But that's not to suggest this be confused with any kind of journalistic endeavor. It's not. And it's certainly not the final word on the subject.

It shouldn't be forgotten that wherever a light shines on a thing from a single vantage point or perspective, it casts a shadow of bias. At various points throughout my chronicling the controversy in Michigan, I was sympathetic and at other times enthusiastic about the way the case seemed to be going. I don't apologize for that. I held out hope to the end (to the conclusion of my involvement anyway) that the compelling evidentiary case—a lot of it good and some not so—Patrick Rusz and the Michigan Wildlife Conservancy compiled might serve as a catalyst for a more substantial state or federal inquiry. So far, it hasn't.

No one is truly objective, especially when the subject revolves around something as bio-politically divisive as the possibility of 150-pound predators living in our midst. When, in the beginning, I tried to write objectively about the mystery of whether or not wild pumas were alive in Michigan and, later, the controversy surrounding the eastern puma in general, there was always a believer or staunch cynic in the crowd insisting that I had left out certain details they considered vital to understanding the real story—vital to shining the light of truth on the case—which is another way of saying that my take on the story was wrong. I never did have a problem with that since it always seemed to me that the people doing the commenting were the extreme personalities who have a stake in being "right" in this debate, the ones who I very much doubt could ever be happy with any reporting on the case unless they had written it themselves.

In August of 2004, the Michigan Wildlife Conservancy released a grainy video of two tawny-colored felines, footage taken by Carol Stokes, the resident of that Monroe County suburb where Rusz took me on our way to the Eastern Cougar Conference in Morgantown, West Virginia. Shot from some three hundred yards away, the video shows the two felines walking along the treeline I recognized on my brief tour of the scene. Curiously, and as is all too typical of this sort of evidence, the footage by itself is of poor quality and so lacking in detail that it's impossible to tell just what kind of cats the viewer is looking at. The conservancy hired Future Media, a local "video forensic firm," to analyze the tape and establish some sort of size reference for the cats. An enhanced version of the Stokes video was posted on the conservancy's Web site with split-screen images of the animals alongside footage of whitetail deer and a nearly six-foot man shot by Stokes over a series of weeks in the same location. During his Web site commentary of the video, Dennis Fijalkowski cites the cats' coloration, tail length, black-tipped tails, and large size (only discernable when juxtaposed with the additional deer and man footage) as proof that the felines in the video are actually two pumas—what the conservancy maintains is an "adult female" and her "nearly grown" cub.

"For the first time in Michigan this video documents two cougars in the same frame," Fijalkowski says in his commentary. "This strongly suggests a breeding cougar population because the cougar is a solitary animal except when raising young."

Following the conservancy's release of the video to the media, the Eastern Cougar Network offered their analysis of the Stokes video on their Web site. Seven of their puma experts/advisors—western biologists and puma experts including Dr. Dave Maehr who pioneered the recovery of the Florida panther—watched the tape and, despite the work done by Future Media to establish scale, flatly deemed the appearance and behavior of the felines in the footage more consistent with house cats than a mother puma and her cub. In the same report, the Eastern Cougar Network also cast doubt on the 2001 Mesick video showing the deer-colored feline moving through the woods in deep snow. Again, "house cat" was the verdict from the experts.

Fijalkowski responded by firing off one of his "cougar trackers" e-mails to conservancy supporters. He was adamant that the Eastern Cougar Network's panel of experts was wrong and also charged that the group was nothing more than "a third-party provider, set up to provide assistance to the state fish and game agencies."

"The state fish and game people were losing credibility with citizens all over the East by their continual criticism and ridicule of honest people that were reporting cougar sightings," the October 15, 2004 memo reads, "So now they have the Eastern Cougar Network, led by a banker from Connecticut, to do the criticism for them."

In another blow to the conservancy's credibility, the Eastern Cougar Network released their investigation into the Chippewa County skull. The report, posted on their Web site in August of 2003, states that the skull more than likely came from Sasha, the Neebish Island captive, currently immortalized by a full-body mount that resides in her adoring owner's living room. Yet at this writing, Rusz and the Michigan Wildlife Conservancy insist that this theory is not conclusive and that the skull, which was found behind a taxidermy shop, came from a wild, perhaps illegally killed, Michigan puma.

Despite the "he-said, she-said" elements of this three-year-long public controversy, Detroit-area citizens weren't taking any chances. In October of 2004, at least two Wayne County elementary schools southeast of Detroit went on lockdown after a spate of alleged sightings in Sterling Heights, Van Buren, and Monroe Township. Thanks to frequent sightings still being reported by visitors and park rangers in the Sleeping Bear Dunes National Lakeshore, the warning signs posted after Eleanor Comings's 2003 close-range encounter remain at all of the trailheads.

Looking at the eastern puma controversy with the hindsight of what has happened in Michigan, I think it's clear that people working outside the system to prove pumas are here have little chance of impressing government wildlife agencies until more than a few bodies turn up. In Michigan, that has yet to occur. Right now too much cynicism and bad-tempered scrutiny exists towards any other type of evidence brought to the table. Skeptics—especially those agency biologists and policy makers who would be responsible for researching and protecting such a controversial carnivore—are extremely intolerant of mistakes. And unfortunately, as the Michigan case illustrates, when the under-funded seekers hazard to play their investigation out in the papers for the sake of public support, there are far too many opportunities for missteps, and knee-jerk public remarks always seem to highlight the divisiveness of the issue rather than to inspire a larger movement to discover what's really out there.

It seems to me that state and federal agencies in the East don't care about pumas right now. And, in my experience, there's no picture, no video, not a hundred piles of puma scat from a hundred different locations that will change that without vast and determined public support. In addition to constantly asking Rusz when he was finally going to move forward with peer review, something he'd been promising reporters since the fall of 2001, I often pressed him for a response as to why the Michigan Wildlife Conservancy didn't band like-minded persons together to wage a real, grass-roots, public advocacy campaign. For instance, why didn't the conservancy use their mailing list and extensive media connections in the state to organize a letter-writing campaign to congressmen, the governor, and MDNR department heads asking that a state-sponsored habitat or social carrying capacity study be done for the sake of pumas? Either that or seek to raise the money and support to conduct one of these studies for themselves.

And what about going over the heads of state biologists and taking their evidentiary case right to the feds? What about the deluge of money and manpower that should be available through the Endangered Species Act for seeking out and/or restoring pumas in the East? Here also is an opportunity to get the public more involved, since before any federal money can begin to flow an urgently needed update of the Endangered Species Act is required, one that recognizes the modern genetic taxonomy of pumas and thereby does away with the current policy that only recognizes two separate subspecies of pumas living East of the Mississippi.

But even then, would that change anything? Given the news from Washington last year, probably not. In May of 2003, the U.S. Department of the Interior announced in a press release that the Endangered Species Act was in effect "broken" and in need of a drastic overhaul thanks to a flood of litigation from plaintiffs (environmental groups) over critical habitat issues affecting thirty-two species nationwide. This means that for now, there's no federal money out there for protecting and restoring any "new" threatened or endangered species. And that means no money for finding or reestablishing puma populations in the East.

I believe there are pumas in Michigan, maybe just a handful. When I started all this, I wasn't so sure. But more importantly, I believe there are still places out there where pumas can live. This is good, since one thing to come of all this is the knowledge that as western populations grow, pumas will continue to migrate East until eventually there will be no denying them.

Whenever I go back over what has happened here, a certain feeling of hopelessness and dread overtakes me—until I remember seeing that puma gliding away from me on a woodsy two-track road. Reflecting on those fleeting seconds, my pessimism is washed away by the sort of peace—a feeling of hope—that maybe the woods out there are still big and deep enough for myths and legends to live.

ENDNOTES

1. East of the Mississippi River only the so-called "eastern cougar," *Felis (Puma) concolor couguar*, and the Florida panther, *Felis (Puma) concolor coryi*, are federally recognized as protected subspecies under the Endangered Species Act of 1973. This distinction is based on Arthur Goldman's taxonomic revision of the species penned in the 1940s in his book, *The Puma: Mysterious American Cat*. In classifying pumas that once roamed the East, Goldman used primarily skull measurements from a dusty collection of museum specimens—only seven skulls in the case of the eastern puma and seventeen for the Florida panther—while also sorting those pumas appearing in the rest of the United States into a confusing jumble of geographically overlapping subcategories: *Felis (Puma) concolor azteca* (Arizona and New Mexico); *Felis (Puma) concolor browni* (the Hualpai Mountains, Arizona); *Felis (Puma) concolor californica* (California); *Felis (Puma) concolor coryi* (Arkansas and Louisiana to Florida); *Felis (Puma) concolor couguar* (Tennessee to lower Michigan); *Felis (Puma) concolor hippolestes* (North Dakota to Wyoming and Colorado); *Felis (Puma) concolor improcera* (southern California); *Felis (Puma) concolor kaibabensis* (Nevada, Utah, and northern Arizona); *Felis (Puma) concolor missoulensis* (Idaho and Montana); *Felis (Puma) concolor oregonensis* (Washington and Oregon); *Felis (Puma) concolor schorgeri* (Kansas and Missouri up to Minnesota, Wisconsin, and the Upper Peninsula of Michigan); and *Felis (Puma) concolor stanleyana* (Oklahoma and Texas).

2. In addition to his own son, Rusz's team of volunteers who located and provided some of the puma scats for genetic testing included Mike Zuidema, the retired MDNR forester, and another longtime believer named Nancy

Gagnon, a staff member and graduate student of forestry at Michigan Technological University who claimed she saw at least one puma on her Houghton County property in the UP where she also later found puma scats.

3. Soon after news of their inquiry into the status of Michigan pumas broke—a move the group insisted was unrelated in any way to their sudden preoccupation with large "charismatic mega fauna"—board members for the Michigan Wildlife Habitat Foundation voted in 2002 to change the organization's name to the Michigan Wildlife Conservancy. Founded in 1983, MWC's began a small non-profit whose self-described mission was to "restore and improve living space for Michigan animals."

4. Pioneered only in the last ten years, mitochondrial and macrosatellite DNA testing chemically isolates cells sloughed off in the digestion process from the lining of the animal's gut. The process is far less time consuming and more conclusive than the old method that required laboratory technicians to painstakingly dissect scat samples and find tiny hairs the puma may have ingested during grooming.

5. Robert Carroll's *The Skeptic's Dictionary* defines "argument to ignorance" or "argumentum ad ignorantium" as one claiming something is true because it hasn't been proven false. An "ad hoc hypotheses," notes Carroll, is any "new scientific theory that is proposed which conflicts with an established theory and which lacks an essential explanatory mechanism."

6. Carroll calls this "communal reinforcement" when "claims become beliefs through repeated assertions by members of a community [or] when the mass media provide tacit support for untested and unsupported claims by saying nothing skeptical about even the most outlandish claims."

7. Todd Lester, president of the Eastern Cougar Foundation, filed through the Freedom of Information Act (FOIA) to find out whatever became of the female puma and her cub. In a bizarre series of twists, Lester discovered that the state either lost or destroyed all results of the necropsy

done on the male to discover its origin. They also misplaced or destroyed the body. Lester also reported that the USFW service "advised" the West Virginia DNR to turn the pregnant female loose in the Cranberry Glades Wilderness because it was an animal listed under the Endangered Species Act. The female and the cub she was carrying were also lost, according to what Lester dug up in his FOIA request.

8. Pumas have an almost bizarre propensity for running afoul of moving vehicles. They've been killed by cars, trains, trucks, motorcycles, and farm tractors. Pumas are so adept at getting themselves hit that Robert Downing—noting the "low but consistent rate of roadkills in Florida and the West"—suggested that "automobile traffic is a search tool of sorts, and that vast areas of the East have, with high probability, already been proven cougar-free based on high traffic volume and the lack of documented roadkills."

9. According to Arthur Goldman's taxonomy work, Michigan was once believed to be the home of two separate subspecies: *Felis (Puma) concolor schorgeri* (the Wisconsin puma) in the Upper Peninsula and *Felis (Puma) concolor couguar* (the eastern puma) in the Lower.

10. This brings up the question of how many other times captive pumas were set loose to breed in Florida. Cases like the one involving Ted Turner, the eco-minded media mogul ba-zillionaire, who in 1988 set two western pumas loose on his sprawling property near Capps. Turner never showed up for trial and paid a measly $1,500 fine. Six months later the male puma became roadkill on nearby Interstate 10, described by Fergus, "in the pink of health" with an armadillo in its stomach. Nobody knows what ever happened to the female.

11. When Central Michigan University took over analyzing scats for MWC, the first thing they needed were scats from other Michigan wildcats, namely bobcat, for comparative analysis.

SUGGESTED READING

For a creature that supposedly does not exist, at first glance there seems to exist a remarkable amount of reading material on the subject of eastern pumas. Depending on what you call the creature (eastern puma or eastern cougar), typing the subject into the computer brings up anywhere from 45,000 to 250,000 hits on the Internet alone. That might seem like a lot until you start reading what's really there. Sighting-inspired newspaper reports from across the country comprise the bulk of it—but because the locale and circumstances differ from week to week, the plain truth is that once you've read one you've pretty much read them all. Information is even thin from a natural history and biological standpoint, especially the latter, which should really come as no surprise since there's never, ever been any research done involving real, live "eastern pumas" . . . and, come to think of it, there never will be. I'm speaking about the subspecies currently (and erroneously) recognized by the people who make the laws—*Felis (Puma) concolor couguar*—a creature that never lived.

There's a glut of information out there about pumas in general. Talk about the so-called Florida panther and the books alone dealing in whole or in part with the subject come close to outnumbering the actual count of animals on the ground. Obviously, the list below is far from a complete summary. There are three stacks of books teetering knee-high beside my desk. Some good, some not so, depending upon what you know (or what you think you know) coming into it. The titles below are the ones I picked off the top and, not surprisingly, they are the ones that during my research I probably drew from the most. Also of relevance are the titles here about red wolves, Colorado grizzly bears, and other thought-to-be-lost species. I included these because the predator may be different, but the politics are the same.

It's been said that much of what is understood about pumas in general comes from "the science of assumption." If this is true, it holds double when talking about pumas in the East. Because the creature is right now little more than an enigmatic idea punctuated by occasional visitations, it follows that a lot of what I learned came from listening to people who thought they understood the beast and the mystery it plays on us. I logged hundreds of hours of spirited conversations and heated debates with believers and nonbelievers about the idea of pumas living in the East. Maybe it's because the debate is so old, but after a while I found the exchanges took on a vapid, dancelike quality where I not only began anticipating all of each side's argumentative steps but also came to think I may have invented a few of my own. At any rate, when it came to ideas and opinions I was diligent about my notes and made sure to give credit to those who said things first, even if it risked interrupting the flow of the narrative.

Bass, Rick. *The New Wolves.* The Lyons Press, 1998.

———. *The Lost Grizzlies.* Houghton Mifflin, 1995.

Bolgiano, Chris. *Mountain Lion: An Unnatural History of Pumas and People.* Stackpole Books, 1995.

Brocke, Rainer H. *Reintroduction of the* Cougar Felis Concolor *in Adirondack Park: A Problem Analysis and Recommendations.* New York State Department of Environmental Conservation, 1981.

Downing, Robert. "The Search for Cougars in the Eastern United States." *Cryptozoology* 3 (1984).

Etling, Kathy. *Cougar Attacks: Encounters of the Worst Kind.* The Lyons Press, 2001.

Fergus, Charles. *Swamp Screamer.* North Point Press, 1996.

Grambo, Rebecca J. (photography by Daniel Cox). *Mountain Lion.* Chronicle Books, 1999.

Hoagland, Edward. *Red Wolves and Black Bears.* Lyons & Burford, 1976.

Olson, Dennis L. *Solitary Spirits: Cougars*. NorthWord Press, Inc., 1996.

Parker, Gerry. *The Eastern Panther: Mystery Cat of the Appalachians*. Nimbus Publishing, 1998.

Petersen, David. *Ghost Grizzlies*. Johnson Books, 1998.

Shaw, Harley. *Soul Among Lions*. Johnson Books, 1989.

Weidensaul, Scott. *The Ghost with Trembling Wings: Science, Wishful Thinking, and the Search for Lost Species*. North Point Press, 2002.

INDEX